Texas

Texas

An American History

BENJAMIN HEBER JOHNSON

Yale UNIVERSITY PRESS

New Haven and London

Published with assistance from the Mary Cady Tew Memorial Fund.

Copyright © 2025 by Benjamin H. Johnson.

All rights reserved.

This book may not be reproduced, in whole or in part, including illustrations, in any form (beyond that copying permitted by Sections 107 and 108 of the U.S. Copyright Law and except by reviewers for the public press), without written permission from the publishers.

Yale University Press books may be purchased in quantity for educational, business, or promotional use. For information, please e-mail sales.press@yale.edu (U.S. office) or sales@yaleup.co.uk (U.K. office).

Illustrations by Weshoyot Alvitre.

Designed by Mary Valencia
Set in Adobe Text Pro type by Integrated Publishing Solutions
Printed in the United States of America.

ISBN 978-0-300-22672-0 (hardcover : alk. paper)
Library of Congress Control Number: 2024938878

A catalogue record for this book is available from the British Library.

This paper meets the requirements of ANSI/NISO Z39.48-1992
(Permanence of Paper).

10 9 8 7 6 5 4 3 2 1

For My Family

It's not necessary to like being a Texan, or a Midwesterner, or a Jew, or an Andalusian, or a Negro, or a hybrid child of the international rich. It is, I think, necessary to know in that crystal chamber of the mind where one speaks straight to oneself that one is or was that thing, and for any understanding of the human condition it's probably necessary to know a little about what the thing consists of.

—John Graves, *Goodbye to a River,* 1960

Contents

Introduction: Burying Stephen F. Austin 1

1. Ancient Worlds 10

2. Castaways in Indian Country 21

3. Entering Indian Worlds 32

4. At the Edge of Empires 47

5. Becoming Mexican 60

6. Becoming Independent 73

7. Being Independent 89

8. Losing Independence 100

9. Border State 112

10. Civil Wars 124

11. A White Man's Country 137

12. Home on the Range 151

13. Taming the Frontier 163

CONTENTS

14. The People's Party 178

15. Fighting for Democracy 192

16. Homefronts 204

17. After Spindletop 216

18. Automobiles and Burning Crosses 227

19. Looking to the Past in Hard Times 240

20. The Good War 254

21. A Giant Reputation 268

22. Civil Rights 283

23. Luckenbach and Beyond 296

24. Urban Cowboys 309

25. An Age of Disquiet 323

Epilogue 337

Essay on Sources 343

Acknowledgments 359

Index 361

Texas

Introduction:
Burying Stephen F. Austin

In most regards, Stephen F. Austin's funeral was like any other funeral. Friends and family of the person being buried come together, dressed in their best dark clothing. Their faces are long, their conversation quiet out of respect for the occasion. Prayers are said, songs sung. A few people speak about the person's life and accomplishments, what his or her time on earth meant to them. If the deceased was a public figure, like Austin, some of these speakers are also prominent people—judges, politicians, generals. Ordinary people, most of whom never met the person being buried, gather outside. They watch as his body is taken to a cemetery and put into a grave, with family and close friends tossing handfuls of dirt on the coffin to mark their loved one's final departure. Newspapers describe the day's events, maybe reprinting the speeches given. The death and funeral become the subject of conversations for days and maybe weeks. Then they fade slowly into the past, perhaps to be remembered again on the anniversary of the person's death or birth, especially if they were important enough to have a holiday established in their honor: think George Washington, Abraham Lincoln, Martin Luther King Jr.

That is more or less what happened at Austin's funeral. He was the person who first brought large numbers of American colonists into what was then (in the 1820s) the Mexican province of Coahuila y Tejas. It wasn't easy. A few years before, his father, Moses Austin, had traveled to San Antonio and secured permission to bring American colonists into what was then a Spanish province. But Moses caught pneumonia on the return trip, dying shortly after returning to his Missouri home. Stephen, not even thirty years old, honored his father's dying wishes and resolved to bring colonists to Tejas. He went to Mexico City and persuaded the Congress of the newly independent nation of Mexico to honor the agreement between his father and the Spanish crown. In little more than a decade, something like 30,000 Americans moved to Texas. In 1836, joined by some of their Mexican neighbors, they rebelled against the Mexican government. After a crushing defeat at an old mission they knew as "the Alamo," they managed to win their independence in the Battle of San Jacinto, not only defeating the Mexican Army but, astonishingly, capturing Mexico's president in the process. Austin served as the new nation's first secretary of state. But only for a few months—he died in late December of 1836, at the age of forty-three.

So of course his funeral was a huge event: his body was put on a horse-drawn wagon and carried to a nearby town. The town's leaders canceled school for the day, and the schoolchildren walked past the casket holding Austin's body, "each one dropping a white flower on the casket as they passed, until the casket was covered with flowers." A prominent doctor addressed the gathered crowd of children and their families. He compared Stephen Austin to the biblical figure Moses, noting that "he was only allowed a glimpse of the promised land to which he had led his people." Austin's body was then taken to the next town down the line, where a similar ceremony was conducted, with schoolchildren once again dropping flowers (this time, roses) onto his casket. The next day, his body reached a large nearby city, where the morning paper printed Austin's portrait in the middle of its front page. Family members watched as prominent elected officials and a seventh-grader lauded their departed relative, emphasizing the suffering that he had endured on behalf of Texas.

As if this was not enough, the body was then taken to the capital city. The police chief and dozens of soldiers in dress uniform received the casket. The political leaders of Texas carried the coffin into the capitol building itself, where that night 3,000 Texans gathered for a memorial service. At this gathering, a choir sang the hymns "How Great a Foundation" and "Infinite Love." A minister deemed Austin a "God-chose and God-inspired man." The state's leading judge thundered that "He whose coffined remains repose in that casket was the great leading pioneer of an advancing civilization in Texas." Austin was not only a hero of Texas, but an exemplary human being; as the judge continued, "we can truly affirm that such was his intellectual organism, his self-poise amid difficulties, and the purity of his private life, that few men in ancient or modern times have equaled him."

The following day, the third day of this prolonged ceremony, children again assembled as Austin's body was brought to the Texas State Cemetery and buried on the highest point of its "Hill of Heroes." It can still be found there today, in the city that bears Austin's name.

All of these ceremonies, events, and speeches are more or

less what happens when famous people die, then and now. But there was one very, very odd thing about this outpouring: it took place not in 1836, when Austin died, but in 1910, seventy-four years later. Austin's reburial began with the strange sight of a hundred people gathering around his original grave, in Brazoria County south of Houston, to watch his body dug up. Since his wooden coffin had long since disintegrated, his skeleton was removed from the earth by hand. Austin's skull was handed to his grand-niece, who held it up so that the assembled crowd could admire it. "The skull was almost perfectly preserved," a newspaper reporter wrote, and "the teeth were in perfect condition, and so lustrous and deep was the natural enamel on them that when the skull was held up to the light the sun shone through them as though they were made of crystal."

Why would you dig up somebody's body, look at its remains, hold all of these ceremonies, and then bury it again?

The Texans who planned all of this were trying to make a statement about their history. They succeeded. The most important story of their past, all of these ceremonies suggested, was the Texas Revolution, when Anglo Texans won their independence from Mexico (there was no mention of the Texas-Mexicans who also participated in the revolt). Since Austin's settling of American colonists in Texas set this in motion, he was the state's key founder. Austin was, as the speakers at the services repeated over and over again, "the father of Texas."

Maybe all of this seems natural and obvious: Austin was a hugely important figure. People who grew up in Texas, like I did, learned about Austin in children's books, heard about him in their classes, saw paintings of him, and maybe went to the state capitol and looked up at his marble statue.

But Austin was not always so widely understood as the "father" of Texas. Indeed, in his final years, most Anglo Texans turned against him: when he ran for president of the newly independent nation in 1836, he received only a scant 10 percent of the vote, far less than the 76 percent that won General Sam Houston the office. Most of the voters found him too brainy and mild-mannered for their taste, maybe a little too much like a teacher or a businessman, and not enough like a soldier. The years that he spent urging his colonists to live in peace with their Mexican neighbors and the Mexican government made him an odd, maybe even suspicious, figure for those who had fought a bloody war against that government and against many of their neighbors. Austin spoke excellent Spanish and had lived with prominent Mexican families, in whose circles he was known as "Esteban."

The educators, politicians, and family members who arranged for the elaborate ceremonies of 1910 didn't mention this more complicated history. They didn't mention plenty of other things: in celebrating Austin as the father of Texas, for example, they moved away from the previous generation's celebration of the Confederacy, the great rebellion of 1861 that saw Texas join most other southern states in seceding from the United States. They didn't mention much of anything that had happened after the 1830s—not how Texas gave up its independence to become a state in 1845, not the Civil War, not the expulsion of almost all Indians from the state, not the flood of immigrants from across the United States and Europe that settled the Lone Star State, not the discovery of oil at Spindletop in East Texas in 1901 that marked the birth of the modern American petroleum industry and had already changed the state dramatically by the time they dug up Austin's bones.

The people who honored Austin in 1910 weren't being dishonest, and they weren't stupid. They were telling a history. And when you tell a history, you have to talk about some things but not others, emphasize some people and some themes while minimizing or ignoring others. If you don't do this, you

6 INTRODUCTION

end up with a jumble, like a map that's too big and detailed to let you navigate.

Like the 1910 ceremonies, this book tells a history of Texas. It is a complicated, and fascinating, story, and a longer one too, since more than a century has gone by since Austin's remains were dug up. Like the people gathered in the towns and capitol in 1910, I have to make decisions about what to put in and what to leave out. Some of my choices are very different from those made by the organizers of the 1910 events. Most important, this book does not claim one single "father" of Texas, or even one key event like the revolution. There were many fathers, and mothers as well.

In part this is because of how long and complicated Texas history is. No handful of people, no single event (even very important ones like the Texas Revolution) can let us understand the past of a place larger than most contemporary nations. This book tells a history of hundreds of years, in which Texas has gone from a set of Indian homelands at the edge of the vast Spanish Empire to a part of Mexico, to an independent nation, to a state in the United States, to a part of the Confederacy, and back to the United States. No one event explains how and why most people in Texas shifted from hunting to growing their own food, or moved from the countryside to big cities, or started driving cars instead of walking and riding horses, to say nothing of the jets many of us now fly in, or the SpaceX rockets now launched from the South Texas coast. So this book pays as much attention to developments before people like Austin showed up in Texas, and to the twentieth and twenty-first centuries, as it does to the nineteenth.

This book is also different from the best-known stories of Texas history because it discusses many different kinds of people. The 1910 ceremonies told a story in which white people were the most important characters, and certainly all of the

INTRODUCTION 7

good guys. Nobody mentioned slavery, even though Austin's settlements brought plantation slavery into Texas, and growing debates over the institution kept Texas out of the United States for nine years. The crowds of schoolchildren lined up to see his casket pass by were carefully separated into Black and white, with the white children in front. The story that they heard about the Texas past centered on the liberation of Texas from Mexico. In contrast, this book shows the deep and enduring connections between Texas and Mexico, from the transfer of agriculture and religious elements from Mesoamerica to the protections for women's property rights in Spanish and Mexican law, to the recent migrations that have made Texans of Mexican descent the largest single group in the state. Similarly, I try to show the extent to which Indigenous, Black, and Asian people shaped Texas history, not only in past centuries but in recent cultural and political changes. As I write these lines, there are more Black elected officials in Texas than in any other state, and the Vietnamese, South Asian, and Nigerian populations number among the largest such communities in the country. This book tries to be a history of all Texans, not just descendants of white southerners like me.

Texas: An American History also has a different attitude toward the past it describes than did the speakers in 1910. When they called Austin the father of Texas, they meant to praise him. Texas history is often meant as celebration, the equivalent of the children's story about George Washington telling his dad that he did chop down the cherry tree. Texas made me who I am and I love the place. There is plenty that I celebrate about its past. But learning about Texas history does not always make me feel good. Some of this history is awful and makes me feel angry, sad, disgusted, and sometimes even ashamed. I think that is what honest history—unlike patriotic myth—does for most readers. So there is plenty of nobility, bravery, and creativity in these pages, but also treachery, exploitation, brutality, and just plain stupidity. That's what people are like, that's the history of the world, that's the history of Texas—the good, the bad, and the ugly.

This book's attitude toward its subject and its wider cast of characters might surprise or even annoy readers who think of people like Stephen F. Austin as the only embodiments of the "real" Texas history. But on another level, I am in sync with the creators of the 1910 ceremonies: Texas is an important, fascinating place with a history that is very much worth understanding. The book is titled *Texas: An American History* because I show in many places how Texas shaped the larger history of the United States. When Americans turn on their laptops, play video games, go to church, vote, eat Tex-Mex, go on a grocery run, listen to music, grill a steak, or watch a football game, they are, knowingly or not, paying tribute to the influence of the Lone Star State. The history of the United States cannot be understood without knowing something of Texas history.

The reverse is also true: major developments in Texas history cannot be understood apart from the larger context of the United States, Mexico, and beyond. This is the case even for chapters of Texas history that are distinctive from the rest of U.S. history, such as the nine years Texas spent as an independent country. In this period, cotton prices, factionalism within Mexico, and divisions in the United States over the expansion of slavery shaped the circumstances in which Texans lived and charted their future. Economic circumstances in Latin America, struggles against dictatorship in Mexico and in Europe, changes in Christianity, the rise of industrial cities with workers who needed to be fed, and wars in Europe and

INTRODUCTION 9

Asia all worked at different times to bring new people to Texas, to foster new kinds of politics, and to change how Texans made their living. Texas has a distinct history, to be sure, that is not the same as the rest of U.S. history. It is also not exceptional—standing outside of the larger patterns of U.S. history—but rather deeply American.

And in a way, Texas is even bigger than that. One of the reasons that it has been so influential is that for centuries it has been not just a place, but also an image. Texas means something to millions of people all across the world who have never even been there. For southern farmers crushed by debt and European revolutionaries hounded by monarchies, it represented a chance to regain lost freedoms; for Mexican leaders and English crusaders against slavery, it represented oppression and treachery. For countless millions across the world after 1963, it evoked a terrible assassination that marked the descent of the United States into stagnation and division. For eastern Europeans and Middle Easterners who grew up watching the television show *Dallas*, it meant wealth, power, and the oil business. Texas is so powerful an image that recently people in Norway started using "Texas" to mean "crazy" or "wild." A police chief describing reckless international truck drivers told a reporter that "it is absolutely Texas" on the big highways, and a schoolteacher explained that "it was totally Texas on the bus this morning." For them, Texas was not just a place, but also an attitude, wild and maybe a little dangerous, but also impressive. Texas history reaches out beyond its borders. Its outsized reputation has sometimes reflected, but at other times inflated or hidden, the real legacies of its histories.

This is a little history of a big state.

PAINTING THE WHITE SHAMAN MURAL

1
Ancient Worlds

If you drive west on Highway 90 out of Del Rio, as I first did on one of many childhood camping trips to Big Bend National Park, stop before you get to the huge bridge over the Pecos River. Pull over onto the shoulder of the highway and bushwack north for about ten minutes until you come to the rim of a narrow and small side canyon that drains into the Pecos. In a little mouth at the canyon's top there is a smooth wall that faces west. This surface's warm cream color contrasts with the colder-looking gray limestone of the exposed canyon walls, seeming to invite you into its shelter.

Enter and look up. You'll see figures looking back at you: five faceless human-shaped beings with rectangular black torsos topped with red squares, carrying what look to be staffs; and a striking white figure three feet high with its arms outstretched, decorated with a thick gray stripe running down its body, flanked by red squiggles that somehow make me think of a priest's robes. Deer and what look like stylized bunches of pine needles (or are they arrows?) join these human-like figures. Other images on the wall are harder to identify. A curved, bulbous oblong thing makes me think of a slug, but why is it painted in yellow, black, and white sections, with a few white circles, and why is it five or six times larger than the white figure? There are also more abstract drawings—most obviously, a semicircle with a red rectangle sticking down and something that looks vaguely like a trailer with three sets of wheels and a bunch of bumps on its top. Are these supposed to represent things, or ideas? What is the significance of the line of small red semicircles or the irregular solid black circles?

Really the whole thing is a mystery. It seems to have been painted all at once, which couldn't have been easy since the composition is twenty-six feet long and thirteen feet tall at its highest. It must have taken months of work, much of it done even before painting could begin. Minerals like manganese and hematite had to be dug, plants like yucca root picked, and carefully mixed with animal fat in the right portions to make the different paints. The fat alone was a precious commodity. In the time these images were painted—somewhere between 1,500 and 4,000 years ago—drought had driven bison from the region, and Europeans had not yet introduced cattle, sheep, and goats. Deer, javelina, and rabbit would have been the only sources of animal fat. Archaeologists who have looked at fossilized human waste report that grasshoppers, snakes, and lizards were more commonly eaten than these larger animals, so they must have been scarce and hard to kill. Furthermore, scaffolding had to be built to reach so high on the rock wall, in a region where the climate since the last ice age had been so arid that wood was never easy to come by. What were the painters trying to say, and to whom? Why was it so important to them to use so many scarce materials? Were the artists trying to placate or honor some ancient deity or deities?

Unpacking the mystery of the White Shaman mural, as it came to be known, is an impossibility. We do not even know what language its creators spoke when they dipped brushes into pigment and carefully painted this complicated scene. Anybody who is reading this book is literate and likely spends most of their time under a roof and between four walls. The mural's creators had no written language and scarce shelter. They never encountered wheat, rice, beef, an automobile, or air-conditioning. The circumstances of their lives are so, so different from ours that it would seem presumptuous to think that as modern people we can know what story their mural tells.

Yet the mural can teach us more than we might think about Texas. The White Shaman site is especially beautiful and haunting. But it is just one of countless places where Native peoples left their marks on the landscape. The region where the Pecos joins the Rio Grande alone has several thousand sites with drawings, some on the scale of the White Shaman mural. What look to the casual eye like little piles of dirt scattered over the uplands of West Texas are actually the remnants of earth ovens, with soil and limestone used to slow-roast otherwise inedible plants like agave, lechuguilla, and sotol. The oldest are 7,000 or more years old. When you know what you're looking for, it's easy to see that Texas is a very, very old place.

If your education was anything like mine, you think of the people who left these traces as "Indians." That is a word used for inhabitants of the western hemisphere by Christopher Columbus, who died thinking that he had made landfall near the subcontinent of India, whose rich trade beckoned western Europeans. Columbus was off by about 10,000 miles, and in any event his voyages took place at least a thousand years after the White Shaman mural was painted. "Indian" was a useful term to distinguish Native peoples from relative newcomers from Europe and Africa (and, later, Asia). But it would not

ANCIENT WORLDS 13

have made any sense to the White Shaman artists. Whatever name they used for themselves would have marked them off from their neighbors, who had also lived in Texas for a very long time.

Some of these neighbors were similar, like distant relatives: their language was probably understandable, and they told similar stories about their origins, made similar paintings, and lived off the land in a similar way, eating plants and small animals and constantly moving from place to place. But others, especially if you traveled farther east and north, deeper into present-day Texas, did not seem like relatives at all. These people spoke different languages, held different beliefs, created different art, and lived off the land in different ways. A few hundred miles to the north of the mural, for example, the abundant bison living off the rich grasslands of the Plains were the main source of food, clothing, and shelter. The residents of this region at the time the White Shaman mural was painted left few traces of their culture, but if they were anything like other bison-hunters, the buffalo was a main character in their stories of how the world came to be.

The many distinct natural environments within Texas help explain the fact that it was home to so many different cultures. The central part of Texas, made up of mixed oak woodlands and open prairies and cut through by many rivers and streams, provided a large range of potential food, from larger animals like deer and bear to edible roots, pecans, and persimmon. Archaeologists can find so many former ovens and trash piles that they believe this region supported far more people than the dry and sparse canyonlands that the White Shaman artists called home. Here the land provided not just more sources of food, but also enough animal bones to manufacture tools such as fishhooks and needles. Farther to the east, more rain falls and forests of pine trees grew. At the time the mural

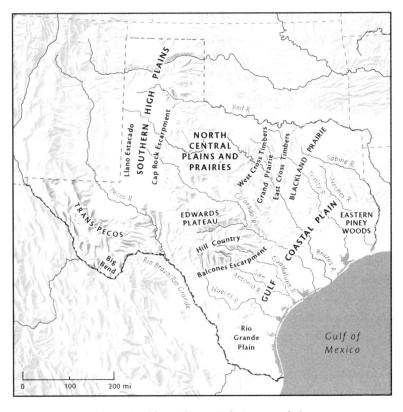

Texas landforms (Erin Greb Cartography)

was painted, this region provided few resources and thus was lightly populated. Until the adoption of agriculture, it was easier to live closer to the coast. Here people moved regularly in order to take advantage of the seasonal abundance of dozens of plants and animals. Pecans, mesquite beans, and prickly pear fruit were important plant foods, while peccary, rabbits, birds, and shellfish joined an occasional bison to provide meat.

People have lived in present-day Texas for at least 13,000 years, and probably more like 20,000 years. Archaeologists

ANCIENT WORLDS 15

keep finding evidence that pushes the arrival of humans to the Americas back further in time. Whatever the correct date, this is an enormous amount of time. If those centuries were compressed to a day, the first Europeans—from Spain—would show up at about eleven-thirty at night. Texas would become a part of the United States fifteen minutes before midnight. I would be born a few minutes before midnight. Counted another way, at least five hundred generations of people have lived in Texas. Only the last nine or so have included names like "Johnson."

No wonder that a lot had changed between the arrival of people and the painting of the White Shaman mural. The first people to call Texas home lived alongside amazing animals that are no longer around: mastodons and woolly mammoths, enormous bison (a quarter to a half larger than the current species of bison), wolves much larger than the largest living wolf, saber-toothed tigers, and beavers that weighed several hundred pounds. They may have seen camels and horses as well. Scientists call these creatures "megafauna." What a sight all of these animals would have been! The sheer size of these creatures made them dangerous, but also alluring. People could eat for weeks or longer on a mammoth if they knew how to salt or dry the meat, or sink it in cold water. The presence of such animals, along with those like deer and elk that are still here today, might have been what lured people east from Siberia into what we now call Alaska, and then down into the center of North America and ultimately to what became Texas.

Did hunters drive these animals into extinction? The timing is awfully suspicious. As in South America and Australia and New Zealand, most large animals went extinct around when people first showed up. Some anthropologists point to climate change or diseases as an explanation and find it hard to believe that small populations of people without modern technology could have driven so many creatures extinct. Others can't shake the idea that it was people. Sure, it must have been risky to try to kill, say, a mastodon when your only weapon was a spear with a sharpened stone tip, to be thrown by hand or with the aid of an atlatl. But we know that people did it, because we have found spear points embedded in the skeletons of megafauna. These stone tips might seem primitive to those of us who live in the age of satellites and the internet, but it took modern scholars a long time to replicate the flaking of flint stones that produced the style of blades they deemed "Clovis" points after the New Mexico town near where they were found. Modern scientists have found that these points are less likely to break on impact, and thus likely to last longer, than sharp rocks that are not worked in this fashion. What might look simple to us wasn't so simple after all.

The Clovis point may have been one of the early exports from Texas, since it seems to have been developed in the southern Plains and spread from there. People also figured out how to take advantage of the herd behavior of some megafauna, to make them stampede over the edge of high cliffs to their deaths. About 10,000 years ago, hunters near the present-day town of Langtry in West Texas killed around 120 giant bison in this way. This site remained in use for centuries. So maybe people did drive megafauna to extinction, or at least helped push them over the edge. Given how long it took some of them to reproduce—mastodons took more than two years to bear their young—it might not have taken as much as it seems to wipe them out.

Whatever the explanation, the disappearance of these giants was one early change in ancient Texas. The growth in numbers of the somewhat smaller, but still impressively large, modern bison might have been the result of these extinctions. The rise of hotter, drier weather that changed more from season to season pushed people to look more to plants rather than meat for their sustenance. (It might have also caused or at least contributed to the doom of the megafauna.) Over time people invented ways to weave baskets, bags, nets, snares, clothing, and sandals, all from what grew where they lived. They made other inventions, too. Perhaps 8,000 years ago, people living on the southern Plains developed another style of chipping hard stones into sharp points for spears and daggers. Anthropologists dubbed this style "Folsom" after another New Mexico town, where one was found embedded between bison ribs. It must have had some advantages, because it spread throughout the western Plains. It's not hard to figure out the appeal of a much later invention, which came to Texas around 1,400 years ago: the bow and arrow allowed hunting at a greater distance, surely making it easier to get dinner without risking your life.

Agriculture—growing plants as crops, rather than seeking them out where they grew by themselves—made even more changes possible. There were not a lot of plants in early Texas that provided enough food to make it seem worthwhile to stay in one place to care for them. But eventually people brought some in. The most appealing crops were corn, squash, and beans. They worked best when planted together in a combination known as the "three sisters." The bean climbed up the stalk of the corn plant, while its roots took nitrogen from the air and put it in the ground where it fed the corn plant. The big leaves of the squash cast a lot of shade, which helped to keep weeds from growing. These three came from the south, in what is now Mexico, where farmers had spent thousands of years replanting seeds from the largest ears of corn and the best beans and squash. The sunflower, attractive for its oily seeds, was one of the few crops to originate in the present-day United States.

Strictly speaking, agriculture has been around for a long time in Texas. Corn was grown in West Texas as early as 4,000 years ago by people who relied on hunting and gathering for most of their food. But it was only much more recently, in wetter eastern Texas, that people decided to center their lives around growing plants. For centuries, in a large region around what is now the intersection of Texas, Arkansas, and Oklahoma, the people who came to be called "Caddo" by Europeans grew corn as a part of a diet based on deer, rabbits, wild turkey, fish, hickory nuts, persimmon, and numerous other plants. About eight hundred years ago they started spending more of their time and energy farming corn, developing strains with more and larger kernels on each cob and suitable for grinding into flour. They were good enough at this to develop a population of hundreds of thousands that was densely settled on farmsteads and in sizable towns. Unlike small, more mobile groups, Caddos built large buildings such as fifty-foot-high homes, and huge mounds where priests conducted religious ceremonies. They buried their leaders in cone-shaped mounds alongside valuable goods like pottery, precious metals, and weapons. Caddo society was very different from the mobile, smaller-scale, and egalitarian culture of the artists of the White Shaman mural.

One thing that all of these societies had in common was that they lived mostly off of the resources of their homelands, making their food, shelter, and clothing from the plants and animals that lived where they did. Yet they were also connected to one another, and even to societies far beyond the boundaries of present-day Texas. Flint from Texas quarries was traded all the way to Minnesota and the Pacific. Much later, corn came into Texas either from the Pueblo Indians of New Mexico or from northeast Mexico (and both of these places got it from southern Mexico, where it was first turned into a crop, about

1,500 miles away from the Caddos who so embraced the import). Caddo possessions show just how far trading networks could reach. They traded their hardwood bows, pottery, and tanned hides for cotton and turquoise from New Mexico, Great Lakes copper from a thousand miles away, and bison from the Plains. And it wasn't just goods that moved, but also people. Speakers of Athapaskan, a very different language than any other in Texas, started moving south from contemporary Alaska and reached the Panhandle by about 1300. They continued hunting bison and learned to grow corn, squash, and beans in river valleys. Texas and Texans have always been tied to other places.

Some of the most important ties were to Mexico. And it's only when you look at those ties that the White Shaman mural begins to make more sense. The archaeologist who spent decades studying this site gained new understandings when she started learning about the beliefs and art of Nahua-speaking people in Mexico, especially the Huichols, a small Indian group that today lives in northwestern Mexico. Conversations with Huichols convinced her that the mural tells one of the central stories of their beliefs. This is an account of a journey that made people, the sun, the moon, and the rest of the world that we know. In many tellings, it involves five ancestral human-like beings. The mural has five hominoid figures painted in black, the color of the primordial world below. They are linked by a white cord that suggests a path or trail. The three-foot-high white figure that gave the mural its modern name, the archaeologist believes, is the moon goddess emerging from one of the travelers as they met with success in the first hunt. The semicircle embodies Mount Dawn, from which all life emerged from the underworld, and what struck me as a slug looks a lot like the fish painted on Huichol pottery to represent the underworld god whose body became plants and animals.

The mural is proof of an ancient religion in an ancient place. It might be hard for me to see right away what story it tells, but there are hundreds of thousands of people living in Mexico who would recognize the figures in the mural and could tell you stories about them. Some Huichols still make a long journey, six hundred miles round trip, every year, to recreate the original hunt that gave birth to the world.

The old and deep past of Texas lives on today.

2

Castaways in Indian Country

The strangers washed up on the beach were a sad sight. They numbered forty, huddled near the wreck of an odd raft made of logs tied together with fraying rope made of long hair of a sort unfamiliar to the men peeking out through the high grass of the dunes a little west of what is now Galveston. The stranded party contained only men. Usually this was bad news, meaning that a group was intent on warfare, taking captives, or both. But these men were in no condition to fight or kidnap anybody. They were wet, nearly entirely naked, and so skinny that it was easy to spot their ribs sticking out, even through their long, dirty beards and the surprising amount of hair on their torsos. Only six of them could even stand up.

It was November 2, 1528. You might say that the European colonization of Texas had begun. A lot of textbooks do. But if so, it was with a whimper rather than a bang. The disheveled and starving men on the beach sighted by Karankawas in whose territory they had unceremoniously landed were the remnants of a large expedition of five ships and four hundred men that had left Spain seventeen months earlier, in June of 1527. The leaders of this expedition hoped to create a Spanish colony in what they called "flowery" ("Florida" in Spanish), a name that they used to describe the entire coast of the Gulf of Mexico from what is now northern Mexico to the contemporary state of Florida. Its leaders, including the treasurer, a Spanish warrior with the aristocratic name Álvar Nuñez Cabeza de Vaca, had high hopes for their venture. Not even a decade had gone by since a similar force landed in Mexico and within a few years put Spain in charge of the domain of the Aztec Empire. The gold, gems, and labor of its millions of new subjects made Spain the world's foremost power. This earlier conquest of Mexico brought Christianity, which Cabeza de Vaca was sure was the one true religion, to the mainland of the Americas. It also made the leader of the invasion, Hernán Cortés, so enormously wealthy and powerful that schoolchildren all over the world still learn his name. Cabeza de Vaca and his companions hoped for similar fame and fortune.

It didn't take too long for hunger and desperation to replace these high hopes. The Spanish were just beginning to learn about the challenges of the Americas. They had no word, for example, for hurricanes, because the Mediterranean and North Atlantic weren't hot and humid enough to give rise to the enormous storms. (They took the name of the storm from *hurakan* in Taino, the language of one of the Caribbean's most populous Native groups.) After stopping in Cuba, the expedition was smashed by a hurricane before it could even leave for the Gulf Coast. It lost two of its ships and sixty of its men. The Spaniards regrouped from the storm and left the following spring, intending to sail west and land on the coast of present-day northern Mexico. But the navigators were unfamiliar with

CASTAWAYS IN INDIAN COUNTRY

the powerful Gulf Stream current, which pushed the ships far to the east. When they hit land, they believed they had sailed across the entire Gulf and landed within reach of earlier Spanish settlements. They were off by about 1,500 miles and had instead landed to their north, near Tampa Bay on the peninsula of Florida.

The people of the Gulf Coast proved to be as challenging as the environment. The expedition quickly ran out of provisions. Their ability to live off the unfamiliar land was limited, so their survival depended on securing food from Indians they encountered. The Natives had little interest in feeding the bumbling, inept, and very un-friendly Spaniards. So they kept their distance as best they could. The Spanish could find no large, densely settled empire with rich agricultural lands, a complex government, or great mineral wealth. There was nothing like the Aztec Empire in Florida to be decapitated and made a part of Spain. The closest the Spanish came was bumping into Apalachee territory after several months of grueling travel. Here there were more towns and extensive cornfields. The Spanish occupied and plundered some of them, but were continually harassed and occasionally killed by Apalachee men. Their numbers dwindled.

They also fought with one another. Their leader ordered the expedition to divide into two. A smaller party would sail the ships along the coast, while the bulk of the men would take the forty remaining horses and strike out over land. This command provoked argument and nearly a rebellion. The two parties never saw one another again, just as Cabeza de Vaca said he feared would happen. Under perpetual attack and growing danger of starvation, the party on land quarreled as well. The mounted men nearly abandoned the others, believing their chances of finding a Spanish settlement to be much greater on their own.

Without regular shelter or food, many fell sick, and dozens died. Finally, the remaining 240 or so camped by a shallow bay in west Florida and began to slaughter their horses. They ate the meat and saved the hair to braid into rope. Believing that staying on land would mean their slow and inevitable deaths, they resolved to return to the sea. They made enormous fires to melt down their crossbows and spurs into crude axes, hatchets, and saws. These were used to chop pine trees into logs, which they lashed together with horsehair rope into four large rafts. Their ragged shirts, tied together with the rest of the hair, became sails. They pushed off back into the ocean, hopeful that they could travel far enough to land in Spanish territory.

The trip on the raft was the last, long stage of the ordeal before the Karankawas found one raft's crew on the beach that cold November day. Dehydration and starvation haunted the men as they worked their way west along the northern coast of the Gulf of Mexico for six weeks. Currents and storms separated the four rafts from one another. "We had been suffering from hunger for many days and had been pounded so much by the sea," wrote one survivor years later, "that the following day many men began to faint... all the men in my boat had passed out, one on top of another, so near death that few of them were conscious and fewer than five were still upright." The surf smashed them ashore.

We know about these events in such detail because Cabeza de Vaca wrote and published a detailed account of them after he rejoined Spanish society. The title, typical of the style of that time, was long: *The account that Álvar Nuñez Cabeza de Vaca gave about what happened in the Indies to the fleet sent by Governor Pánfilo Narváez from the year 27 to the year 36 that re-*

turned to Seville with three of his company. It was widely read in the Spanish-speaking world after its publication in Spain in 1542 and later translated into Italian, English, and other languages. This book offered the first detailed descriptions of the people, plants, animals, and geography of what became Texas. Texas remained extremely difficult for outsiders to reach, but anybody who read his book could learn about "vipers that kill men when they strike" (rattlesnakes) and furry "cows" with curved horns (bison). You might say that its publication marked the birth of Texas literature, even though Cabeza de Vaca never used the word "Texas" because it hadn't been coined in Spanish, English, or any other language.

The different peoples who already lived there knew Texas well and loved their home deeply. Outsiders found it a strange and terrifying place. The Karankawas who found the Spaniards treated them with kindness and generosity, bringing the large party fish, cattail roots, and freshwater for days. The Spaniards wanted to go back to Cuba, and again launched their raft into the ocean, only to have it sink in the heavy surf. Three drowned in the accident, with the others washed up on shore "as naked as the day they were born," looking "like the picture of death." They presented such a sad sight that Karankawas sat down and cried with them. Fearing death if they remained on the beach and seeing no real choice, Cabeza de Vaca proposed that the Spanish ask the Indians to take them into their lodges and give them shelter. Some of his companions, knowing of Aztec ritual sacrifice in Mexico and remembering their earlier fighting with Natives, protested. They feared that the Karankawas "would sacrifice us to their idols."

Five doubters remained on the beach. The rest of the party walked slowly inland, escorted by Karankawas who "provided for four or five large fires to be placed at intervals" so that even this short trip would not kill the castaways. A lodge warmed by roaring fires awaited them in the Karankawa village. The party remained on edge, but in the morning after they were again fed fish and roots, "we were a little reassured and lost some of our fear of being sacrificed." It turned out that the Spanish were the only ones to consume human flesh that winter. The "five Christians who had taken shelter on the coast," Cabeza de Vaca remembered, "became so desperate that they ate one another one by one until there was only one left, who survived because the others were not there to eat him."

Soon enough, things weren't much better for the group taken in by the Karankawas. Their weakened condition left them ill-prepared to survive the harsh weather and limited food of the following winter. Sixty-five of the eighty died. Their hosts, so generous at first, grew tired of their presence. The strangers were inept hunters with bow and arrow and knew nothing of the traps, baskets, and underwater fences the Karankawas used to catch fish. Feeding so many extra men in the always lean winter and early spring must have been a burden. Moreover, the cannibalism of the Spaniards who stayed on the beach left the Indians "so shocked that they would have killed the men had they seen them begin to do this." And soon enough the Karankawas came down with some kind of stomach ailment, perhaps dysentery from the decomposing bodies of the Spanish dead, or another disease brought by the Europeans to which they had not been previously exposed and were thus very vulnerable. Half of them died over the next few months. Those remaining had had enough. "They thought that we were the cause of their deaths, and were so sure of it that they plotted among themselves to kill those of us who had survived," Cabeza de Vaca reported. "When they were about to carry out their plan," one man intervened, declaring "that they should not believe that we were causing them to die, because, if we had power over life and death, we would spare our own and not so many of us would have died helplessly." Cabeza de Vaca survived only because the rest listened to this man's counsel.

Several years of a tenuous existence with the Karankawas and their neighbors followed. Cabeza de Vaca described the first year of his life in the region as very much like the life of a slave. He worked constantly, digging for cattail roots, carrying firewood, and hauling water. This work was pretty much the same as what most Karankawas did. But the aristocratic Spaniard, so used to giving orders and commanding the labor of others, found it extremely difficult. (One of his fellow survivors, enslaved in North Africa by the Spanish and given the name "Estebanico" by his captors, must have found the work was not so different from what he was used to when the Spanish were his masters.) And the foreigners were subject to taunting and violence at the hands of children and adults alike. They were frequently slapped and beaten, and a number were killed. After more than a year, however, Cabeza de Vaca's situation improved when he moved to a neighboring group and found that his status as an outsider made it easy to travel between the territories of different groups, bringing goods produced in one region, like shells from the coast, to other places and exchanging them for red dye and mesquite beans.

Eventually, he and the other three survivors of the expedition (Estebanico and two other Spaniards) reunited at the southern tip of Texas and began a long walk south along the coast toward the Spanish settlements that they had sailed toward years before. This was when the strangest and most unexpected part of Cabeza de Vaca's story began. The four foreigners, at first castaways and then slaves, became healers and widely adored mystical figures. As early as their time near Galveston, Indians had occasionally asked them to make the sign of a cross or say a prayer over a sick person. As the four headed south from the Rio Grande deeper into what is now northeastern Mexico, the Avavare people who took them in asked for their sick to be healed, offering deer meat and cactus in exchange. Avavares who suffered from headaches found that the sign of the cross removed their pain. Word of such powers spread. Members of other nearby groups who "were crippled and in very poor condition" came, were blessed, and "went away as strong as if they had never been sick." Soon "our fame spread throughout the area, and all the Indians who heard about it came looking for us so that we could cure them and bless their children." By the last portions of their long walk through northern Mexico, the travelers were greeted as heroes or shamans. Locals guided them from one settlement to another, where they were provided with abundant food and comfortable lodging, and showered with gifts. "These people were so awed and excited that they rushed to reach us and touch us," Cabeza de Vaca wrote of one large town of a hundred lodges. "The press of the crowd was so great that they nearly squeezed us to death. They lifted us and carried us to their lodges without letting our feet touch the ground . . . They spent the entire night dancing."

We do not know exactly why so many Native people saw the Spanish castaways as healers, since they did not write down their reasons. It wasn't because the four outsiders had any special knowledge or skills. Mostly they prayed and made the sign of the cross over the sick. (Once Cabeza de Vaca used a flint knife to remove an arrowhead lodged near a man's heart. Centuries later, this inspired the Texas Surgical Society to choose a cow's skull as part of its logo, referring to the English translation of his name.) In an age when Africans, Europeans, and Indians alike drew no sharp lines between the natural and divine or spiritual world, it made sense to think that outsiders might have access to gods or powers that you did not. The ecstatic masses who greeted the four had never seen anybody from Europe or Africa before. Their bodies, hair, the languages they spoke, and their incredible stories of coming from far-off lands across the ocean set them apart.

A modern person with faith in science would attribute their healing to the power of suggestion—the sick wanted to be healed, they believed the strangers had powers, and so their bodies responded accordingly. Cabeza de Vaca, a devout Christian who lived before the invention of modern science, attributed his power to the kindness of God. "[W]e all asked God, as best we could, to restore their health, since He knew that that was the only way for those people to help us, so that we might escape form such a miserable life," he wrote. "And God was so merciful that the following morning they all awakened well and healthy. They went away as though they had never been sick." The Spanish nobleman, lost for so long, began to hope that his newfound power was part of God's plan to "bring me out of captivity."

The mystery of the healing is joined by another: why, as they headed down the Gulf Coast toward the Spanish settlements they had originally sailed for years earlier, did they abruptly turn west and instead start walking inland? Had they continued south, they would have rejoined Spanish society soon, probably within two weeks. Yet they instead chose to extend their time away, traveling for over a thousand miles more, across deserts and two mountain ranges, before they approached the Pacific coast of Sinaloa.

Here the four knew they were approaching the borders of the Spanish Empire. They saw an Indian man wearing a forged belt buckle on his necklace. Then they came across abandoned campsites with stakes for tying up horses, still possessed exclusively by the Spanish who had brought them from Europe.

It had been almost nine years since they left their homes. The three Spaniards were thrilled that they would soon rejoin their people and again see their families. (Perhaps Estebanico shared their excitement, or perhaps he dreaded the prospect that he would soon exchange his status as a respected healer for that of a slave.) But all was not well: the Spanish in Sinaloa were burning villages, destroying crops, and carrying off Indians as slaves to work in their fields and mines. "We traveled far," Cabeza de Vaca remembered, "and found the entire country empty because the people who lived there were fleeing into the mountains, not daring to work the fields or plant crops for fear of the Christians."

Cabeza de Vaca and his Spanish companions had come to conquer and to rule. (It's hard to think that Estebanico, as a slave, had a choice in the matter.) They were the first people from Europe and Africa to see Texas. They left little mark on the place. Sixty years would pass before the Spanish government sent an expedition into Texas, and 130 before it could establish even a tiny permanent settlement. On the other hand, their suffering and the years of living with different Indian peoples had transformed the four men. Their Indian companions could not believe that they were from the same people as the slavers with lances and horses. "They said instead that the Christians were lying," Cabeza de Vaca wrote, "because we had come from the East and they had come from the West; that we healed the sick and they killed the healthy; that we were naked and barefooted and they were dressed and on horseback, with lances; that we coveted nothing but instead gave away everything that was given to us and kept none of it, while the sole purpose of the others was to steal everything they found, never giving anything to anybody."

He never stopped being a Christian or a Spaniard, and gladly served the crown for the rest of his life. Yet Cabeza de

Vaca's memories of living with Indians in Texas made him a more humane man. In 1540, four years after his return to Spanish society, he was appointed governor of a province that includes parts of present-day Argentina, Uruguay, and Paraguay. Here Cabeza de Vaca tried to be a different kind of conquistador, walking barefoot ahead of his soldiers, offering gifts to Guaraní Indians in an effort to establish friendly relations and to eventually Christianize them. He didn't have much luck. The Guaraní didn't want to join Spanish society, and the Spanish colonists found it profitable to act more like the slavers in Sinaloa than the castaway healer who had been appointed to lead them. Soon enough the colonists revolted against Cabeza de Vaca and sent him back to Spain in chains to face dozens of criminal charges. He spent most of the rest of his life struggling to establish his innocence and to vindicate his actions.

Cabeza de Vaca and his four companions hadn't changed Texas. They were like a little wave that splashed up on a rock and then washed back into the ocean. But Texas had transformed them.

3
Entering Indian Worlds

The conquest of the Aztec Empire in the 1520s and of the Incan Empire the following decade (in the midst of Cabeza de Vaca's long stay in Texas) made Spain the world's great superpower. Its fleets sailed the world, bringing American silver and Aztec corn to China, Chinese fabrics to its territories in the Philippines and Latin America, and kidnapped Africans to the mines and plantations of the Americas. Wheat, sugar, cattle, sheep, goats, and horses brought by the Spanish changed the fabric of daily life for millions—the food they ate, the clothing they wore, the landscapes they lived in. Tobacco, previously unknown to Europe, Asia, and Africa, became the world's first great consumer good, bringing a dangerously addictive buzz and the outrage of staid elders to such far-flung places as England, Turkey, and Japan. Corn from Mesoamerica and potatoes from the Andes enthralled farmers the world over, providing the nutrition for a sustained population boom in the eastern hemisphere. On the other hand, the diseases the Spanish brought with them to the Americas and the Pacific, like smallpox, malaria, and the flu, killed so many countless millions that this episode of human history was as horrific as it was wondrous. In 1588, about thirty years after Cabeza de Vaca died, Spain sent an enormous fleet to invade the then smaller and weaker nation of England. Catholic Spain wanted to bring Protestant England to heel. If it hadn't been for a freak storm that scattered and smashed the armada, the history of Texas and the rest of North America could have turned out very differently. I might be writing this in Spanish.

Yet Texas remained on the edge of Spain's new western domain, within its sight, but out of its reach. The vastness and mysteries of Texas that had swallowed up Cabeza de Vaca and his companions continued to frustrate Spain for centuries. An exploring party led by Francisco Vázquez de Coronado headed east from the current location of Albuquerque, New Mexico, crossing what later became the Texas Panhandle in search of cities of gold that Natives kept telling him were farther away. Coronado didn't realize it, but he came within a few hundred miles of another Spanish expedition, one led by Hernando de Soto that started in Florida and reached Caddo towns in the piney woods of East Texas. The Spaniards burned houses and seized captives as they proceeded. The relentless opposition of the Caddo prompted them to turn back to the east, where the survivors built crude boats that they floated down the Mississippi River to the Gulf of Mexico. They crawled along the Texas coast, with no idea that they were retracing Cabeza de Vaca's ill-fated voyage of the previous decade.

Spanish invasions had more success elsewhere. By the 1600s, Spain had expanded its American empire far from its centers of power in the Caribbean and Mexico City. Despite prolonged military resistance from nomadic peoples, the town of Zacatecas, in contemporary north-central Mexico, became a center of world silver production. Mining and processing silver ore were so dangerous and labor-intensive that the Spanish turned to slavery to provide the necessary manpower. For generations they mounted slaving raids, of the sort that had so disturbed Cabeza de Vaca, over a huge space. They also looked for places hospitable to conquest and settlement. A thousand miles to the north of Zacatecas, expeditions of hundreds of armed men (some Spanish, most Aztec and Tlaxcalan Indians incorporated into the empire) reached the lands of the Pueblo Indians in the northern Rio Grande valley. Here, finding arable land and relatively dense Native populations, they established settlements and built churches. This area they named "New Mexico" because the agricultural towns of permanent adobe and stone buildings seemed more like Mexico City than the nomadic communities of the Mexican north or the Great Plains. On the far side of the Gulf of Mexico, similar expeditions implanted small colonies and numerous missions in Florida. Here a chain of churches stretched east more than 250 miles to the Atlantic coast, and up the seaboard into present-day South Carolina. The Spanish also explored the area around New Mexico, crossing the Great Plains of the present Texas Panhandle and state of Kansas to the east, and reaching deep into Arizona to the west. Voyages launched from the west coast of Mexico reached far up the North American coast, mapping some of California's harbors.

In Florida and New Mexico, Spaniards could not do entirely what they willed to the Native peoples, who greatly outnumbered them. But their military might was formidable enough when they needed to call upon it. The residents of Acoma, one of New Mexico's western pueblos, learned this in 1599. They grew tired of the constant demands for food and

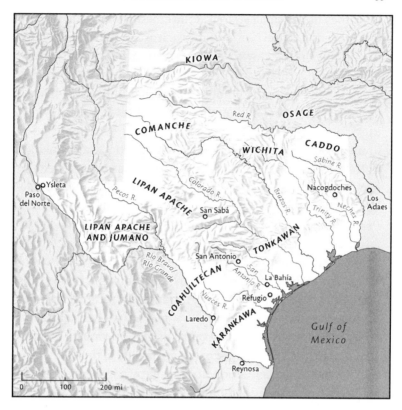

Indigenous and Spanish Texas (Erin Greb Cartography)

the violence from the Spanish soldiers stationed in their midst. Acomans killed eleven soldiers and drove the rest from town. But Spanish soldiers, mounted on horses and protected by steel armor, returned, killing five hundred men and perhaps three hundred women and children. The Spanish commander ordered that all surviving Acoman men over age twenty-five have one foot cut off. Acoman captives were sentenced to decades of servitude. It took two generations to rebuild the town.

In comparison, the Spanish touched Texas only lightly. In

36 ENTERING INDIAN WORLDS

1659, they built a small church at the crossing of the Rio Grande they called Paso del Norte, because it was a convenient stopping point on the way to New Mexico. A few Spanish colonists cleared farms nearby and soon another small church was erected. Such were the humble beginnings of El Paso–Juárez, now a city of several million that straddles the border between Mexico and the United States. These small beginnings grew dramatically in 1680, when a coordinated rebellion of Pueblos in New Mexico killed hundreds of Spaniards and expelled the rest from the region. A few thousand Spanish and allied Indians fled down the Rio Grande some three hundred miles to El Paso. Here they grouped into five settlements, surrounded by farms and ranches. Many of these people remained after the Spanish gradually reasserted their authority over the Pueblo towns in the next decade. The Spanish authorities treated this region as a part of New Mexico. Although the settlements were on the south side of the river—that is, on the Mexican side of today's border—the shifting course of the Rio Grande eventually put one of them, Ysleta, on the north side of the river. Thus the first continuously settled European town in Texas began as spillover from the more populous and strategically important New Mexico.

So in the late 1600s, the Spanish Empire had no real presence in the enormous swath of territory from El Paso in the west to the ranches of northeastern Mexico in the south and the missions of the Florida panhandle to the east. Spanish priests working to establish missions downriver from El Paso, near what is now the town of Presidio, in the late 1680s were thus startled to hear Jumano Indians mention other Spaniards, far to the east in the territory of the Caddos. How could this be? They offered pages ripped from a book and a drawing of a ship with writing on the back as evidence.

But the writing was in French, not Spanish! This infor-

ENTERING INDIAN WORLDS 37

mation made Spanish authorities see that their lack of presence in Texas might become a huge problem for their still-growing empire. At the time, France and Spain were at war back in Europe. And France was another rising imperial power, competing with Spain and England for territory and trade in the Americas. It established "New France," a set of small colonies, fur-trading posts, and a few missions in northeastern North America and was expanding it just as Spain was reconsolidating control over New Mexico after the Pueblo Revolt. Gradually its skillful diplomatic and trade connections with Native peoples allowed France to extend its power into the Great Lakes and the upper Mississippi Valley, even as other expeditions founded colonies and established profitable trade connections in the Caribbean, South America, West Africa, and India. If France created a colony in Texas, and especially if it allied with Caddos, it would drive a wedge between Spanish Florida and New Mexico. Eventually, it might threaten both. If the French could link a new presence on the Texas Gulf Coast to their initial bases in the Great Lakes and the continent's northeast, they might even be able to turn themselves into North America's leading European power, perhaps someday threatening the rich silver mines of northern Mexico.

So Spanish leaders turned their attention to the vast territory that would later be called Texas, again not for its own sake but rather because of its connections to places like New Mexico that were already important to them. They searched frantically for the French colony or encampment that the priests in West Texas had been told about. Five naval expeditions crawled up the Texas coast, peeking into inlets and river mouths. Eventually a Spanish ship came upon the wrecks of two French ships near Matagorda (south along the coast from present-day Galveston). But it was one of the six overland expeditions, led by the Coahuila governor Alonso de León, that found the actual settlement in 1689 along a creek that fed into Matagorda Bay. He breathed a sigh of relief to see only a handful of crude buildings. Exposed human remains, scattered clothing and pots, and wind-blown papers testified to the failure of what he had feared would become a bastion of French power.

The French effort to found a colony on the Texas coast turned out to be as much of a disaster as the expedition that left Cabeza de Vaca stranded and starving on the Texas coast a century and a half before. René Robert Cavelier, Sieur de La Salle, its leader, had left France in command of four ships and more than three hundred people, including women and children. His intention was to establish a military outpost near the mouth of the Mississippi. This was a bold incursion into the Spanish-controlled Gulf of Mexico and would have created the possibility of linking up with the French settlements on the mainland, by way of the Mississippi River. But they missed the river's mouth and instead made landfall hundreds of miles to the west, in what is now Texas. Infighting prompted one of the ship's captains to abandon the expedition and sail back to France. The crops they planted failed and colonists grew sick and began dying. Nearby Karankawas, whom La Salle had treated poorly from the beginning, began attacking. A mere forty colonists survived when La Salle led seventeen of his men northeast in a desperate attempt to cross Caddo territory and then head north to French posts in Illinois. His soldiers mutinied and killed him; a few survivors made it all the way to New France. A decisive Karankawa raid killed the surviving adults at the Gulf Coast encampment, taking children and adopting them into their society.

The Spanish interest in Texas outlived this failed French venture. De León traded with the Karankawas for the return of the French children. He came back the next year, 1690, first burning the pitiful remnants of the French fort to the ground and then establishing contact with the region's Indian peoples to ensure that they had not fallen into the French orbit. The size and wealth of the Caddo population made them particularly important. The fact that they were now trading directly with French outposts on the Mississippi River rattled de León. So he made a long march northeast to Caddo country, giving symbols of Spanish authority to a village leader and leaving behind eighteen men and boys. The Spaniards, three priests among them, started building a church in hopes of persuading the Caddo to adopt Christianity.

The start of prolonged Spanish contact with the Caddo changed little at first; Caddos continued to live as they had before. Within a few years, however, they grew irritated by the Spaniards in their midst. The priests had no goods of any real value, and the lack of women among them raised Caddo suspicions. Harassment and violence toward local women confirmed these fears, so a few years later they sent the Spanish packing. Yet this first prolonged encounter was, literally, the beginning of "Texas." The soldiers and priests heard their Caddo hosts use a word that they wrote down as "Techas," "Tejas," "Tayshas," and the like. It seems to have meant "friend" or "ally." Spanish authorities started using the word to refer to Caddoan peoples, and soon the entire region. "Tejano" came to mean a Hispanic resident of Texas. Later, English speakers pronounced the x as a hard sound rather than something like "ch" or "ha," and the word "Texas" as we know it was born.

Texas continued to appeal to the Spaniards as a buffer between their valuable northern territories and the French. A few decades later, increased French ties with Caddos prompted a reluctant Spanish government to overcome its fear of overextending its resources. Larger expeditions left Coahuila, again setting up missions among Caddos (this time with Spanish women and children along). A midway point was needed to break up the more than six-hundred-mile journey it took to reach Caddo territory from Coahuila. And so in 1718, along the San Antonio River, the governor of Coahuila established Mission San Antonio de Valero (later the Alamo) and the Villa of Béxar (later San Antonio).

We know about these events because Spanish and French authorities generated written records that are still available to us, centuries later. Caddos, Apaches, Jumanos, Karankawas, and others relied on the spoken word and rituals to transmit information and thus had no need for paper and writing. So while it is easy to tell the European side of this story, the question of how Natives understood these developments remains unclear. How were they impacted by the Spanish and French who visited them and occasionally settled in their midst?

In some ways Native peoples paid the outsiders less attention than we tend to think from the vantage of the twenty-first century. The Spanish and French looked different from the neighbors they were used to, and they had novel and useful goods that were previously unknown—iron tools, armor, firearms. But they were few in number and initially in no position to threaten the societies already in place in Texas. The sight greeting a French priest visiting a Caddo village in 1686 sharply contrasted with the wrecked ships, crumbling buildings, small churches, and crude farms of El Paso and the abandoned forts along the coast. "This village," he wrote, "is one of the largest and most populous that I have seen in America. It is at least twenty leagues long . . . in hamlets of ten or twelve cabins, forming cantons, each with a different name. Their cabins are fine, forty or fifty feet high, of the shape of beehives." Despite European prejudices, he found that the Caddos "had nothing barbarous but the name."

ENTERING INDIAN WORLDS

The priest was not alone in being impressed by Texas Indians. Most of us today think of Indians as "losing" their culture, being forced to exchange their languages for European tongues like Spanish and English, trade their clothing for western garments, and settle down in permanent houses. But in seventeenth-century Texas, things were just as likely to go in the other direction. One of the few Frenchmen who survived La Salle's failed colony and made his way back to New France recalled that two sailors had abandoned the outpost and "perfectly inured themselves of the customs of the Natives. They were naked, their faces and bodies with figures tattooed on them like the rest." Like many immigrants throughout history, at least some of those who traded European customs for Indigenous ones seem to have profited from their decision. Spanish soldiers reported that another Frenchman who left La Salle's settlement had joined a nearby Coahuiltecan group—and become the chief of their village. Other French deserters found refuge in Caddo towns. They lived in large houses with the extended families of Caddo leaders, were "streaked with paint after the fashion of the Indians," and married and fathered children with Caddo women.

These men enjoyed a level of material comfort and possibilities for family life that they could not have had they remained in the impoverished and overwhelmingly male European outposts. The gravitational pull of Caddo culture and institutions was visible even in the 1730s, when the Spanish boasted a much larger and ongoing presence, with a fort, several churches, scores of soldiers, and handfuls of priests. Caddos welcomed the priests but declined to convert to Christianity, leaving the work of the missions and the attendance at Catholic mass to the Spaniards alone. The Spanish soldiers and few civilian settlers had trouble growing corn, so they started spending more of their time herding livestock and trading surplus animals with French Louisiana to the east and with other Native groups of the Plains. In other words, their economy looked more and more Caddoan, and less and less Spanish. So did their buildings—"huts of stick and grass," lamented a visiting Spanish inspector. Even the presidio, or fort, looked like a Caddo building, not a Spanish one. Caddos felt no obligation to learn much Spanish, but priests learned two distinct Caddoan dialects. Since Caddos would not come to their churches, they traveled to Caddo homes to preach the gospel, perform Christian baptisms for those who would accept them, and offer blessings for healing. In this they resembled Caddo *connas,* holy men who performed rituals and healed the sick. Were the Spanish converting the Caddo, or were the Caddo converting the Spanish?

Yet no matter how partially or slowly, the reach of the Spanish Empire changed life for the Caddos and their neighbors. For one thing, there were fewer of them than there had been before. Archaeologists estimate that the total population of Caddoan peoples living in the region where western Louisiana and Arkansas, southeastern Oklahoma, and East Texas converge reached a high of somewhere around 250,000 in the early 1500s. By the 1690s, when the Spanish initiated sustained contact, only about 15,000 Caddos remained, organized into the three confederacies of Hasinai, Kadohadacho, and Natchitoches. The culprit was disease. The greater population sizes and densities of Europe, and the long history of swapping diseases with domesticated animals like pigs, cows, and chickens that were not present in the Americas, exposed Europeans to a greater number of diseases for generation upon generation. Indigenous populations hosted far fewer diseases, and therefore people like Caddos were very vulnerable to diseases brought from across the ocean. Caddos had repelled de Soto's murderous rampage in 1542, but ailments such as smallpox, measles,

ENTERING INDIAN WORLDS 43

and the flu brought by this unwelcome visitor swept through the southeast of the continent. We can only wonder what it was like to live through the suffering and chaos brought by such epidemics.

Not all changes were so grim. The Spanish brought animals to North America that had never before lived there, at least not since the earliest days of human habitation of the continent. The Indigenous peoples of Texas were quick to realize the advantages of greater speed and mobility that horses offered in warfare, long-distance trade, and communication with neighbors. It didn't take long for horses to escape the control of the Spanish. Beginning early in the seventeenth century, Native nations across southern and western Texas traded mounts from New Mexico and raided into Nuevo León, Coahuila, and Nueva Vizcaya. So quickly did horses spread east and north that by the 1680s French visitors to Caddo country found horses in every hamlet. Some bore Spanish brands, but more were bred and raised by Caddos themselves. Contacts with the Spanish world also enriched agriculture. Jumanos and Apaches found new kinds of corn and squash that the Spanish brought to the Pueblo world to be appealing additions to their own fields. Indians living in San Antonio's missions added cantaloupe, watermelons, wheat, sugar cane, lentils, sweet potatoes, and peaches—all brought to the Americas by Europeans—to the traditional native staples of corn, squash, and beans. These plants and animals allowed Native people to have more and better food, raised by themselves or exchanged across trade networks made more robust by horses and mules.

Although Caddos, Apaches, Karankawas, Wichitas, and many others easily dealt with Spanish and French interlopers, the peoples of South Texas had a more difficult time. In this region Spanish power was greater. Over the previous century, diseases and slave raiding brought massive disruption to the present-day Mexican states of Coahuila, Nuevo León, and Tamaulipas. Populations collapsed by 90 percent. Many survivors fled north into Texas, joining Coahuiltecan and coastal bands in a complicated and shifting mixture of people. Here, Indians continued to move around with the seasons, but lived in larger and more ethnically diverse settlements than they had before. Although "Coahuiltecan" became the term most often used to describe them, and Coahuilteco the language that allowed them to speak with one another, for generations before the arrival of the Spanish, Native peoples in this region lived in hundreds of different shifting bands that spoke tongues from at least seven distinct language groups. The change brought by colonialism made South Texas society even more complicated. Even a partial list of names for distinct ethnic groups that come down to us from Spanish written sources in the 1700s hints at this complexity, as peoples with deep roots in the region were joined by those fleeing violence and disruption elsewhere: Aranama, Bidai, Cantona, Cavas, Caynaaya, Cholomé, Cíbola, Emets, Ervipiame, Jumano, Mescale, Pamaque, Pampopa, Papanac, Pastía, Payayas, Sana, Tohana, Yojuane, Xarame.

One sign that there was a different balance of power here than in Caddo country to the east was that Indians moved into missions. Many accepted Christian baptism, attended mass, learned Spanish, and eventually started marrying Hispanic settlers and taking Spanish surnames. Nevertheless, in important ways the missions were Indian as well as European institutions. Spanish authorities bestowed positions of mayor, councilman, sheriff, and the like on Native men who were recognized as leaders by their own groups. They relied on Natives to serve as masons, carpenters, and blacksmiths. These craftsmen incorporated Indigenous designs like birds, flowers, plants, circles, waves, and long, curving lines into the church carvings and paintings. Priests wanted their Indian congregants to settle down and live permanently in the mission communities, growing crops for their food as the Spanish did. But for generations many Native groups resisted this, instead coming and going with the seasons, using the Spanish outposts for protection against Apache and Comanche raiders and at other times continuing to live according to the old ways by hunting and fishing.

In 1777, as British North American citizens waged a war for independence from Britain, Father Agustín Morfi mounted a horse and left Mexico City. He headed north in the company of Teodoro de Croix, the military man who had just been named commander general of northern New Spain. Croix was worried by how weak Spanish power was on the huge northern frontier that stretched from Sonora in the west to Texas in the east. The apparent inability of Spanish soldiers and settlers to protect themselves from Apache and Comanche attacks particularly troubled him. So he wanted to see the frontier for himself. Morfi came as the chaplain, the priest charged with ministering to the souls of Croix and his entourage.

They spent almost a month in Texas in early 1778. What they saw only confirmed their sense of Spanish weakness. "Though we still call ourselves masters," wrote Morfi after his return, "we do not exercise dominion over a foot of land beyond San Antonio." San Antonio itself was hardly an image of Spanish might. Morfi described the fort there as "surrounded by a poor stockade on which are mounted a few swivel guns, without shelter or defense, that can be used only for firing a salvo." (Three years later, a storm destroyed even this sad wall.) At that time, Croix estimated that the Spanish could summon two hundred soldiers at most from across the entire province. Comanche, Tonkawa, Caddo, and Wichita leaders could mobilize a total of perhaps 10,000 men.

More than a hundred years had passed since a Spanish mission erected at Paso del Norte brought an ongoing European presence to the place that had come to be called Tejas. Cabeza de Vaca's landing near Galveston was nearly two and a half centuries in the past—about as long as the United States has been a country. Europeans had explored Texas, created a name for it, and changed the ways its inhabitants lived. But they remained a small minority, at the mercy of its numerous and very different Native societies.

A NEW CIVILIZATION

4
At the Edge of Empires

Teodoro de Croix's inspection of Texas in 1777–78 came out of a larger effort to reorganize Spain's entire frontier in North America. The crown recognized that conditions in the huge stretch of territory from Texas to California posed unique challenges to its power and reach. This region attracted few settlers, and priests and soldiers remained vastly outnumbered and overmatched by Indian peoples. So the Spanish government created a new jurisdiction, the "Provincias Internas," or "Internal Provinces," which it hoped would lead to the strengthening of its hold on the north. Croix became its first commander general. A Spanish soldier since age seventeen, he had distinguished himself in combat across much of Europe. He came to New Spain in 1766 when his uncle became viceroy. The Spanish government hoped that his military experience and time as governor of Acapulco would prepare him for the challenges of the north.

They did and they didn't. On one hand, Croix and his

successors brought important changes to Spanish Texas in the late 1700s. For a time, Spanish settlements in Texas grew in size, number, and prosperity. They even made some diplomatic and trade deals with some of their most powerful Indian neighbors that helped both sides. On the other hand, these small gains were overshadowed by conflicts with two expansive young powers—Comanches coming down from the north and a young United States to the east. Divisions within Spanish Texas only made these challenges more severe, with Hispanic Texans fighting one another as part of a larger struggle for Mexican independence from Spain. In 1821, little more than four decades after Croix's efforts began, the rebels won and founded the nation of Mexico. The fighting left the province of Texas on life support, the new nation's weakest and most vulnerable region.

In the early 1700s, the first leaders of Spanish Texas, heartened by the dramatic expansion of Spain's realm in the Americas, approached the challenges of solidifying their northern frontier with great confidence, sometimes arrogance. Indians were supposed to accept Spanish rule, which meant converting to Christianity and working for missions or for Spanish nobles as laborers and servants. When these Spanish leaders worried about other, competing empires, they worried about France and England. By the 1770s, however, Spaniards had learned that Indian power could not simply be wished away. One scoffed at the idea that a fort in Indian territory would persuade Apaches and others to respect Spanish might, joking that it would be as useful "as a ship anchored in the mid-Atlantic would be in preventing foreign trade with America." Croix not only understood the limits to Spanish power, but also soon realized that

AT THE EDGE OF EMPIRES   49

he had to contend with a new rival, one that was in fact overtaking Spanish power in Texas.

"They are a people so numerous and so haughty that when asked their number, they make no difficulty of comparing it to that of the stars," wrote a Spanish officer a few years before Croix's visit to Texas. "They are so skillful in horsemanship," he continued, "that they have no equal; so daring that they never ask for or grant truces; and in the possession of such a territory that, finding in it an abundance of pasturage for their horses and an incredible number of cattle which furnish them raiment, food, and shelter, they only just fall short of possessing all of the conveniences of the earth, and have no need to covet the trade pursued by the rest of the Indians whom they call, on this account, slaves of the Europeans."

This increasingly powerful group was new to Texas, newer than even the Spanish. Their ancestors a few generations back lived as bands of hunters and gatherers moving about the Great Basin in what is now Utah and Nevada alongside other Shoshone people. At some point in the 1600s they began adopting horses, introduced to North America by the Spanish, and then moved out of the Rocky Mountains and onto the Great Plains. Spanish authorities in New Mexico first took note of them in 1706. Although they called themselves "Numunu," or "the people," the Spanish adopted the Ute word "Komántica," or "anybody who wants to fight me all the time," into "Comanche," the name they would be known by to the outside world.

Comanche numbers and power grew explosively. By the 1730s, Spanish accounts suggested that they had at least one horse per person. This wealth in livestock allowed them to carry larger tipis and more trade goods than they had been able to when they had only dogs as domesticated animals. They could also more easily move in search of bison herds and grazing grounds for their horses. Hunting from the back of a horse was so much more efficient than running on foot that Comanches could easily kill more bison than they needed for their own use of meat and hides. Over time they became increasingly specialized, realizing that it was more profitable to trade meat and robes (and captives taken in war) to Pueblo, Spanish, and Caddo towns for food than to grow it themselves. Over a few generations, Comanches became so focused on hunting bison that they avoided eating birds and shunned fish. In time they gathered and farmed so little that they stopped using many specialized words for plants. Why work in fields when you could trade for produce, or just attack towns and take what you needed by force of arms? Their new way of living also made them hard to attack, since they had no fields or permanent towns to defend.

By the 1750s, Comanches pushed into the plains of the Texas Panhandle and Edwards Plateau, coming within easy reach of San Antonio. At this point they numbered between 10,000 and 15,000—in other words, three to five times the population of the Spanish settlements of Texas. By 1780 there were more Comanches than the combined populations of Spanish Texas and New Mexico. They were vulnerable to the same diseases that devastated so many Indian peoples. Indeed, a few years after Croix's visit a smallpox epidemic swept through eastern Comanches, taking several thousand lives. But they were healthy, smart, and rich enough to limit the frequency and size of such epidemics. Increasingly they avoided visiting San Antonio, Nacogdoches, and other towns to trade, instead making merchants cross long distances on the Plains to visit them. These visitors would be inspected for signs of illness before being allowed to trade, reducing the threat posed by disease.

The rise of Comanche power changed the politics of much

of the North American continent. Apache people, whose territory stretched from South Texas all the way to Sonora, lost the most in this reshuffling of power. They were less decisive in casting their lot entirely with horseback bison hunting. They eventually became skilled horseback warriors and hunters, but chose to maintain the fields of corn, squash, and beans that they planted in river bottomlands. Comanches valued the same habitat as winter shelter and pasture for their burgeoning livestock. They were better armed and more mobile than their Apache foes, who began retreating to the south and were forced to rely more on raiding Spanish and Indian neighbors to make their living. So the mid-1700s saw a dramatic rise in violence between the two Native groups.

Ironically, the real success of the Spanish settlements in ranching only made them more inviting targets. Some of San Antonio's earliest arriving soldiers established herds of cattle and horses as large as two hundred, but the missions were the early drivers of the livestock industry that would later come to symbolize Texas. Their sheep, goats, horses, and cattle became so abundant that they spread out far from the missions themselves and required the construction of widely dispersed corrals, utility buildings, and shelters for ranch hands and their families. Missions and private ranchers branded their herds, some of which reached the thousands, with distinct patterns to show ownership. Many animals escaped and reproduced, living wild on their own. In an otherwise economically backward province, the booming stock populations were an attractive commodity for the Spanish government to tax—and for Indians to take.

The dramatic and rapid defeat of a joint Apache-Spanish venture made it clear just how powerful the Native foes of Spanish Texas had become. In 1757, Spaniards built a mission and fort more than a hundred miles northwest of San Antonio in the San Sabá valley, in territory traditionally under the control of Apaches. The venture was part of a tentative agreement between Spanish and Apache leaders, in which Apaches gained Spanish military support in exchange for promises to adopt Christianity, live in permanent towns, and become full-time farmers. Comanches, Taovayas, Tonkawas, and Caddos didn't like the looks of this, and soon assembled a large force comprising several thousand warriors, many armed with French rifles. They surrounded the fort and mission, setting fire to and destroying the latter. Their actions seemed designed to strike fear into the Spanish and Apache people: livestock were slaughtered, Christian ornaments and paintings were destroyed, and a decapitated priest's body was left on the church altar. "I consider it impossible to reduce and settle these Apache Indians," an unnerved priest concluded, "even with the aid of the King's forces." A Spanish commander was more blunt about what the defeat meant: "our destruction seems probable." A few years later, the Spanish abandoned the fort, and the alliance with Apaches lay in shambles.

Impressive as this show of military force was, economic power was at least as important to the extension of the Comanche domain into Texas as was warfare. Through other Indian intermediaries on the eastern plains, they began trading horses, bison robes, and Apache captives with French Louisiana in exchange for firearms (such as those on display in the sacking of San Sabá) and iron tools. This network meant that they were soon better armed than their Spanish and Native adversaries in Texas and New Mexico. One Spanish governor warned in the 1750s that the arms trade was "our great detriment, especially since this Kingdom is so limited in armaments and its settlers too poor to equip themselves and too few to sustain the burden of continuous warfare." In 1803, the French sale of its claims in Louisiana to the United States only strengthened the Comanches' trading position. Now they had access to American guns and manufactured goods. And the huge expansion of slave plantations in Louisiana, Mississippi, and Alabama meant that Americans needed tens of thousands of horses and mules to plow their fields, power the machines that cleaned cotton and processed sugar, and transport these commodities to ports. Comanches were happy to meet all of these needs, funneling their own mounts to the Americans, or better yet, raiding the herds of Apache or other Indians, driving them east to sell to the Americans or to intermediaries like the Caddo. An amazed observer in northwestern Louisiana reported seeing more than 3,000 horses and mules procured by Comanches change hands in one town's market in a single month.

Croix, longtime soldier that he was, looked first to a military solution to the Comanche problem. He was appalled that Spain pretended to defend its 1,800-mile-long northern frontier with a mere 2,000 soldiers. So he changed the placement of some of the Spanish forts and pleaded with the crown to provide more troops. He also realized that frontier warfare differed from European conflicts, where large armies were assembled to meet one another in decisive pitched battles. In North America, wars were fought in small skirmishes and rapid engagements. So Croix eliminated the requirement that all Spanish soldiers be equipped with leather armor (which weighed eighteen pounds), a lance (three pounds), and shield (four pounds). This made his units more mobile and less costly to equip, allowing the crown to support more soldiers for the same amount of money.

Yet he soon realized that there were limits to the military force that Spain would ever be able to marshal. His early dreams of an all-out offensive were dashed when a war with England diverted a potential infusion of Spanish soldiers. He knew from New Mexico and San Antonio leaders that individual Comanche bands could be attacked and defeated with smart leadership and surgical strikes. But the Comanches collectively were far too powerful to make war on. Indeed, shortly after his arrival in Texas, eastern Comanche leaders succeeded in cutting off livestock drives from Spanish settlements to markets in Louisiana, ensuring that this profitable trade would remain in their hands. So Croix and his successors turned to treaties and trade instead. In 1785, they dispatched emissaries to Comanche territory, bearing tobacco, cloth, knives, and other valuable goods as gifts. Eastern Comanche leaders known to the Spanish as Camisa de Hierro (Iron Shirt) and Cabeza Rapada (Shaved Head) assembled a large gathering in the Red River valley to negotiate with the Spanish envoys. They were receptive to Spanish proposals to offer annual gifts ("equivalent to the pillaging . . . they make when they are at war," admitted one of the Texan envoys privately), create licensed traders to exchange manufactured goods for hides, and unite against the Apaches. In exchange, the Comanches agreed to stop attacking Spanish Texas and to return captives taken in previous raids. Special buildings and warehouses were constructed in San Antonio to house visiting Comanche delegations and the generous gifts for them.

The peace treaty held for decades. Lipan Apaches, already pushed south to the scrublands of South Texas and beyond, were the big losers in this alliance between the desperate Spaniards and increasingly ambitious Comanches. This was an uneven treaty, one that in practice recognized the inability of Spanish settlements to stand up to Comanche military power and trading networks. Europeans like Croix looked down on Indians too much to admit it, but by 1800 Texas was more a part of the Comanche Empire than it was of the Spanish Empire.

Comanche power was not the only threat to Spanish Texas. A few decades after the bargain with the Comanches, Texas came into the orbit of another young nation. In the early 1800s, Napoleon, the emperor of France, found his nation hard-pressed by warfare in Europe and a revolution of the slaves who generated so much wealth on the sugar plantations of Haiti. Convinced that Louisiana was more trouble than it was worth, he sold it to the young United States in 1803.

France did not actually rule or even occupy most of the vast territory in question—it was under the control of a host of Indian nations, who fought tenaciously for their homelands in the decades that followed. But the sale had important consequences for Texas, and right away. The sale granted the United States control of Louisiana and its principal city, New Orleans, which lay at the mouth of the enormous Mississippi River and thus provided potential access to the commerce of a huge swath of North America. American businessmen, settlers, and the slaves that plantation owners brought with them flooded into Louisiana. Within a few years its population was twenty to twenty-five times as large as that of Spanish Texas. Where did American territory end and Spanish territory begin? Thomas Jefferson's administration claimed that the Louisiana Purchase stretched all the way west to the Rio Grande, which would have made Texas and half of New Mexico part of the United States. Spanish authorities thought this was ridiculous, but privately worried about what "the most ambitious, restless, unsteady, caviling and meddlesome government on earth" (as one referred to the United States) might do with a disputed border separating them from a province that Spain could barely populate and defend. The crown continued to forbid trade with the United States, to little avail along the Texas-Louisiana border. Eventually the two nations settled on the Sabine River—which currently marks most of the border between the states of Texas and Louisiana—as the proper line. But this legal formality brought little security to the leaders of Spanish Texas, who arrested Americans trespassing on their territory as part of American mapping expeditions or in search of wild livestock. Both sides wondered if the rapidly expanding United States would someday swallow up Texas.

For some residents of Spanish Texas, the United States was more of an inspiration than a threat. Texas lay at the edge of the Spanish, French, and Anglo-American worlds, but the residents of its Spanish settlements were nonetheless caught up in the great political changes of the early 1800s. Like their leaders, Spanish Texans worried about the threats of being swallowed up by Comanches or Americans. At the same time, they grew increasingly frustrated with their own government. The successes of the American, Haitian, and French Revolutions in the previous decades demonstrated the deep appeal of the idea that people should rule themselves by creating their own government and making their own laws, rather than obeying a monarch. With the Spanish crown occupied across the Atlantic in a struggle for its own survival against invading French armies, republican movements exploded across Latin America. The struggle for Mexican independence came into the open in September of 1810. Far from Texas, in a town north of Mexico City, parish priest Miguel Hidalgo issued a proclamation that condemned Spanish rule and called for an uprising against the government. Soon his armies were on the march, winning key victories in central Mexico.

The revolt gained significant support in Texas. In January 1811, former soldiers in San Antonio led by Juan Bautista

AT THE EDGE OF EMPIRES 57

de las Casas arrested the Texas governor and declared themselves in support of Hidalgo's movement. Royalist forces soon organized and struck back, capturing las Casas, executing him for treason, and placing his decapitated head on display in the central plaza as a warning to other would-be revolutionaries. Both sides recognized that the position of Texas on the border between the United States and Mexico made it strategically important to the course of the rebellion even if it was so lightly populated. Royalists closed the border to Americans and tried to keep residents from crossing it, for fear that rebels would buy arms and gather recruits. Bernardo Gutiérrez de Lara, a blacksmith from a town on the south bank of the Rio Grande, managed to do exactly this. In New Orleans and western Louisiana he recruited and armed a small force of several hundred Tejanos, other exiled Mexicans, and sympathetic Americans. In August 1812 they crossed the Sabine into Texas and easily captured Nacogdoches when most of its garrison came over to their side. Its ranks swollen by Tejanos who cast their lot with independence, Gutiérrez's army marched west, defeated royalist forces, and captured San Antonio.

In April 1813, in the days after Gutiérrez's army took San Antonio, a council of thirty citizens issued proclamations that Texas was independent of Spanish rule and had become a state of "the Mexican Republic." "The bonds that kept us under the domination of European Spain," they declared, "are forever dissolved; that we are free and Independent; that we have the right to establish our own Government and that henceforth all legitimate authority arises from the Pueblo in whom this right Only belongs." They articulated the same ideas of equality as had republicans in the United States, France, and Haiti: "Men were all Born free and all have one common origin. They are shaped in the image of their Creator, the only one they should humble down to." Spanish rule they condemned for denying them the right to govern themselves, failing to foster economic prosperity, and denying those born in Texas the right to hold high office in the army, government, and church. These complaints were similar to those made all across Mexico. So was the glowing reference to the American Revolution launched in 1776, in which the "Pueblo of the United States freed itself from the yoke of Tyranny and declared its independence . . . [resulting] in its prosperity and current splendor." The distinct position of Texas as a border province came out in the criticism of Spanish restrictions on trade and "all communication with other Nations," a veiled reference to American Louisiana.

These lofty ideals were more easily stated than put into effect. Very soon the rebellion was crushed with overwhelming force. Armies loyal to the Spanish crown captured and executed Hidalgo and defeated rebels on battlefields across Mexico. Recognizing the danger of leaving Texas in republican hands, the Spanish government sent an army of nearly 2,000 under the command of Joaquín de Arredondo marching north from Laredo. A somewhat smaller republican army met them on August 18, 1813, in a sandy oak forest twenty miles south of San Antonio near the Medina River. Arredondo and his officers, including a young man named Antonio López de Santa Anna, lured the rebels into a foolish attack on his entrenched cannons and cut their army to pieces. Perhaps one thousand men died in the battle of Medina, in what remains the bloodiest clash ever fought on Texan soil.

Arredondo's overwhelming victory ensured that Texas would remain in the royalist fold. "The ever victorious and invincible arms of our Sovereign, aided by the powerful hand of the God of War," he boasted, "have gained the most complete and decisive victory over the base and perfidious rabble commanded by certain vile assassins, ridiculously styled a general and commanders."

The royalist victory came at a high price, leaving Spain's claim to control Texas at all in question. Several hundred people whose families had sided with the rebels fled San Antonio in fear of retaliation. By wagon and horseback, but mostly on foot, they began a desperate dash east toward Louisiana, carrying whatever they could, knowing that the Spanish Army would not want to start a conflict with the United States by entering its territory. Arredondo's treatment of a conquered San Antonio confirmed their fears: he imprisoned most of the remaining population in crude holding pens. Men were chained together and sent to work on roads, public buildings, and farms in work gangs, while women and children from suspect families were confined near the main square and forced to work for his soldiers. Over a span of two weeks, every day Arredondo had firing squads execute three men in public. He was intent not only on conquering a rebellious Texas, but on terrorizing and humiliating it.

Arredondo's next step was to send cavalry units east, to pursue the town's refugees and subordinate the other Spanish outposts in Texas, La Bahía and Nacogdoches. These units killed perhaps several hundred of the fleeing Tejanos, running them down and lancing them from horseback or capturing and shooting them. When Arredondo entered Nacogdoches, he found it a ghost town of three families. He ordered them to return with his army to San Antonio, where he had all imprisoned men shot, the women put to work, and the children left to fend for themselves on the streets. He had kept Texas from remaining in insurgent hands, but only at the cost of killing perhaps a quarter of its Spanish population and forcing another quarter into exile in the United States and Comanche territory. Nacogdoches was abandoned, La Bahía left in tatters. A devastated San Antonio, populated by around 2,000 people, was virtually all that remained of Spanish Texas in 1813.

ESTEBAN AND ERASMO

5
Becoming Mexican

Esteban was proud to be a Mexican. Although he grew up in another country, he moved to Mexico in 1821, the year of its independence from Spain. He moved for the reasons that most migrants do: he saw more opportunities for bettering his station in life in another country. Mexico was good to him. It was, he told his fellow immigrants four years after he moved, "the most liberal and munificent government on earth to emigrants."

Esteban was good to Mexico, too. He felt that immigrants like himself owed an obligation to their new country. They didn't need to give up who they were—speaking their native tongue to one another was fine, and he was proud of his ethnic heritage. But he understood that people like him were newcomers to a country that rightly belonged to others. "I would say to Texas, you must all harmonise [*sic*] . . . with the Mexican population," he urged his fellow migrants from the United States. That meant learning to speak Spanish and ac-

BECOMING MEXICAN 61

cepting that "the Roman Catholic faith is the religion of this nation," even though most immigrants were Protestants. He followed his own advice, becoming fluent in Spanish in just a few years. At public gatherings he hoisted Mexico's flag, read its constitution, and led a pledge of allegiance to it. When the time came, he would bear arms in defense of his adopted homeland.

Close personal ties with Mexicans allowed Esteban to integrate himself in his new home. Erasmo Seguín, one of San Antonio's leading citizens, befriended him on arrival. Esteban's younger brother lived with the Seguín family for a year while Esteban was away in Mexico City on business. Erasmo Seguín's son Juan spent extended periods in Esteban's home, taking the opportunity to study English. A few years later, when his brother lost his life to yellow fever, Esteban was devastated. He became very sick himself and was on the verge of death for several weeks. Normally a private man reluctant to express strong emotions, he turned to another prominent Tejano friend from San Antonio, José Antonio Navarro, to express his grief once he had recovered. Esteban never married, but some of his fellow immigrants—Peter Ellis Bean, Samuel Davenport, and James Bowie among them—married Mexican women from the families that made up Esteban's social circles in his adopted homeland.

Esteban has been remembered in history by the name he was given at birth, and would be known by to the wider world after he later rebelled against Mexico: Stephen F. Austin. Austin's life as Esteban, a successful and loyal immigrant to Mexico for the better part of fifteen years, lets us see how for a time Mexican nationalism worked in Texas. Ambitious outsiders like Austin cooperated with native Tejano leaders to make the most of the opportunities offered by the young republic. They built up the state's economy and population, and along with them the self-confidence of its citizens. For a time, they even negotiated one of the thorniest issues created by the arrival of so many American settlers—slavery.

The prospect of land ownership and wealth drew Stephen to become Esteban. His father, Moses Austin, died back home in Missouri in 1821 after a grueling round trip to San Antonio. The elder Austin had traveled to then-Spanish Texas in search of a land deal after an economic downturn wrecked his mining and banking business in Missouri. Moses proposed to bring three hundred American families to Texas, for which he would be compensated with an enormous land grant. After his death, his son took up this proposal and successfully pitched it to authorities of the newly independent Mexico.

It was a way to honor his father, and to make his own fortune. Stephen's decision later became the start of a powerful Texas mythology: Moses saw the promised land, but it was left to others to bring his people there.

The younger Austin entered Texas just as Mexico gained its independence from Spain. Independence came by a curious route. In 1821, Agustín de Iturbide, a Spanish general who had fought republican insurgents for the past decade, struck a deal with the rebel commanders he was supposed to crush. Both sides agreed on Mexican independence—the key goal of the rebels—but in a very conservative form, providing that Mexico would be a constitutional monarchy with Catholicism as its official religion. It was a chaotic beginning to the country. Iturbide had himself crowned as emperor, but was quickly overthrown in a revolt in the name of a full republic, in which Mexican citizens would elect their leaders.

Mexican independence was won in battles in the country's interior, not in its vast and lightly populated northern stretches. But for Texas, independence came as victory and vindication for the freedom-loving northerners who had sacrificed so much in the previous decade. José Félix Trespalacios served as the first Mexican governor of Texas. He was originally from Chihuahua, where as a member of a local militia he had joined republican forces fighting to overthrow Spanish rule. Captured and imprisoned as a traitor, Trespalacios escaped and fled to New Orleans, where he supported rebel efforts to take Texas. He sailed back to Mexico to rejoin battles for independence. This loyal service to the cause and his familiarity with the north earned him appointment as governor of Texas.

Trespalacios dramatically allied himself with Tejano struggles for self-government. Heading north from Mexico City to San Antonio to assume office in 1822, he stopped at the Medina River. There he ordered the dignified burial of the still-exposed remains of some of the one thousand patriots who had died for an independent and free Mexico in 1813. "A cross carved in the trunk of [a] live oak indicates the site of the grave," wrote one observer. "Placed at the height of a man's head, renewed from time to time by the soldiers of the presidio who carve it as deep as the wood, it seems to be freshly engraved."

The governor's early pronouncements showed the appeal of independence and the hopes that it awakened. "You are free," he wrote to his fellow Mexican citizens of Texas in his first proclamation. Spanish governors gave orders and demanded obedience, but Trespalacios told Texans that "[you] may criticize my actions" and "suggest to me that which will lead to the best decisions in matters in which we are all concerned." Spain had tried to limit contact with the outside world, but the new governor saw that Mexico was connected to the wider world. He thought that Texans should take advantage of those connections: "You are going to freely engage with other

Nations, and I hope that your social virtues will instill confidence and make credible this new nation that will soon appear on the face of the Universe." This first proclamation was handwritten and copied in ornate script and read aloud in town halls and from church steps.

The government of Texas was broke from the beginning. But Trespalacios insisted on spending money on one very important item. He dispatched a trusted deputy to New Orleans to buy a printing press "to facilitate the spread of the arts and Enlightenment." Brought by boat to Matagorda Bay and then hauled overland to San Antonio by seven mules, the press was only the third ever to be in Texas. Trespalacios used it to issue another proclamation, a single large sheet printed in both Spanish and English. Here he announced the coming of a new day for "the advocates of light & reason, the friends of the province of Texas, and the Mexican Empire" and heralded the dawning of an age in which "man was raised to his true dignity . . . in the enjoyment of his unalienable rights." This could be considered the start of the first educational campaign in Texas, in which the state's leaders committed to the free exchange of information and ideas.

These words, and their printing in English, showed that the new leaders of Texas were open to outsiders, especially Americans. The later wars and conflicts between Mexico and the United States, and the later mistreatment of people of Mexican descent in Texas, make it easy to forget how much the founders of both nations admired one another. Latin Americans fighting for the creation of self-governing republics saw the United States as a model. Americans had defeated the mighty British Empire and created a stable political system where the laws were enforced and leaders who lost elections left office peacefully instead of turning to violence to stay in power. Many Americans, in turn, applauded the rise of movements for self-rule and independence to their south in the 1810s. Hundreds of American babies and several towns, for example, were named after the South American revolutionary Simón Bolívar, whose portrait was sometimes displayed next to George Washington's at American diplomatic receptions. Austin changed nationalities and went by a new name with his Mexican friends, but he did not have to discard his values when he moved to Mexican Texas. The way he saw it, he had simply moved from one free country to another.

The leaders of Mexican Texas were eager to attract outside settlers. Their Spanish predecessors had considered many colonization plans, from luring 10,000 Swiss farmers with promises of land to uprooting Tlaxcalan Indians from central Mexico and resettling them on the Texas frontier. Recovery since the brutal civil wars of the 1810s was so slow that it made such population schemes seem appealing, maybe even essential. San Antonio's city council wryly observed that "Since 1813, when this Province was reconquered" by royal authorities, Texas "had advanced at an amazing rate, towards ruin and destruction." The basic problem was the same that Spanish authorities had always faced—a lack of population, or rather non-Indian population. The scorched-earth policies by which the Spanish government had fought revolution only made the problem worse, by killing so many Tejanos and driving more into exile. This self-sabotage not only limited any prospect of economic growth, but left Texas even more vulnerable to Comanche military power.

As exciting and cherished as it was, Mexican independence actually left Texas in a worse position vis-à-vis Comanches than it had been in under Spanish rule. The peace deal the Spanish had made with Comanches back in 1785 depended on the regular shipment of goods from central Mexico to San Antonio. This involved a long and uncertain supply chain that stretched from Mexican ports far overland and across the Rio Grande and the Nueces River. Civil war in Spain and mass warfare in the struggle for independence cut off these essential goods. Faced with a partner that could not live up to its obligations, and droughts that reduced buffalo herds on the southern Plains, Comanches broke the peace. Waves of attacks on ranches south of San Antonio resulted in the loss of lives, the slaughter of cattle, and the capture of thousands of horses. Over the ensuing decade, Comanches extended their raiding south across the Rio Grande, into Nuevo Santander, Coahuila, and Nuevo León. Independence brought no relief from this onslaught, since the new government had money for neither more soldiers nor a resumption of the gifts that had once satisfied the powerful Comanche. San Antonio's city council complained to the central government that "many early settlers and their descendants have been sacrificed to the barbarians, and not a few others have died of hunger and pestilence, which have caused havoc in this part of the republic due to the inaction and apathy of those who govern." The young nation's maps said that Texas was a part of Mexico, but they might as well have said it was a part of Comanchería.

Getting hundreds or even thousands of Americans to move to Texas seemed like one way to solve this problem. San Antonio's leaders made this point to Mexico's leaders over and over again. "Immigration is, unquestionably," they wrote in one message, "the most efficient, quick, and economical means we can employ to destroy the Indians and to populate lands they now occupy . . . This goal can only be achieved by freely admitting these enthusiastic North Americans so they may live in this desert. They are already experienced in dealing with the barbarians in their native land, where they have done similar work."

BECOMING MEXICAN
67

But why would Americans want to move to Texas, so poor and ravaged by war? Economic opportunity has always been one of the main reasons people are willing to pack up their belongings, gather their families, and move vast distances to strange countries where they don't even speak the language. By the 1830s, it was easier to become a landowner, and to own more land, in Mexican Texas than in most of the United States. The government of the United States offered its public lands at $1.25 per acre in the 1820s, a price that was out of reach for most farmers hurt by an economic collapse that began in 1819. Private lands in Mississippi and Alabama with easy access to river shipping could cost as much as $50 per acre, a sum that only the wealthiest could afford. Austin offered land in Texas for only 12.5 cents per acre, for up to 177 acres per family. Americans could gain economic security, prosperity, and one day maybe even wealth by moving to Mexican Texas.

They did have to make sacrifices for their hopes of future prosperity. Especially if they had been doing all right back in the United States, these migrants found that living in frontier conditions in northeastern Mexico deprived them of some of the comforts and goods they enjoyed. Manufactured items and agricultural products brought from abroad were scarce. Buildings, even the few hotels in existence, were more likely to be constructed of logs fit together than milled lumber and nails. There was no glass available for windows, and coffee was hard to come by. Visitors at hotels were often served their meals on the ground of a patio or a breezeway between buildings. Those wanting mattresses or pillows were advised to bring their own, or to gather moss for padding and comfort. Cornmeal was much easier to get than milled wheat flour.

On the other hand, in some ways these colonists were wealthy. Wild game was abundant and the land fertile, so these new Mexicans ate well: "fresh bread, venison, wild turkey, beef, fowl, eggs, milk," in one traveler's description. And they were rich in other ways, too. This is what impressed Esteban's cousin Mary Austin Holley, who visited Texas in the early 1830s and wrote about her experiences for American newspapers. "Artificial wants are entirely forgotten, in the view of real ones, and self, eternal self, does not alone, fill up the round of life. Delicate ladies find they can be useful and need not be vain. Even privations become pleasures: people grow ingenious in overcoming difficulties . . . they discover in themselves, powers, they did not suspect themselves of possessing." Like the Tejanos they joined, American settlers in Texas celebrated their hardiness and self-reliance.

The slaves they brought with them were not celebrating. Like their white owners, these people came from the U.S. South, especially the states of Louisiana, Arkansas, and Alabama that were close to Texas. White slaveowners were moving rapidly west from eastern states such as the Carolinas and Virginia, drawn by rich soils that produced enormous cotton harvests. In these states and the part of Texas that Austin was settling, the land was so fertile that investors sent their money there to start new cotton farms. The result was that many white families who did not move west made profits by selling their slaves to those who did, even if that meant separating husbands from wives and children from their parents. For these migrants, the path to Texas was a trail of tears.

It was obvious from the beginning that Americans drawn to Texas were going to bring slaves with them. When Moses Austin first visited San Antonio to propose a colony, he brought an enslaved man named Richmond with him. The elder Austin also traveled in the company of a fellow American slaveowner who was trying to recover Marian, Richard, and Tivi, who had

BECOMING MEXICAN 69

fled his Louisiana plantation hoping to find freedom in Texas. Slavery was an important aspect of Esteban Austin's first colony. As Austin wrote to a Tejano friend, "the primary product that will elevate us from poverty is Cotton . . . and we cannot do this without the help of slaves."

Three years after its establishment, slaves made up a quarter of the settlement's population. One settler, Jared Groce, brought ninety slaves with him and soon established a very profitable cotton plantation in the bottomlands of the Brazos River. Even white settlers who did not own slaves often paid their owners for slave labor. The laws that Austin drew up for his settlement protected these practices with organized violence. White colonists were supposed to capture, whip, and return enslaved people found away from their owners without a written pass. Nobody was allowed to do business with a slave without their owner's permission. And if you harbored a slave or helped one to escape, you could be sentenced to hard labor and fined an amount so large that it would bankrupt you for life.

A lot of Mexicans did not like this at all. They fought for their freedom from Spain because they believed that they should rule their own lives. Why should the same right be denied to slaves? By the 1820s, when Austin began bringing Americans into Texas, the enslavement of people of African descent had virtually vanished from Mexico, with only a few thousand still held in bondage in a nation of six million people. Many political leaders in the early years of independence wanted to ban it outright; as one congressman said, slavery is "inhumane and against all right" and Mexico should "abolish it for all time." Others, including the Tejano leaders who had befriended Esteban Austin, were not as enthusiastic. They worried that banning slavery outright would keep Americans from populating the desperately weak north. These leaders managed to keep laws about slavery vague enough for Austin and his friends to bring slaves to Texas, sometimes under the guise of being "servants" who had contracts with settlers that made them work for decades. When Mexico implemented a new constitution in 1824, it put a lot of power in the hands of the state rather than the national government. This arrangement gave Austin and his Tejano friends more cover to bring slaveowners and their human property to Texas. It might not have been fully legal, but nobody was going to stop them.

The settlers that Austin had brought sometimes worried about the debates over slavery in Mexico. But for the most part, they could go about their business without fear of interference. A New York land speculator traveling through Austin's settlements in 1831 casually noted the presence of "negroes, held as slaves, though the laws of Mexico forbid it." Whatever the law said was no match for the customs and practices of the white Americans who had moved to Texas, since "the whites are generally in favor of slavery and ready to sustain the master . . . the province is so distant from the capital, and had been for some time so little attended to by the government, that the laws on this subject were ineffectual."

This traveler, like others who wrote about Texas in this period, did not think to ask the enslaved what they made of their odd legal status. But you can find clues that slaves knew about these debates. At least some of them knew that if they could flee the areas where white Americans had settled, and make their way to San Antonio or even farther south across the Rio Grande, they could gain their freedom. A slave named Jim, brought to a plantation in the first wave of settlement in Austin's colony in the early 1820s, "openly announced his determination to leave, and, acting on impulse, threw down his hoe and started away." His owner's son aimed a rifle at Jim and ordered him back to work. Jim continued, so the son shot him in the back, killing him. Years later, when the Mexican Army came near to fight rebelling American immigrants, many of the plantation's slaves fled and found their freedom in Mexico.

Just five years after he moved to Texas, at the end of 1826 and start of 1827, Esteban's loyalty to Mexico was tested. The Mexican government authorized a fellow immigrant named Haden Edwards to bring as many as eight hundred families from the United States to the area north of Austin's colony, around Nacogdoches. Things went bad fast. There were already settlers living in the area, a mixed group of French, Spanish, Mexican, and American farmers and ranchers. Edwards demanded that they provide legal documentation for their claims to own land and informed them that their land would be sold to outsiders if they could not do so. Very few residents had these documents, so they feared that Edwards would take their lives' work from them. Newcomers and older residents voted for different candidates for the mayor of Nacogdoches, resulting in complaints to the governor. Mexico's president became alarmed. This looked like foreigners coming in and taking lands from law-abiding Mexican citizens, instead of respecting the law and becoming good Mexicans. So he canceled the plans to bring in more settlers and ordered that Edwards be expelled from the country.

Edwards didn't back down. He gathered a posse, captured Nacogdoches, and then declared the existence of an independent "Republic of Fredonia." Faced with a rebellion, the Mexican government assembled soldiers in San Antonio and Goliad and began marching east. Esteban called Edwards's forces "a party of infatuated madmen" and formed a militia from the American immigrants living in his settlement. They joined the soldiers, marched into Nacogdoches, and put down the rebellion. Edwards fled to Louisiana. Esteban spent several weeks in East Texas, reassuring residents of the good intentions of the Mexican government, which pardoned all but the revolt's leaders. Esteban had been born in the United States, but he had become a loyal citizen of Mexico.

AUSTIN IN THE DUNGEON

6

Becoming Independent

Stephen F. Austin sat in a prison cell in Mexico City. He had been seized by Mexican soldiers in January of 1834 in Saltillo, the capital of the state of Coahuila y Tejas, while heading back home to Texas from the capital of Mexico. The soldiers dragged him back to Mexico City, where he had just gone to speak directly to the leaders of Mexico's central government about what Texas needed to continue to prosper. There he was thrown into a dungeon of three-foot-thick stone walls with no windows and light only from "a very small skylight in the roof which barely afforded light to read on very clear days when the sun was high." Austin was shuffled from prison to prison until December, when he posted a bond and agreed to remain in the capital. Mexico's government let him go only in July 1835. It took him a few more months to get back to Texas, this time traveling on ship by way of New Orleans.

It was an unlikely turn of events: Austin was arrested only six years after he proved his loyalty to his adopted homeland by helping to crush Haden Edwards's Fredonian Rebellion. He was accused of trying to start a revolt against the Mexican government, which he had served loyally for so long. Austin had only intended to advocate for a separate state government for Texas (rather than continue in a union with Coahuila), but authorities in Mexico City found his conduct treasonous. Soon enough, Texas did rise in rebellion and Austin was named the commander of its ragtag army. He and the other leaders of the breakaway state argued with one another about how to fight as the Mexican government sent a large army to capture them. The Texan army was undisciplined and poorly led. It lost two big battles—one famously at the Alamo, an old church and Indian mission on the edge of San Antonio, and the other at Goliad a bit farther south. Pretty much everybody thought that their revolution had failed, and almost all of the settlers began fleeing to the United States. But in April of 1836, the Texas rebels defeated the invading Mexican Army and captured Mexico's president. In one of the most improbable set of events ever, Texas became an independent country.

This is a strange story. If it were written in a novel, I might not believe it. It is strange because Texans made up only a tiny proportion of a large country and it was very unlikely that they would win a war against Mexico's huge army. It is also strange because most of the leaders of Texas—immigrant Americans such as Austin and his Tejano friends the Seguíns—did not want independence until all of their other choices ran out. At times, the Texan army even flew the Mexican flag to show that they remained loyal to their country if not its leader.

Texans have told the story of their revolution over and over again since it happened. I learned it as a child growing up in Houston, Texas, and have read versions of it in newspapers and books, and seen it in countless movies. The story of the Texas Revolution—especially the heroic stand at the Alamo—

is an inspiring story of an underdog triumphing against all expectations. It has great heroes: Stephen F. Austin, Sam Houston, James Bowie, William Barret Travis, and Davy Crockett. They became something like the saints of Texas history and made Texas the stuff of legend in much of the world. Texans kept telling this story even after they joined the United States in 1845, not even ten years after declaring their independence. It's understandable that defying such incredible odds made them feel brave, heroic, maybe a little bit different from other Americans. But the explanation of why they rebelled and what happened to all of the people living in Texas because of their victory is not so simple, and depending on how you look at it, might not be so noble.

It is hard to say exactly when the Texas Revolution began. Some people think that once thousands of Americans moved to Texas, it was just a matter of time—that they weren't going to accept being governed by leaders far away in Mexico City. There were Mexican officials at the time who worried as much. In 1828, concerned by the Fredonian Rebellion, the Mexican government dispatched a commission to investigate the conditions along its border with the United States. Its leader, General Manuel Mier y Terán, was alarmed at how un-Mexican the American settlements in Texas seemed. He found Mexican influence in these areas to be "almost nothing." American settlers spoke English, maintained English-language schools, and sent their children back to the United States for higher education. Mexicans spoke Spanish at home and in schools, were Catholic, and followed news and fashion trends from Mexico. Except for a few leaders like Austin, American settlers seemed unfamiliar with Mexican culture and politics. All of this made him worry that the continued immigration of Americans to

Texas would lead to secession and to Texas becoming a part of the United States. "Texas," he warned his government, "could throw the whole nation into revolution."

At the same time, Mier y Terán also found evidence that Mexico's system was working. He admired the American colonists. Those who came with Austin and other leaders who had received permission to settle immigrants were "for the most part industrious and honest, and appreciate this country." He wished that they had more to do with the long-standing residents of Texas, but also found evidence of unity between immigrants and established Mexican families. The former called themselves "Texians" and the latter "Tejanos," reflecting not only the differences between the two groups but also their similarities. Both groups expressed "a most evident uniformity of opinion on one point," that Texas needed to be administered as its own state rather than as part of the combined state of Coahuila y Tejas. Travel to Coahuila's capital of Saltillo was time-consuming, expensive, and (because of Comanche and Apache attacks) dangerous. In a sense, Texans were united by their frustration with their state's governance. They were all vulnerable to corrupt local officials who took advantage of the great distance from central authorities to extract bribes to conduct routine business.

Both Tejano and Texian leaders wanted the Mexican government to continue allowing new settlers to come in from the United States and elsewhere. This immigration raised concerns in Mexico City that the country was letting in too many Americans. Austin and other leaders managed to bring about 10,000 settlers by 1830, who then outnumbered the Tejano population several times over. But American settlers had taken Texas off of economic life support, creating a large enough population to better withstand the onslaughts of formidable Comanche military power. Especially because they sold cotton on the world market through New Orleans, these American settlers also offered economic opportunities to Tejano merchants. Selling goods or land to American immigrants was one of the few ways for Tejanos to make significant amounts of money in Texas.

It was an open secret that enslaved people and the institution of slavery came with American migrants. Austin's colony "was formed for slavery and without it her inhabitants would be nothing," observed one Mexican official. One reason that the most politically active and influential Tejanos, such as the Seguín and Navarro families of San Antonio, wanted their government to continue to welcome Americans was that they had started to profit from the enslaved people the Americans brought with them. José Antonio Navarro became a slaveholder at about this time, leasing and buying people who worked as cooks and ranch hands. The San Antonio merchant José Casiano actually had Austin purchase several slaves for him in the early 1830s. Other merchants started thinking about making the large investments to build cotton gins in Texas and even in Coahuila, betting that slavery would continue to grow in Texas and might even spread to other parts of Mexico.

With time, more and more Mexican authorities began to agree with Mier y Terán's warning that the rapidly growing American settlements in Texas were not being incorporated into the fabric of Mexico. Mexico's Congress passed a law in 1830 that dramatically limited further migration to Texas, voiding contracts with empresarios that had not been fulfilled, banning the importation of slaves into Texas, and providing for the creation of military forts and customs houses on Mexico's coasts and borders to better assert control over them. These measures were not enough to satisfy Mier y Terán. Fearing that political divisions in Mexico were intractable and would lead to prolonged national chaos, the agitated officer put on his dress uniform, braced his sword against the walls of a ruined church near the Rio Grande, and ran himself through the heart. "What will become of Texas? Whatever God wills," he wrote in his last letter.

Austin, his Tejano allies, and his colonists all saw these moves against immigration and slavery as threats to the whole enterprise of settling Americans in Texas. Almost all Americans enticed to move to Texas, wrote one such colonist to Austin, "are from Slaveholding states—they have enrolled themselves in your register under the firm conviction that slavery would be tolerated, and they would be secure in the ownership of those brought by them." Even more alarming to slaveholding colonists was that their human property followed these developments closely. "These slaves are beginning to learn the favorable intent of the Mexican law toward their unfortunate condition and are becoming restless under their yoke," observed one Mexican official. Frightened masters turned to more brutality to maintain control of their human property. "And the masters, in the effort to retain them, are making that yoke even heavier; they extract their teeth, set on the dogs to tear them to pieces, the most lenient being he who but flogs his slaves until they are flayed." Austin wrestled with the question, but could see no way out. The 1830 law "seems to be to destroy in one blow the happiness and prosperity of this colony," he wrote in despair. The trip to Mexico during which he was arrested was his effort to reverse the law's implementation and renew immigration into Texas from the United States.

If the 1830 law could not be reversed, what were Texans to do? Was the answer to break with Mexico, either to declare independence or seek to make Texas part of the United States?

Some American immigrants began speaking openly of these possibilities. And, just as had happened before the United States declared its independence in 1776, fighting with the government broke out. In fall 1835, Texians fired on a Mexican naval ship that had been sent to enforce taxes on imports and exports. Soon thereafter, American immigrants in the town of Gonzales refused to surrender a cannon left by the Mexican military to be used against Comanche raids, instead skirmishing with the soldiers sent to retrieve it. No one was killed in these small clashes, but all understood that they raised the prospect of armed revolution.

But Austin, other early-arriving settlers from the United States, and Tejano leaders like the Navarros and Seguíns thought that they could find a solution within Mexico instead of by breaking away from it. One ray of hope for them was that Texas wasn't the only part of Mexico fed up with the central government in the 1830s. Protests against the centralization of power under Santa Anna, a longtime army officer and now the president, erupted across the country in 1834 and 1835. They were particularly strong in the north, where ideas of local autonomy and republican self-rule had been powerful since the later years of Spanish rule. Santa Anna sent military forces to the capitals of Zacatecas and Coahuila y Tejas to quash this unrest, but the Texans knew they had allies throughout Mexico. One of the leading opponents of Santa Anna, Lorenzo de Zavala, resigned his diplomatic position in protest and came to Texas to help organize opposition to what he viewed as a dictatorship.

So it is not surprising that Austin did not advocate for revolution or independence when he returned to Texas after his imprisonment. Instead, he urged Texians to elect representatives and send them to a "consultation" in light of what all assumed was to be a major deployment of the Mexican Army in

Texas to quash political dissent. "[I]t is our bounden and solemn duty as Mexicans, and as Texians," Austin proclaimed, "to represent the evils that are likely to result from this mistaken and most impolitic policy in the military movement." Some delegates to the Consultation, especially those who had recently moved to Texas and therefore had no history of working and cooperating with Tejanos and other Mexicans, wanted to declare independence and fight for it. But a majority opted for Austin's course of remaining loyal to what they saw as the legitimate government of Mexico for as long as possible. Texans, said the declaration issued by the Consultation, "hold it to be their right, during . . . the reign of despotism, to withdraw from the Union, to establish an independent Government . . . but that they will continue faithful to the Mexican government so long as that nation is governed by the Constitution and Laws." They hoped this approach would maintain the support of Tejanos and liberals across Mexico in resisting Santa Anna's army.

The Consultation's statement was compelling as political rhetoric, but it failed to set up an effective basis for resisting the massive military force headed to Texas. Instead, chaos reigned: the provisional governor they selected was in favor of revolution and independence and fought constantly with a more moderate council made up of representatives from across Texas. The delegates named Sam Houston, a former governor of Tennessee who had experience as an officer in the U.S. Army, as the commander-in-chief of their army. But the delegates did not give Houston authority over volunteer forces, who continued to elect their own officers and follow their own direction. And war was upon them: shortly before the convention met, in October of 1835, General Martín Perfecto de Cos led an army of 650 men into San Antonio. They occupied one of the missions there, known as the Alamo. The most important settlement in Texas was now in the military control of the central

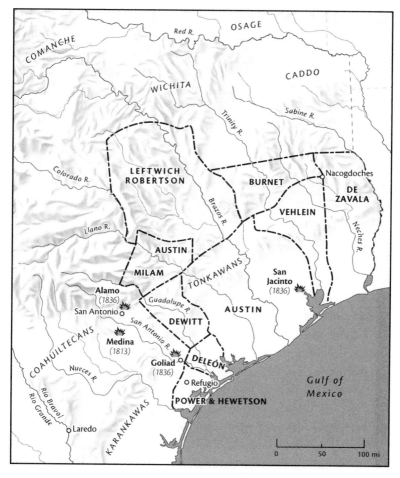

Revolutionary Texas, with Mexican land grants (Erin Greb Cartography)

government. Santa Anna, the nation's president, was en route at the head of a larger force.

A ragtag Texan army formed near the city out of small bands, including more than a hundred Tejanos from San Antonio and Victoria, a slightly smaller group loyal to the former slave trader and land speculator James Bowie, and volunteers arriving from the United States to join what they hoped would be a revolution. They laid siege to Cos's force in the Alamo. This motley crew was passionate and energetic, and armed with longer-range rifles than the Mexican Army. But the Texan army looked more like a rabble than a military force capable of defeating Cos's soldiers in San Antonio, let alone the much larger forces marching north to crush the revolt. "Words are inadequate to convey an impression of the appearance of the first Texas army," recalled one veteran, Noah Smithwick, decades later, remembering the torn clothes, beaver hats, broad sombreros, moccasins, leather shoes, and array of random weapons and farm animals that the Texans brought with them into San Antonio. The assemblage did not really act like an army, either. Soldiers debated orders before choosing whether or not to follow them. Men came and went as they pleased, alternately bored by the long siege, attracted by the prospect of a real battle, and enjoying the drinking and fun with their fellow soldiers. "In the name of almighty God," Austin pleaded with the convention, "send no more ardent spirits to this camp."

In the siege's second month, Austin ordered an attack on the Alamo, believing Cos's force to be demoralized and hungry. His officers told him that most of the army would not obey the order. A frustrated Austin left the scene, accepting the convention's charge that he travel to the United States to seek support for the rebellion in his home country. More men left the army, returning to their homes. Austin's replacement in (supposed) command at the scene received more reports of despair in the Mexican ranks, and ordered an attack. Again officers balked, and then several hundred more soldiers melted away from the Texan forces. The Texas government ordered a withdrawal of its army from San Antonio, but a furious settler named Ben Milam rallied the volunteers, crying out, "Who will

BECOMING INDEPENDENT 83

follow old Ben Milam into San Antonio?" Three hundred of
the Texans, including dozens of Tejanos led by Juan Seguín,
stormed the city. After several days of heavy fighting—in which
Milam himself was killed—Cos surrendered. San Antonio was
now in rebel hands.

Yet the Texans continued to be long on rhetoric and
drama, and short on organization and strategy. General Sam
Houston thought it foolish to plan to defend San Antonio
against the even larger invading forces on their way, preferring
instead to gather and train an army farther east on the Brazos
River. He wanted as much time as possible to prepare to fight
Santa Anna's army and ordered the destruction and abandon-
ment of the Alamo. At the same time, more men trickled into
the garrison. Most notable were the already famous former
Tennessee congressman Davy Crockett and the attorney and
former Alabama militia leader William Barret Travis, the latter of whom was appointed commander by the Texas government. James Bowie, elected by volunteers as commander, was
particularly impressed by the improvements made to the mission's defenses by Texian volunteers. He thought the rebels
could hold the fort for a time and thereby delay the advance of
the Mexican Army. They dug into the old church compound.
By some accounts, they flew the Mexican flag with "1824" on
it, the same flag that the tiny Texan navy boasted. This invoked
the liberal constitution under which Texas had been settled
by Americans and ensured the loyalty of Tejanos disgusted by
Santa Anna's dictatorship but who still saw themselves as Mexican patriots.

Soon this small band of fewer than two hundred was
surrounded by several thousand soldiers led by Mexican president Santa Anna. The second siege of the Alamo had begun.
Whereas the Texans had released Cos and his soldiers when
they took the Alamo, Santa Anna flew a red flag from San

84   BECOMING INDEPENDENT

Antonio's church, meaning that all defenders would be killed unless they surrendered. Travis, Crockett, and their compatriots remained defiant. Travis sent a message out through Mexican lines addressed "to the people of Texas & All Americans in the world," urging them to come to the aid of the besieged garrison but vowing to fight even if no more arrived. "Victory or Death" was the letter's conclusion.

This was powerful rhetoric. Travis's letter was reprinted in newspapers across the world and became a kind of holy scripture of Texas nationalism, read in Texas history classes and memorized by generations of schoolchildren. It also helped to push the Texians away from their earlier caution. It was harder and harder to imagine remaining loyal citizens of a nation conducting such merciless warfare. On March 2, with the Alamo still under siege, elected delegates announced that they were now fighting for independence. Their declaration was modeled closely after the U.S. Declaration of Independence of 1776, indicting the Mexican government for failing to live up to its promises to colonists and for violating its own constitution. All of the declaration's sixty signatories were white Americans, save for Tejanos Francisco Ruiz and José Antonio Navarro and the Mexican liberal Lorenzo de Zavala.

The delegates then wrote a constitution, which they also modeled closely after the U.S. Constitution, creating separate legislative, judicial, and executive branches. Some elements of the new system did reflect the influence of Spanish and Mexican legal traditions. Early Texas law, for example, gave greater protections to homesteads from taxation, to people in debt, and to women as property holders than did U.S. legal codes. And the constitution made it clear that Tejanos would be citizens of the new country.

Black people were another matter altogether. The constitution left no doubt that, for the Texan rebels, independence meant the continuation of slavery. In fact, it meant the institution's strengthening, because now the laws and government would clearly support the institution. As much as today's Texans talk about their revolution, they usually leave this part out, because it makes it hard to think of the revolution as a simple and glorious triumph of freedom. The new constitution said that "all persons of color who were slaves for life previous to their emigration to Texas, and who are now held in bondage," would remain enslaved for life. Still unnerved by the acts of the Mexican legislature that had outlawed slavery, the new leaders of Texas prevented its government from ever following a similar course. "Congress shall pass no laws to prohibit emigrants from bringing their slaves into the Republic with them . . . nor shall any slave holder be allowed to emancipate his or her slave or slaves without the consent of congress." Furthermore, the authors of the constitution made it illegal for any "free person of African descent, either in whole or in part" to live in Texas without an act of Congress explicitly allowing them to do so. In short, Black people had no rights in Texas.

The Texan rebels had declared themselves for independence and laid out a blueprint for the independent country they hoped to create. But they still lacked a credible way of achieving it. Unknown to the delegates as they began drafting the constitution, the defenders of the Alamo had been overwhelmed in a frontal assault by the vastly larger Mexican Army. Almost all of the mission's defenders died in combat, along with hundreds of the attackers. The survivors were a few combatants (almost certainly including Davy Crockett), the wives and children of some of the defenders (both Tejano and Texian), and a few enslaved men (including "Joe," owned by Travis, and "Sam," who belonged to James Bowie). True to his word, Santa Anna condemned the surviving combatants to death, overruling his more humane officers who wanted to treat the captives

86   BECOMING INDEPENDENT

as prisoners of war. He had the bodies of the slain Texans burned on two enormous funeral pyres, while the more numerous Mexican dead were buried or thrown into the San Antonio River. The stench of death hung over the town.

The overwhelming defeat at the Alamo was not even the biggest blow to Texan hopes. Receiving word of the fall of the Alamo, General Sam Houston ordered the large force of four hundred under the command of James Fannin at Goliad to join him in retreating eastward. Doing so would have brought the Texan army up to about eight hundred—still badly outnumbered, but perhaps enough to defeat the Mexican Army in battle at the right place and time. But Fannin dithered for a week before finally packing up to begin his march. Weak oxen pulling cannons and baggage slowed his march to a crawl. After only six miles, he stopped for rest in the middle of an exposed prairie, ignoring the pleas of his men to march until they reached a more defensible line of trees. Mexican cavalry surrounded the exposed force. The Texans fought back, but they were surrounded and out of water. The next morning, they surrendered. On Palm Sunday, Mexican officers carried out Santa Anna's orders, executing nearly four hundred prisoners.

The disaster outside of Goliad was the second crushing defeat—and the second massacre of surrendered men—for the Texans in three weeks. At this point, everybody thought the Texas Revolution had failed. American settlers in Texas packed up what belongings they could and fled east toward the United States, abandoning their dreams. "The desolation of the country through which we passed beggars description," remembered Noah Smithwick of the mass flight that came to be called the Runaway Scrape. "Houses were standing open, the beds unmade, the breakfast things still on the tables, pans of milk moulding in the dairies. There were cribs full of corn, smoke houses full of bacon, yards full of chickens that ran after us for food, nests of eggs in every fence corner, young corn and garden truck rejoicing in the rain, cattle cropping the luxuriant grass, hogs, fat and lazy, wallowing in the mud, all abandoned." To Smithwick, it seemed that even the pets knew something terrible was happening. "Forlorn dogs roamed around the deserted homes, their doleful howls adding to the general sense of desolation. Hungry cats ran mewing to meet us, rubbing their sides against our legs in token of welcome."

What looked like a disaster for white settlers appeared as an opportunity for their slaves. When Mexican armies entered Texas in the fall of 1835, one of the wealthy settlers wrote to Austin informing him that he and other masters had crushed a slave revolt: "the negroes on the Brazos made an attempt to rise . . . near 100 had been taken up and many whipd nearly to death some hung etc." In the Runaway Scrape, many slaves ran the other way, south and west toward the Mexican Army and freedom. Ann Thomas recalled that four of her family's six slaves fled to the Mexican Army, "being promised their freedom on doing so," she assumed. At least fourteen enslaved people similarly escaped their owners in Victoria in April, as so many Texans were fleeing east. Any independence that these individuals gained came from leaving Texas.

Thrilled with his victories at the Alamo and Goliad, Santa Anna did not think that the upstart rebels could resist him. "It's a dangerous thing to despise your enemy," noted a Texan officer of the dictator's overconfidence. Santa Anna made the fateful mistake of dividing his forces. Four different armies headed east in search of the Texan government and Houston's army. One of the detachments found Houston's army, but could not cross the rain-swollen Colorado River to attack it. Houston again retreated east, camping for two weeks at Jared Groce's

88   BECOMING INDEPENDENT

plantation on the Brazos. Here his men rested and drilled, joined by hundreds more Texan refugees and newly arrived Americans. When Santa Anna led one army toward the Texan government, Houston saw his opportunity (or, claimed his detractors, was forced into fighting by his angry and restless soldiers). The Texans raced toward a crossing at Buffalo Bayou east of what is now Houston, taking up a strong defensive position in an oak grove at a ranch called San Jacinto. The Mexican army of 1,200 outnumbered the Texan force of 900. Its officers were thus not expecting the Texan attack that came in the midafternoon of April 21. The Texans—including a cavalry detachment led by Juan Seguín, who had left the Alamo before its fall in search of reinforcements—overran the Mexican lines. They spent most of the rest of the day killing their opponents. Half of Santa Anna's army was slaughtered and he was captured. "The dead Mexicans lay in piles," remembered one veteran.

Mexico still had far more soldiers in the field than the rebel province did. But the captive Mexican president ordered his generals to retreat west. Summer rains, disease, and months on the trail decimated the remaining Mexican forces. Texians and rebellious Tejanos returned to their houses, farms, and ranches. Against all odds, the Texas Revolution had succeeded. What began as an effort to preserve what Austin and other American immigrants and Tejano leaders such as the Seguíns had achieved as loyal Mexicans ended in the birth of a new country, the Republic of Texas.

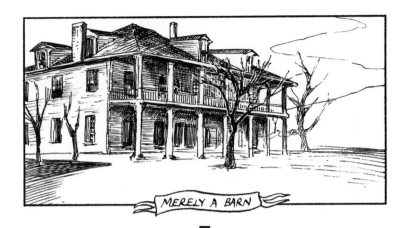

MERELY A BARN

7
Being Independent

The Texas Revolution was a drama, and not just for those living through it. Austin's imprisonment, the sieges and massacres of survivors at the Alamo and Goliad, and the shocking Texan victory at San Jacinto were all sensational news on both sides of the Atlantic within weeks. Texans realized what an asset this story could be, painting themselves as courageous freedom fighters. "We were a little band," Sam Houston said when he became the first president of the Republic of Texas, "contending for liberty; they were thousands, well appointed, munitioned, and provisioned, seeking to rivet chains upon us, or extirpate us from the earth."

Yet the next chapter in this gripping story remained unclear. Would the Texas Revolution become part of American history, with Texas joining the United States? Or would Texas remain the lead character of its own drama as an independent country? Or—equally likely—would Mexico, still vastly larger than the Lone Star Republic, get its act together and reconquer its lost province? Would Native peoples maintain their power and territory, or be conquered or expelled by whatever government ruled Texas? What would these and other possible fates mean for slavery, which still made slaveowners rich despite growing opposition to it across the world?

As with the Texas Revolution, we know how this story ends: with the incorporation of Texas as the 28th state of the United States in 1845, less than a decade after it gained its independence. But like the success of the Texas Revolution, this was not the only possible outcome. And what was a triumph for some was a great loss for others.

The Republic of Texas had its independence, but not much else. About 30,000 Anglo Americans (the records of the early republic are not the best, so we cannot be precise about population numbers) were joined by almost 3,500 Tejanos as citizens with legal rights under the constitution. Many Tejanos doubted whether the majority population would respect their rights, despite the loyalty and bravery that leaders like Juan Seguín had shown on the battlefield. As many as 5,000 slaves, almost all belonging to Anglo Texans, rounded out the republic's population. Since the richest Americans were less likely to move to Texas, these slaves lived in small groups on the farms of their owners rather than on larger plantations as was the case back in the United States. Enslaved Texans resented their bondage, being torn from their families and friends back in the United States, and knew that freedom was theirs if they could cross to Mexican territory. Nearly 15,000 Native people—Comanches were still the most numerous and powerful—lived inside and on the edge of the new country, and were intent on preserving their territory and livelihoods. Mexico, with a pop-

BEING INDEPENDENT 91

ulation of more than seven million, refused to recognize the legitimacy of the Texas government. The country's leaders laughed at Texan claims that the length of the Rio Grande, which started in what is now southern Colorado and cut in half the Mexican state of Nuevo México, was the rightful border. And they hoped and planned for a reconquest of the breakaway province.

The government that Anglo Texans and their Tejano allies created was not very well equipped to deal with so many challenges. The nation's capital was the small hamlet of Columbia on the lower Brazos River. A wooden house was used for the Congress to gather, but congressmen and other visitors had to sleep outside on the ground or on crude wooden pallets. Stephen F. Austin, who became secretary of state after Sam Houston crushed him in the presidential election by more than ten to one, lived in an unheated shed attached to one of the town's private homes. He suffered from recurrent fevers that may have been caused by malaria. Within months of assuming his new office, he came down with pneumonia and died, in December of 1836, at only forty-three years of age.

Soon the new government relocated to the new town of Houston, lured by the promises of developers to provide land and buildings for the nation's government at no cost. Here the legislature met in an actual two-story capitol building ("merely a barn," sniffed one French visitor), and Sam Houston worked out of a shack with a small shed to house official papers. Poor drainage meant trudging through ankle-deep mud for most of the year. A lack of housing and swarms of mosquitos made life in the new capital unpleasant and even outright dangerous. Dysentery, yellow fever, and malaria were frequent visitors. At one point, Houston ripped out some of his wooden floor for firewood. One congressman wrote to his wife that "we live like hogs."

Governments need money to operate. The Texas government had none. It already owed more than a million dollars to Americans who had funded the secession effort. It needed money to pay off this debt, raise an army, set up county governments to enforce the law, run some courts to resolve legal disputes, and pay its officials. But since no other countries recognized its legitimacy, it could not borrow from banks in the United States, England, or anywhere else. So it issued its own treasury bills, which foreign investors were reluctant to purchase. It tried taxing imports—the most important way that national governments across the world raised money at the time—but many of its own citizens just smuggled goods across the border with the United States, which the Texan government could not afford to police. At least a third of the republic's citizens refused to pay the direct tax on property to which their government next turned. As a result, its remaining soldiers were poorly paid and barely fed, high officials went for years without any salary, and citizens who wanted mail had to hire private carriers to transport it. The one commodity Texas had in abundance was land. But it could afford to hire only one person to staff the office charged with the enormous task of weighing sometimes conflicting claims to millions of acres administered by three governments (Spain, Mexico, and now Texas) and issuing titles that would allow that land to be bought, sold, and used as collateral for debts.

The obvious weakness of the Texas government created a dynamic in which foreign nations and the republic's own citizens looked on it with contempt, making its success even less likely. Texas "may still be considered a mere experiment upon independence which the loss of friends or of a single battle may disperse to the winds," wrote back an agent sent by the U.S. government. His British counterpart's description of the government as "a band of outlaws who occupy Texas" was a bit more scathing, but no more so than one Anglo Texan's portrayal of it as "perhaps the most imbecile body that ever sat judgment on the fate of a nation."

The obvious way to solve these many problems was to join the United States. Becoming another state of the Union would entitle Texas to the defense of the U.S. Army and eliminate the import tax charged on its cotton in New Orleans and other American ports. Even more Americans would be willing to move to Texas, bringing their slaves and other valuable property with them. The land-rich but cash-poor earlier arrivals could quickly become wealthy simply by selling some of their land to their new neighbors. And almost all were from the United States, so statehood would have been the resumption of a familiar identity and legal status—as Houston put it, "to be reunited to the great Republican family of the North." The election in September 1836 that made him president also included a proposition that the government seek annexation. It passed overwhelmingly. The Houston administration quickly pursued it, sending representatives to Washington, D.C., to make the case to what they hoped would be a sympathetic U.S. government.

Yet the United States declined. President Andrew Jackson, concerned by the weakness of the Texas government and the prospect of war with Mexico, was not willing even to extend formal diplomatic recognition. And he was not at all sure that he could get the congressional votes needed for annexation, because, as the Texan delegates soon realized, their case for joining the Union was entangled in the most divisive question in American life, one that within a generation would rip the country apart: slavery.

An institution that was present in British colonies before the birth of the United States in 1776 (and in many societies long before that), by 1836 slavery had come under sustained

94   BEING INDEPENDENT

moral and political attack. The same beliefs in human equality that prompted the leaders of Mexico and other newly independent countries in the rest of Latin America to outlaw the practice had gained traction in the English-speaking world as well. The northern parts of the United States had outlawed slavery in preceding decades. And in 1833, just a few years before the Texas Revolution, England had outlawed the practice in all of its domains. Abolition, as the organized effort to end slavery was called, was a worldwide social movement that Texas could not escape. Yet slavery remained highly profitable where it was still practiced. White Americans in the South, like their counterparts in other slave societies such as Brazil and Cuba, developed sophisticated economic practices such as mortgages and insurance based on slave property, and, like the Republic of Texas, actively defended the institution. They were powerful enough in the U.S. Congress to ban even discussion of petitions against slavery, enraging abolitionists and enflaming public opinion.

American abolitionists despised the Texas Revolution and the government it had created. Benjamin Lundy, one of the country's most important abolitionists, had a deep history with Texas and soon became the most vocal opponent of admitting it into the Union. Given the importance of slavery to the Lone Star Republic's economy, and the extensive protections its constitution gave to slavery, Lundy and his allies knew that Texas as a state would send pro-slavery representatives and senators to Washington, thereby strengthening the hand of slaveholders in American politics. Amazingly, Lundy had lived in the small Missouri town of Herculaneum around 1820, when Moses Austin and his son Stephen also lived there. He must have known them. Lundy was also very interested in Texas, but as a place where free Black people and emancipated slaves might move and live in dignity and freedom. By the time of the Texas

Revolution, he had received tentative approval from the Mexican government to settle a colony of emancipated slaves in the province, where they could live and be free. The revolution's success dashed those hopes.

Lundy and his allies wrote about Texas in newspaper articles and books that were read not only across the United States, but more widely in the English-speaking world. They told a story about Texas that in some ways was similar to the one told by Texas partisans, marveling that a disorganized, chaotic army of frontier rabble had been able to wrest independence from the vastly larger nation of Mexico. But for abolitionists, the rebellious Texans were the villains rather than the heroes, because they were enslavers. The revolution was the triumph of oppression, not freedom. "The immediate cause and the leading object" of the revolution, Lundy proclaimed, was a "settled design, among the slaveholders of this country, (with land-speculators and slave-traders,) to wrest the large and valuable territory of Texas from the Mexican Republic, in order to re-establish the SYSTEM OF SLAVERY; to open a vast and profitable SLAVE-MARKET therein; and, ultimately, to annex it to the United States." The charges prompted northern congressional representatives, including former U.S. president John Quincy Adams, to mobilize against annexation. For the time being at least, Texas could not join the United States.

The abolitionist attacks created an image of Texans that has lasted just as long as the heroic story of the Alamo. For Lundy and his circles, white Texans embodied the worst qualities of the United States—ignorance, crudeness, a refusal to accept legitimate authority, and, above all, the violent domination of others. This is an image of Texans that has barely changed over time and has lasted until today. One abolitionist cartoon was typical in its portrayal of "Young Texas in Repose"—a dirty man with unkempt hair, a broad-brimmed

96 BEING INDEPENDENT

hat, a long Kentucky rifle, and a Bowie knife, a whip next to him, with the words "incest," "rape," "murder," "fraud," and (repeated several times) "slavery" inked on his arm. "Young Texas" lounged on a slave whose hands were chained and back disfigured from being whipped. To welcome a state led by such men into the Union would be to betray, as Lundy put it, "the great fundamental principles of universal liberty—the perpetuity of our free republican institutions—the prosperity, the welfare, and the happiness of future generations." For him, the fight over Texas was a fight for the United States and whether it could ever be a country with freedom for all.

With annexation stopped for the moment, Texas was left to chart its course alone. Sam Houston was well suited to lead a country with so much going against it. Very much like Stephen F. Austin, he had come of age in a world where the United States and white Americans could not simply do as they pleased to others. Indian nations in particular were powers to be reckoned with. Houston grew up in Tennessee with Cherokee neighbors, with whom he lived for years at a time when he grew tired of his own family's demands. His adoptive Indian family gave him the name Colonneh, or Raven. His affection for them was lifelong; when Houston quit the governorship of Tennessee in scandal, he departed to Indian Territory, again living with his Cherokee friends. There he dressed as his Indian neighbors did, and married a Native woman. These connections were very helpful during the Texas Revolution. Houston negotiated a treaty with Cherokees led by Duwali, or "Chief Bowl," in East Texas who had been expelled from the United States. In exchange for a guarantee of their right to own land in the new republic, Cherokees stayed out of the war, allowing Houston's army to deal only with Mexican forces.

Now that Texas was its own country and he was its president, he thought that continuing this pattern was key to Texan diplomacy. Whites and Indians could and should live in peace, Houston insisted. He sought treaties and alliances with the Indian nations of Texas, urging Texans to "abstain on our part from aggressions, establish commerce with the different tribes, supply their useful and necessary wants, maintain even-handed justice with them." The result would be that "natural reason will teach them the utility of our friendship." Under his leadership, the Republic of Texas was not as successful in striking an arrangement with Comanches as it had been with Cherokees. But the country avoided an all-out war with either them or Mexico, did not go further into debt, and began the extraordinary growth that would see its population nearly triple by 1840.

Mirabeau Lamar followed Houston as the Lone Star Republic's second president in 1838. Lamar also emphasized the need for military security as well as a resumption of migration from the United States and the economic growth that the latter would bring. But he was either more optimistic or more reckless than Houston, depending on how you look at it. Lamar urged Texans to dream big. Like almost all white Texans, Lamar was from the United States and had even served two terms in the senate of his native Georgia. Yet he didn't want Texas to become part of the American dream, but instead to chart its own course. If Texas joined the United States, it would be "the grave of all her hopes of happiness and greatness," and Lamar would "feel that the blood of our martyred heroes had been shed in vain." Under his leadership, Texas followed in the footsteps of slightly older republics such as Mexico and the United States. It adopted a new flag—featuring a large five-pointed star that is still familiar all over the world today—and celebrated its own holidays, with March 2 as its independence day and April 21 dedicated to marking the glorious victory over Mexico at San Jacinto.

Texas was growing into its own country, with its own symbols, mythology, and patriotism. Lamar thought it could not just survive, but grow powerful. Texas produced a key good of increasing value to the world—cotton. Lamar thought this would lead nations like Great Britain to ignore the charges of abolitionists and instead establish formal diplomatic relations and trade agreements. There was a "high destiny" awaiting Texas, he told his fellow citizens. He foresaw a nation that would survive its infancy and grow into a "vast extent of territory, stretching from the Sabine to the Pacific . . . embracing the most delightful climate and the richest soil in the world," and predicted that its "mountains of mineral yielding their vast treasures to the touch of industry [and] luxuriant pastures alive with flocks and herds, and her wide fields whitening with a staple commodity" would make it an economic powerhouse.

Lamar celebrated the hardscrabble pioneer virtues and fighting spirit of Texans—or Texians, as he preferred to call the republic's citizens. But he also thought that a well-funded education system would serve the young country well. At his urging, its Congress set aside some of the enormous landholdings claimed by the nation to fund its primary schools, with the hope of starting a state university in the future. The lands set aside were later used to fund Texas A&M University (established in 1876) and the University of Texas (founded in 1881). Education, Lamar believed, would not only enhance the culture and "morals" of Texans, but enhance its agriculture and contribute to its military might. And it would keep Texans living in freedom. "A cultivated mind is the guardian genius of Democracy," he concluded, "the only dictator that freemen acknowledge." The University of Texas at Austin adopted the

Latin translation of Lamar's line about a cultivated mind as its motto.

Propelled by a fighting spirit, a powerful national mythos, and high ambitions, surely Texas could overcome the obstacles that it faced and survive, perhaps even thrive, as an independent country.

8

Losing Independence

President Lamar was right to see Texas as a huge force in history. The republic didn't just shape the destiny of its inhabitants; soon it redrew the entire map of North America. Yet it did not do so as its president envisioned—by succeeding as its own country—but by failing the test of independence. Lamar dragged Texas into a series of unnecessary wars with its neighbors that it had no chance of winning. These conflicts deepened divisions within Texas society and sunk its government deeper and deeper into debt. Seven years after Lamar became president and prophesied a Texas empire stretching west to the Pacific, Texas gave up its independence and became another of the United States.

The contrast between Lamar and Houston is a curious one. Houston is a part of the Texas pantheon in a way that Lamar is not—I grew up near a Lamar High School, but like most of my generation, I didn't really know who he was until I studied Texas history. We all knew about Houston and his glorious defeat of Santa Anna. Yet where Houston succeeded by being cautious and understanding the limits of his own power—retreating from the Mexican Army despite howls of protest, and striking deals with Indian neighbors, to name two examples—Lamar had the brashness and confidence to the point of arrogance that came to be associated with the Texan persona.

Lamar's policy toward Indians is a good example. Lamar and his supporters viewed Indians as one of the great obstacles to the fulfillment of their visions. Where Houston recognized Native power and hoped that treaties and fair treatment could bring security, Lamar saw Indians as a threat that could be eliminated only by violence. Indians were "debased and ignorant savages" who were making "disastrous and cruel warfare upon our neglected border settlements." He could not see that Indian peoples had "any just cause of complaint" for their treatment. Negotiating with them or hoping for peace in return for fair treatment had failed because it just made Texas look weak. "As long as we continue to exhibit our mercy without shewing our strength, so long will the Indian continue to bloody the edge of the tomahawk, and move onward in the work of rapacity and slaughter," he proclaimed at his inauguration.

Lamar lived up to these promises, plunging the republic into expensive and bloody wars with Indians. He sent an army of five hundred to remove Cherokee settlers in July of 1839 from their homes outside of Nacogdoches. Cherokees, along with Shawnee, Kickapoo, and Delaware friends and family, fled in advance of the army, knowing that they did not have the numbers to defeat it. The soldiers caught up to them near present-day Tyler. They killed Duwali, scalped him, left his body to rot, and as a final act sent his hat, originally given to him by Sam Houston, to Houston in order to ridicule him and his closeness to Cherokees. Duwali's people scattered to Arkansas, to Indian lands north of Texas in what the U.S. government had come to call "Indian Territory," and to Mexico. They were victims of what would today be called "ethnic cleansing," or maybe even genocide. "The white man and the red man cannot dwell in harmony together," Lamar bluntly stated. According to him, Indians should be eliminated from Texas, whether that meant pushing them beyond its borders or simply killing them.

This was easier said than done. Comanches proved too formidable for Lamar to kill or expel. They were no longer as powerful by the 1830s as they had been before. Bison populations on the Texas Plains were in decline, not from hunting by Americans, but rather from a complicated environmental crisis created by the wealth and power that Comanche society had built over the previous century. Since bison hides remained valuable trade goods, Comanches could garner wealth by hunting them, even if they killed more bison than were born in a year. Horses and mules, which were valuable because they could carry people and property but also because they could be traded for cash, guns, and other manufactured goods, were also vivid signs of Comanche wealth. By the 1830s, most Comanche families probably had ten to twenty horses. Rich households held dozens or even hundreds. In these families, men had multiple wives, with those they married later performing the difficult work of processing dead buffalo skins into flexible hides. This involved washing the heavy skins, attaching them to a rack to dry, scraping excess fat and meat from their insides, and then preparing a paste from other parts of the dead bison to pound into the hide to make it flexible and soft. The fact that Comanches used a special word to refer to these lower-status wives, which roughly translates into English as "chore-wives," tells us something about how hard this work was.

LOSING INDEPENDENCE   103

The wealth that this kind of labor created was bad news for the bison: horses and mules crowded them out of the river bottoms that provided shelter in winter and may have passed along livestock diseases such as anthrax. Whatever the cause of the decline of bison numbers, the result was that Comanche society was not as resilient as before, and was notably slower to recover population numbers after epidemic diseases than it had been in the early 1800s. Their military position was weaker as well—Cheyenne and Osage pressured them from the north, and what one Texas newspaper described as "a kind of exterminating war" with Cherokees, Shawnees, and other refugee people expelled from the United States broke out in the 1830s.

Yet they were still a force to be reckoned with, able to assemble thousands of fighters and move rapidly. Indeed, in the 1830s and '40s, Comanches extended their reach farther and farther south, taking livestock and captives from Mexican ranches and towns as far south as the city of Querétaro (more than five hundred miles south of the Rio Grande). The raids were brutal, but attackers were careful not to entirely destroy the ranches. To some Mexican observers it looked a lot like they were being harvested by Comanches—they would feed, raise, and train horses and mules only to see most of them taken north year after year. What was terrorizing for Mexicans was lucrative for Comanches. The livestock taken from northern Mexico allowed them to have larger herds than could be supported by the overgrazed Texas Plains, while the human captives they took were adopted and helped to maintain their population numbers. And this extension of Comanche power kept the Mexican government preoccupied with defending its remaining northern states rather than trying to reconquer Texas. For as much as Texans came to hate Comanches, in an odd way Comanches helped them tremendously.

Texas settlers were better armed than Mexican ranchers

and the cotton they grew was of less interest than Mexican livestock. So the Republic of Texas did not bear the brunt of Comanche might. But Lamar's aggressive policies did bring Comanches and Texans into a bloody conflict that neither side won. In March 1840 a Penateka Comanche band led by Muk-wah-ruh accepted an offer from Lamar's government to come to San Antonio to exchange some of their captives and negotiate some kind of peace deal. Comanches brought only one white captive with them, a teenager named Matilda Lockhart, who observers reported was covered in bruises and sores from torture. The Texans decided to hold Native envoys hostage in the house where they were meeting. Soldiers came into the room, Comanches resisted, and the Texans opened fire. A dozen Comanche leaders were killed in the room, with another eighteen killed outside alongside three women and two children they had brought to demonstrate their sincerity in seeking a peace treaty. Seven Texan combatants died.

The war between Texas and Penateka Comanches that followed was destructive but not decisive. A charismatic leader known to Texans as Buffalo Hump gathered a Comanche and Kiowa army of five hundred. In August they laid waste to a big chunk of South Texas, coming down the Guadalupe River valley heading southeast. In addition to attacking isolated farms, the Comanche force surrounded the town of Victoria, where they captured hundreds of horses and mules. Several white farmers and their enslaved laborers were killed, and about fifty defenders massed in the town's center with "panic-stricken citizens," as one witness remembered, "speculating with agonizing suspense upon the fate that would probably befall us." Luckily for them, the Comanches only burned one home and then moved down the river valley to the town of Linnville on the coast, capturing more livestock and trading goods as they went. When they reached Linnville two days later, the residents were able to flee on ships into the Gulf of Mexico. From the deck they watched the looting of their town.

Having retaliated for the murder of their families and taken possession of thousands of horses and mules, the Comanche force began a long retreat northwest toward the Plains and the territory over which they still had unrivaled control. Texan volunteers ambushed them outside of Lockhart, killing perhaps eighty. A Texan invading force entered Penateka territory that fall, killing dozens of Comanche men. The Republic of Texas could not, on one hand, expel or exterminate Comanches, as it had Cherokees. Indeed, Texans so feared Comanche power that for several years after the sacking of Linnville they all but abandoned Austin, the new capital that Lamar had unwisely selected despite its isolated and vulnerable location. On the other hand, Texas was populous and well-armed enough to fight Comanches to a draw. In the contest for control of Texas, for the first time in a century, Comanches were no longer the most powerful force.

President Lamar hoped to expel Indians from Texas altogether. He approached relations with Mexico with a similar swagger. The Republic of Texas claimed the Rio Grande as its western boundary. This claim was a stretch, since the Nueces River had been the southern boundary of Mexican Texas, and the republic had no control of the stretch of land between the Nueces and the Rio Grande known as the "Nueces Strip." As part of his vision of a Texas that stretched all the way to the Pacific, Lamar took it seriously. And he meant the whole Rio Grande, which stretched all the way north through the middle of the Mexican territory of New Mexico.

New Mexico was a very different place than Texas. Only a handful of American residents lived in a territory where Spanish-Mexican settlements founded in the early 1600s, a full century before Spanish Texas, were nestled among dozens of long-standing Pueblo Indian towns, forming a distinctive society with their Comanche, Navajo, Ute, and Apache neighbors. Until the huge influx of white Americans into Texas in the 1830s, New Mexico had always been more populous than its southeastern neighbor and certainly more important to Spain.

Lamar thought it should be part of Texas, and although he had never even seen New Mexico, he knew there was discontent with the rule of a distant government based in Mexico City that was unable or unwilling to prioritize the needs of the northern frontier. So Lamar thought maybe New Mexicans would want to join the republic and become Texans. Even if not, perhaps they would trade with the Lone Star Republic. The Texan Congress was unwilling to fund an expedition, fearing that it would bankrupt the republic and provoke Mexico to invade. Lamar pressed ahead anyway, assembling a group of merchants who brought goods worth $200,000 (more than $6 million in the 2020s) and a volunteer military force. Lamar prepared a proclamation that he wanted read to the citizens of Santa Fe. Overconfident to the point of being pretentious, it referred to "our late glorious revolution . . . made secure by a wise and liberal constitution," and offered to "receive the people of Santa Fe as a portion of the national family," or at least to open up trading relations.

The expedition turned out to be a disaster, its three hundred members crawling across the sometimes rugged terrain between Austin and Santa Fe, becoming lost, being forced to eat their own mounts and dogs to avoid starvation, and limping into New Mexico in September 1841, nearly four months after they departed. Out of food and in poor health, they gladly surrendered to the soldiers that New Mexico's governor had waiting for them. The Texans were imprisoned and marched to Mexico City, some 1,400 miles away.

A similar invasion of Mexico the following year turned out to be just as much of a failure. A volunteer army of seven hundred Texans crossed the Nueces River and captured Laredo, which was north of the Rio Grande and thus within the territory claimed by Texas. Its supposed mission accomplished, the army's general ordered the force to disband. Most of the volunteers, fueled by ambitious visions of growing Texan power, refused. Instead they crossed the Rio Grande and captured the small town of Mier. A Mexican army attacked them, taking most prisoner. The captives were forced to draw from a jar of beans, with the result that those who drew one of seventeen black beans were executed. The rest were marched to Mexico City. So ended the dreams of a Republic of Texas defeating its enemies and expanding into an empire of its own.

One of the commissioners that President Lamar sent with the doomed Santa Fe expedition was José Antonio Navarro. Navarro, one of the leaders of Mexican Texas who had done the most to welcome Stephen F. Austin and make his endeavors successful, was one of the three Mexican signatories of the Texas Declaration of Independence. His inclusion in an expedition intended to bring tens of thousands of Mexican citizens into the Texan fold shows that some leading white Texans at the time thought there was an important place for people of Mexican descent in the republic. Texans like Lamar saw families like the Seguíns, Navarros, and Ruizes—relatively wealthy, happy to command the labor of Black and Native slaves—as their counterparts and even equals. Many American men who had moved to Texas in the Mexican period were married to women from these families. Lorenzo de Zavala, one of Mexico's leading liberal figures, served as vice president of the

108   LOSING INDEPENDENCE

Republic of Texas during its struggle for independence. Juan Seguín was rewarded for his service on the battlefield against Santa Anna by being elected to the republic's Senate, and then as mayor of San Antonio in 1840. In this sense, the Tejano–Anglo American alliance that had given birth to Austin's settlements in Texas and that had won the Texas Revolution survived into the republic.

But it was getting weaker and weaker. The more recently arrived a white American was, the more likely they were to show little understanding, interest, or respect for Mexican residents. Unlike Austin and other arrivals a decade earlier, they showed little desire to learn Spanish or socialize with Tejano neighbors. Indeed, some did not want people of Mexican descent to have any rights in Texas. In Nacogdoches, where the small Tejano community was soon badly outnumbered, American immigrants petitioned the Texas government to strip them of the right to vote and serve on juries. Land claims and legal disputes became the center of new conflicts. White law enforcement officers often refused to investigate claims of violence or theft against Tejanos. The legal system was very slow in confirming title to land ownership; in Nacogdoches, for example, virtually all Tejano families had owned land before the revolution but less than a fifth were able to have their ownership legally confirmed under the republic. "At every hour of the day and night," Juan Seguín later remembered, "my countrymen ran to me for protection against the assaults of extractions of those adventurers." Tejanos were losing the independence for which so many had fought the Spanish crown and Santa Anna's dictatorship.

At times, these tensions grew into large-scale violence. In Nacogdoches in 1838, several hundred angry Tejanos and members of several Indian groups took up arms and rallied behind Vicente Córdova. Córdova was the town's former mayor and had earlier petitioned the Texas Congress about the violation of Tejano property rights. He and his followers announced that they were ready to shed "the last drop of blood" they had in defense of their "individual rights." They were dispersed by the Texan army, and Córdova fled to Mexico.

Juan Seguín was forced on a similar path. After a Mexican army briefly occupied San Antonio in March of 1842, he became the target of charges that he had betrayed the republic to Mexico. Many threatened to kill him for this supposed crime. He resigned as mayor and fled to Mexico. "I had to leave Texas, abandon all for which I had fought and spent my fortune, to become a wanderer." Seguín blamed the rabble of San Antonio—"the scum of society . . . many bad men, fugitives from their country, who found in this land an open field for their criminal designs." But he was also abandoned by the leaders of the Republic of Texas. One general, for example, dismissed Seguín as "unfit for command." Seguín, who had done as much as anybody to settle Americans in Texas and free it from a ruthless autocrat, found himself "a foreigner in my own country."

Soon enough, Seguín's homeland would belong to another country. The prospect of annexation had always appealed to the Anglo majority of the Republic of Texas. The republic's difficulties only made incorporation into the United States seem more appealing: the expense of Indian wars drove the government deeper into debt, making its money all but worthless. And the sharp decline of world cotton prices in the early 1840s—at a point when cotton was nearly 90 percent of its exports—worsened economic conditions in Texas. "We are in collapse," admitted Sam Houston's secretary in a private letter. Even Mirabeau Lamar, the champion of independence and dreamer of Texan empire, came around to support trading independence for statehood.

Changes in politics in the United States created an opening for annexation just big enough for Texas to squeeze through. The Tennessee Democrat James K. Polk ran for the presidency of the United States in 1844 on a platform of unapologetic expansionism, even at the risk of war with Great Britain over where the border with Canada would be in the Pacific Northwest and war with Mexico over Texas. Earlier that year, a treaty annexing Texas to the United States had been voted down in the Senate by more than two to one, but Polk championed it nonetheless. This ensured that he won the support of southern states, where the political establishments were coming to value the protection and extension of slavery above all other issues. Polk won enough northern states to squeak to victory. If his opponent, who did not support the annexation of Texas, had won a few thousand more votes in New York, or had storms hit New York City on election day and resulted in fewer Democratic voters going to the polls, Polk would not have become president. As a result, Texas would have been forced to remain independent, likely coming to resemble Latin American nations like Argentina, torn by mutually hostile political parties (Lamar's expansionists and Houston's realists) and dependent on export crops such as cotton, with values that rose and fell sharply.

Heartened by Polk's victory, pro-annexation senators renewed their push. Previous annexation plans had assumed that a treaty—which had to be supported by two-thirds of the Senate—was required. This time, pro-annexationists took the legally questionable but practically clever step of proposing a simple congressional resolution, which needed only majorities in the U.S. Senate and House of Representatives. The measure passed by 120 to 98 in the House, and 27 to 25 in the Senate. Texas became the twenty-eighth state on December 29, 1845, joining a country that would soon go to war with itself over the very question of slavery that had previously kept Texas out of the Union.

9

Border State

The proponents of annexation believed that giving up independence would bring Texas greater prosperity and security. They were correct. Americanization brought strong economic and population growth and enormously changed the balance of power between Texas and Mexico. Yet it did not lessen divisions within Texas, especially over such questions as slavery and the status of Tejanos. Texas became stronger, wealthier, and more confident in itself, but it was no more unified as a part of the United States than it had been as an independent country.

When Texas stopped being the Lone Star Republic and became the Lone Star State, it started a continental war. In 1846, the newly inaugurated U.S. president, James Polk, sent soldiers across the Nueces River, knowing full well that they were entering territory that had never been part of Texas. When Mexican soldiers attacked them near Matamoros, Polk had the excuse for the war that he wanted. By 1848, American forces had captured much of the country and occupied its capital, forcing Mexico to surrender the enormous swath of territory that stretched from Texas to California.

In a sense, the war was an opportunity for Texas to strike back at Mexico. White Texans enthusiastically enlisted in the war effort. American officers were struck by their aggressiveness. Sometimes they were appalled, as with the general who complained that the Texan recruits "have scarcely made on expedition without unwarrantably killing a Mexican. There is scarcely a form of crime that has not been reported to me as committed by them." The war was a triumph in military terms for the United States, in part because much of the Mexican north, shell-shocked from decades of Comanche and Apache attacks and furious at their own government's inability to halt them, offered little resistance. Yet the war was not popular with the American public, especially the increasingly powerful abolitionist movement. A young congressman from Illinois named Abraham Lincoln first came to prominence by arguing that the attack on American forces took place in Mexico, not Texas. Decades later, the former general William Tecumseh Sherman visited the site of the battle and was confused as to how the long stretch of plains and brush that greeted him could have been the cause of such a momentous event. "We should go to war again, to make them take it back," he joked.

Debates over the legitimacy of the war and the correct location of the southern Texas border did nothing to dampen the appeal Texas held for settlers. Now that there was no prospect in sight that Mexico would invade and regain its breakaway territory, people flooded into Texas, boosting property values and sparking strong economic growth. The non-Indian population grew from about 142,000 in 1847 to more than

604,000 in 1860. Three-quarters of these new migrants came from other southern states. About a third of the population was enslaved. These bondsmen made up an outright majority in thirteen counties. This migration was so huge and slaves were such a large part of it that there were more enslaved people living in Texas by 1860 than there were people of any kind living there in 1846. The warnings of Benjamin Lundy and other abolitionists that the annexation of Texas would mean a huge expansion of slavery had come true.

American southerners and their human property were not the only new Texans, however. The legend of the Texas Revolution, especially of the Alamo, had already gained the Lone Star State international fame. The reputation of Texas as a land of abundance and freedom spread even farther. The largest source of migrants from outside the United States were the German-speaking lands, especially the countryside in the north and west near the Netherlands and Denmark. Small numbers of Germans came when Texas was under Mexican rule, drawn to Austin's colony by letters and newspaper articles praising the low price and high fertility of the land. Many more came after the war, since, as an organization dedicated to recruiting German migrants put it, "Texas has . . . become a link in the biggest and most secure chain of states in America, and on this mighty foundation is striding towards" a bright future. In addition to the pull factor of economic opportunity, there were events that pushed many Germans to leave their homes. Monarchies violently crushed revolutions seeking democratic self-governance throughout Europe in 1848 and 1849. Fleeing for their lives, these revolutionaries found not just security but freedom in Texas. A northerner visiting the Hill Country town of Sisterdale in 1854 was told that "there is hardly a gentleman in this company . . . that German tyrants . . . have

BORDER STATE 115

not condemned to death, or to imprisonment for life." Freedom
and opportunity seemed all the sweeter for having escaped such
a fate. "No kind of obstacles are put in a man's path, and he is
free to earn his livelihood in the most varied ways," wrote a
Prussian schoolteacher in his widely published and read diary
in 1849. "No restraining labor laws keep a man from trying his
hand at one thing or another. Your mind and spirit are given
great latitude and freedom. You can turn in any direction without encountering fetters or obstacles."

Germans were at most 5 percent of the state's population
in the 1850s. They made up a much smaller group than the
hundreds of thousands of Anglo and Black arrivals from southern states, though there were more German Texans than Tejanos. But almost all Germans settled in a belt from Houston
and Galveston in the east to Hondo in the west, with the area
of densest settlement in the Hill Country north and west of
San Antonio. Here they made up a heavy majority. The result,
as is so often the case with large-scale migration, was the creation of a society within a society, with distinctive food, music,
language, culture, and politics. Many observers referred to
Germans as a "race" different from (white) Texans, Mexicans,
Indians, and Blacks. One northern traveler was struck by "the
great variety of the crops" and the neatness of German fields,
which "contrasted favorably with the patches of corn-stubble,
overgrown with crab-grass, which are usually the only gardens
to be seen adjoining the cabins of the poor whites and slaves."
You could tell where Germans lived at a glance, just from
their houses, which were made of timber with plaster or brick
rather than nailed boards. "I have never in my life, except, perhaps in awakening from a dream, met with such a sudden and
complete transfer of associations," wrote the traveler of entering the German region.

Germans also held different beliefs than most other free migrants to the state. Because so many fled places ruled by monarchs and marked by violence between Catholics and Protestants, German nobles gave up titles (as when Baron Otfried Hans Freiherr von Meusebach took the name "John") and avoided Christianity altogether. "Freethinkers," as those skeptical of religion called themselves, supported democracy and reason over religious authority and hierarchy.

The relations between some Comanches and Germans showed the potential for German distinctiveness to create a very different society in Texas. In the 1840s, remarkably friendly relations arose between Comanches and German settlers in Fredericksburg. Comanches profited by selling deer meat and bear grease to the new arrivals, who were too poor and isolated to purchase the wheat flour and pork that they were used to eating. The town's postmaster, Theodore Sprecht, wrote that Comanche bands regularly stayed in town, sometimes sleeping overnight in the homes of German settlers; German men hunted in the countryside without fear of attack. Sprecht's vision of the future of Texas was as a place of harmony between Indians and white settlers, where good treatment and prosperity gradually persuaded the Comanches to remain in place and take up farming. In 1847, Comanche leaders Mopechucope, Buffalo Hump, and Santa Anna met with a German, Anglo, and Tejano delegation and worked out a peace treaty that for a time made the region an island of calm in an ocean of violence. John Meusebach, the settler delegation's leader, praised the virtues of peaceful coexistence and racial fusion. "When my people have lived with you for some time," he told the Comanche men, "and when we know each other better, it may happen that some wish to marry . . . I do not disdain my red brethren because their skin is darker, and I do not think more of the white people because their complexion is lighter."

Most Germans also viewed slavery very differently than did their Anglo neighbors. Although some owned slaves, many more hated the institution. One German settler, for example, went on and on and on about the beauty of the landscape and the fertility of the soil in his letters back home. But he railed against "the curse of slavery," which "the Germans bristle against . . . as it is contrary to the holiest right of man—freedom!" Slaveholders looked on the Germans with suspicion, fearing that they would aid runaway slaves. In 1854 a convention of Germans in San Antonio denounced slavery as "evil," but also rejected federal "interference" in state policies. Germans never started the kind of revolution against Texas slaveowners and their government of the sort that many had participated in back in Europe. Even so, the prominence and success of their settlements became quietly subversive, suggesting that new arrivals to Texas could prosper while respecting the humanity and rights of their Black and Indian neighbors.

The presence of an international border with Mexico posed a greater problem for slaveowners. The strengthening of slavery in Texas and the conflicts with Mexico had only deepened enslaved peoples' views of Mexico as a land of freedom. Human beings who were property north of the Rio Grande belonged to nobody but themselves on the south side. The flight of slaves from the South to freedom in the North or in Canada has become a well-known story to Americans, invoked by the phrase the "underground railroad." Much less well remembered is the story of escaping to freedom in Mexico. "There wasn't no reason to run up North," remembered the former slave Felix Haywood decades later. "All we had to do was to walk, but walk South and we'd be free as soon as we crossed the Rio Grande. In Mexico you could be free," he told his interviewer. "They didn't care what color you was, black, white, yellow, or blue. We would hear about [those who fled] and how they were going to be Mexicans. They brought up their children to speak only Mexican." Travelers and journalists visiting northern Mexico testified that they frequently saw escaped slaves, often in the company of their families.

Most of the enslaved in Texas lived far from the border, in the humid cotton-growing regions of eastern and central Texas, but many were willing and able to make journeys of hundreds of miles to reach freedom. Some came from Louisiana and Arkansas, and in at least one case, incredibly enough, from North Carolina. The dangers they faced in fleeing show how much they wanted to be free. "If they escape immediate capture by dogs or men," a northern traveler wrote of those brave enough to flee, "there is then the great dry desert country to be crossed, with the danger of falling in with savages, or of being attacked by panthers or wolves, or of being bitten or stung by the numerous reptiles that abound in it; of drowning miserably at the last of the fords; in winter, of freezing in another, and at all seasons, of famishing in the wilderness from the want of means to procure food."

The promise of freedom offered by the border was real enough to make flight much more common in Texas than in the South as a whole. Texas slave masters understood this threat. One warned that "unless something be done to arrest the escape of slaves, this class of property will become valueless in Western Texas." The wealthiest and most powerful Texans were all slaveowners—only one in four Texans owned slaves, but that quarter of society held three-quarters of the wealth. They used their influence to make sure the state government did all it could to stop their slaves from stealing themselves. In 1855, for example, the state governor authorized Texas Ranger officer James Callahan to form a company to fight Lipan Apaches and recapture fugitive slaves. Callahan's band of more than a hundred crossed into Mexico, where a mixed army of Mexicans, Seminole Indians, and Black people ambushed them. Callahan fled back toward the border, stopping in the town of Piedras Negras and burning much of it to the ground before returning to Texas soil. State officials tried to get the United States government to help, by securing a treaty with Mexico that would make the Mexican government responsible for deporting escaped slaves back to Texas. Mexico's government refused to sign.

One reason that slaves were so successful in escaping to Mexico was that some in the free population were willing to help them. Slaveowners looked on Germans as more likely to feed and even hide escaped slaves than other people of European descent, and feared Mexicans and Tejanos even more. In the 1850s, white residents of three Texas counties voted to expel all residents of Mexican descent as a precaution against slave uprisings.

The wealthiest and most powerful residents of northeastern Mexico had their own worries about what the border was doing to their society. Many of the largest estates used debts to keep workers on their property—constantly advancing them money for food and shelter, then using the debt to command their labor in an arrangement that some observers compared to slavery. Wages were higher in Texas than in Mexico, and debts could not be collected across the border, so ranch hands and farmworkers began moving north in large enough numbers to frustrate their employers. Major landowners in Mexico's northeast blamed the fugitives to Texas for draining manpower and money from their region. Like slaveholders in Texas, they enlisted their government to complain about runaways and to get the government on the other side of the river to arrest and send them back. The Texas stretch of the U.S.-Mexico border was controversial from the beginning, bringing what some thought of as chaos and theft and others experienced as freedom.

Enslaved people, exiled German revolutionaries, Comanches, white slaveowners, humble white farmers far too poor to own anybody, Mexican migrants, Tejanos: the state of Texas was home to many different kinds of people, a land of opportunity and freedom for some, a place of bondage and oppression for others. These divisions in 1850s Texas had the potential to cause not just conflicts and violence, but outright warfare. This became clear in 1859, when Juan Cortina visited Brownsville. Cortina, who grew up running cattle on both sides of the lower stretches of the Rio Grande, saw a sheriff beating an older man who had worked on his ranches. Cortina shot the sheriff, rode out of town with his victim, then returned several months later at the head of at least fifty men and seized control of the town, emptied its jails, and executed four whites whom he said had murdered Mexican residents but never faced justice.

The dramatic seizure of Brownsville and the darkly florid proclamations that Cortina issued ("our personal enemies," he threatened in one, "shall not possess our lands until they have fattened it with their own gore") commanded the attention of Texas. An alarmed governor dispatched the Texas Rangers to combat him. The federal government of the United States was concerned, too; it sent army units and eventually held congressional hearings about the uprising. Parts of the Mexican Army saw Cortina as a threat and joined the effort to suppress the uprising, but Cortina was not intimidated. Other Tejanos joined his forces, swelling his ranks into the hundreds. The resulting conflict came to be known as "Cortina's War." A few months later, an American army officer reported that "the

BORDER STATE 121

whole country from Brownsville to Rio Grande City, 120 miles
... has been laid waste, the citizens driven out. Business as far
up as Laredo, two hundred and forty miles has been inter-
rupted or suspended for five months."

Cortina attracted so many followers because his experiences of land loss and oppression were shared by so many Tejanos. Cortina was born in Camargo, a town on the south side
of the Rio Grande, in 1824 into a prominent ranching family.
Texas independence came when he was still a boy, but it made
little difference to how his family lived. Although they raised
cattle on lands mostly to the north of the river, in the territory
claimed by Texas, Mexican rule and law remained in force all
the way to the Nueces River until the U.S.-Mexico War in 1846.
The fact that his home and ranchlands were now in Texas
brought few changes at first. Almost all of his neighbors were
also Mexicans who had chosen to remain in Texas. They still
went to the same (Catholic) churches, spoke Spanish at home
and when they did business, used Mexican pesos instead of
U.S. dollars even with white American merchants, and crossed
the Rio Grande to buy and sell cattle, go to dances, and visit
friends and family. They considered Texas their home—their
families had, after all, been there long before people speaking
English and German showed up. And Texas offered them opportunities. For a time, Cortina worked for the U.S. Army hauling cargo with his horses and expanding his own livestock
herds. His brother was elected to be the county's tax assessor.

Cortina's opponents on both sides of the border portrayed him as an illiterate outlaw and a violent thug who hated
Texans and Americans. But Cortina and his followers did not
object to the United States or to being American. Indeed, he
said, the "Mexicans who inhabit this wide region, some because they were born therein, others because since the treaty
of Guadalupe Hidalgo they have been attracted to its soil by

the soft influence of wise laws and the advantage of a free government," believed "that only in the reign of peace can [they] enjoy, without inquietude, the fruit of [their] labor." What drove them to take up arms was that newly arrived Americans were using fraud, the court system, and the police to steal their lands. When his homeland became part of Texas, Cortina pronounced, "flocks of vampires, in the guise of men came and scattered themselves in the settlements, without any capital except the corrupt heart and the most perverse intentions." Mexicans living in Texas had the right to take up arms, because "many of you have been robbed of your property, incarcerated, chased, murdered, and hunted like wild beasts, because your labor was fruitful, and because your industry excited the vile avarice" of the newcomers.

Cortina offered an olive branch to Anglo Texans as well, expressing the hope that "the good sentiments" of Sam Houston, who had just won an election for governor, would mean that the "good inhabitants of the State of Texas" would look on Texans of Mexican descent "as brothers" and support the "legal protection" that they deserved. This moderate approach, however, failed to win the day. Defeat in a large battle in Rio Grande City in the waning days of 1859 forced him to retreat to Mexico with his followers, though it was not the last that Texas would hear from the man who had come to be known as the "Robin Hood of the Rio Grande."

This period of Texas history was thus bookended by wars—the conflict between the United States and Mexico set off when Texas became a state, and Cortina's failed uprising. One of the commanders of the U.S. military forces sent to defeat Cortina arrived in South Texas after participating in the capture of abolitionists who had seized a federal arsenal in Harpers Ferry,

Virginia, in the hopes of setting off an uprising that would end slavery. That man, Colonel Robert E. Lee, would soon play a leading role in another, much larger war that would bring enormous changes to Texas.

10

Civil Wars

Texans who lived through slavery in bondage held vivid memories of their liberation. "I well remember when freedom came," Preely Coleman told her interviewer in Tyler in the 1930s, seventy years after the fact. "We was in the field and master comes up says 'You is all as free as I am.' There was shouting and singing and before night we were all the way to freedom." Jacob Branch, interviewed the same year, could also picture the day clearly, though he was nearly ninety years old. For him it was the end of a drama that had gone on for years. A few years before emancipation, the plantation near Beaumont he lived on had been shaken by artillery bombardments from nearby battles. "After the war starts," he remembered, "lots of slaves runned off to get to the Yankees." Those who could not reach Union soldiers during their brief incursions into the Texas coast and Louisiana took advantage of wartime turmoil and the exodus of so many able-bodied white men to head to the Rio Grande. One day, Branch's owner assembled his slaves and read the "freedom papers" to them, proclaiming that they were all "free as hell." Branch's stepfather Charlie was "so happy he just rolled on the floor like a horse and kicked his heels."

The joy that Coleman, Branch, and countless others felt that day was a long time coming. It had been made possible by generations of the enslaved fleeing to freedom wherever they could find it—the northern states, Canada, or Mexico—and then writing and speaking of the horrors of rape, murder, child theft, and endless work they endured. Abolitionists insisted that the only way to end these outrages was to end the institution of slavery itself. Ironically, the leaders of the slave South ended up helping them: in 1861, eleven southern states left the United States, convinced that remaining in it threatened the practice of slavery, and they formed the Confederacy. At first the United States went to war to restore the status quo—a union with slavery. The Confederacy very nearly won the war, and probably would have killed the United States had it done so. But Confederate armies were defeated in 1865, and by then slaves and abolitionists had made the war a crusade to end slavery. The institution died with the Confederacy. Freedom came for four million Americans, 250,000 of whom lived in Texas.

Texas has been remembered as the western flank of the Confederacy. If you go to the amusement park Six Flags Over Texas outside of Fort Worth, you can see the Confederate flag waving alongside Spanish, Mexican, French, American, and the Lone Star banners. Many white Texans fought hard for the Confederate cause, and later generations honored their efforts by telling stories of their exploits, putting up statues all over the state, and naming schools and military bases after their generals. Secessionists won the vote to leave by an overwhelming margin, more than three to one. Only 18 of 122 counties voted to remain in the United States, clustered together in heavily German areas of central Texas and parts near Oklahoma where only a small number of slaves and slaveowners lived.

But it is too easy to call Texas a Confederate state and leave it at that. Texas did not just enter the U.S. Civil War on one side. The vote was so lopsided because so many were not allowed to vote. Jacob Branch would surely have voted against starting a war to keep him and his family enslaved. If you add the enslaved population—a third of the state in 1861—into the vote, Texas was split right down the middle over whether to leave the United States. And this rough calculation does not even account for the fact that many white, German, and Tejano voters were physically kept from the polls or scared into supporting secession by massive violence. Many, many Texans rejected the Confederacy and celebrated when it was defeated. The divisions within Texas—between enslaver and enslaved, white and Mexican, German and Anglo—had grown more and more violent since Texas joined the United States. They blew up when Texas tried to leave it, in some cases leading to civil wars within the Civil War.

It is revealing that Confederates had to push Sam Houston, the surviving hero of the Texas Revolution, out of the way in order for the state to secede. Houston, serving as governor at the time, had no patience for secession. Secessionist leaders wanted a convention to be called so that the state could follow other southern governments in leaving the United States. An act of the legislature was needed to call such a gathering. Houston refused to call the legislature into session, hoping thereby to avoid disunion. In a way he fought secession as he had fought Santa Anna's armies two decades before—by retreating, then waiting and watching, hoping for a chance to make a stand and seize an unlikely victory. This time it was not to be. A convention gathered despite his wishes, so he finally called the legislature into session. Once an election confirmed the convention's decision to leave the United States and join the Confederacy, state officeholders were required to swear an oath of loyalty to the Confederacy, as of March 2, 1861—Texas Independence Day. Houston refused, and was deposed as governor. He was a slaveowner, but placed a higher value on his loyalty as an American than he did on owning human property. The extreme toll of the war started by men like those who removed him from office—700,000 dead—took many by surprise, but Houston had years earlier presciently expressed his fear that political battles over the extension of slavery would bring "fields of blood," "scenes of horror," and "mighty cities in smoke and ruins."

What led the representatives of white Texans to shove aside the last great hero of the Texas Revolution, one of the fathers of independent Texas? Texans have never been noted for being particularly subtle, and Lone Star Confederates made it clear why they did what they did. "We hold as undeniable truths that" Texas and other southern states "were established exclusively by the white race, for themselves and their posterity," secessionists proclaimed at their convention. "The African race," they announced, "was rightfully held and regarded as an inferior and dependent race." Slavery, based on an open belief in white supremacy, lay at the heart of Texas society, and united it with the other southern states, since Texas joined the United States "as a commonwealth holding, maintaining, and protecting the institution known as negro slavery . . . a relation that had existed from the first settlement of her wilderness by the white race, and which her people intended should exist in all future time." Indeed, in some ways the Republic of Texas had been a kind of starter kit for the Confederacy, creating a legal system that went beyond tolerating slavery to

128   CIVIL WARS

throwing the full weight of the government behind it. Breaking with the United States to join the Confederacy was in a sense to remain true to the political traditions of Anglo Texas. And secessionists left no doubt as to the reason for their departure: those who believed in "the debasing doctrine of the equality of all men, irrespective of race or color" had taken over the federal government and now threatened slavery, still the engine that drove the Texas economy.

Houston's refusal to support such principles was the exception rather than the rule. White Texans fought for the Confederacy in great numbers. As many as 90,000 Texans, including some of my ancestors, served in the Confederate Army, a huge percentage of the white male fighting-age population of some 100,000 to 110,000. Most of the fighting took place outside of Texas. John Bell Hood's "Texas Brigade" became the most famous Texan unit in the war, fighting as part of the Army of Northern Virginia, commanded by the leading Confederate general Robert E. Lee. The brigade fought effectively in key battles. In 1862 it led a charge that turned back Union forces threatening to take the Confederate capital of Richmond, Virginia; later that year, Hood's men joined the Confederate invasion of the North and fought at Antietam and Gettysburg. More than half of its soldiers were killed, wounded, or captured in a single day at Antietam. Those who survived went on to fight in the decisive battles of the war, as the Confederacy failed to stop American forces from invading Virginia and seizing Richmond. Over the course of the war, the brigade suffered a casualty rate of 61 percent. Overall, as many as a quarter of Texans who fought for the Confederacy gave their lives to the cause, somewhere around 20,000. This was the largest loss and greatest suffering proportionate to population since the warfare and destruction of the 1810s in the struggle for independence from Spain.

CIVIL WARS 129

For a time, the war seemed to offer Texas the chance to resurrect Mirabeau Lamar's dreams of a western empire. A few months after Texas joined the Confederacy, small units of mounted Texan forces seized the town of Mesilla in New Mexico, near what is now Las Cruces. They proclaimed the creation of the "Confederate Territory of Arizona," stretching all the way from Mesilla to the California border. Texas Confederates thought that seizing this territory would not only force the Union to fight them in the far west, but also turn it into a route for a future rail connection to the Pacific, allowing Texas and the rest of the Confederate States of America to take advantage of the commerce of the Pacific world, especially China.

Confederate forces controlled only southern New Mexico, particularly the area around Mesilla. They were soon reinforced by three regiments organized in San Antonio and given the name the "Army of New Mexico," which like Confederate Arizona was more of an expression of hope than a military reality. This army, like the expedition of 1842 sent by Texas president Mirabeau Lamar, invaded New Mexico. Seeking to capture Albuquerque and Santa Fe, it was met by Union forces recruited in Colorado and northern New Mexico, the part of the state that had resisted the earlier Texan invasions. New Mexico's governor tapped into widely shared loathing of Texans and raised an army of 5,000 to ensure the state could fend off the Confederacy. In March of 1862, Union and Confederate forces met at Glorieta Pass, between Santa Fe and Las Vegas, New Mexico. They fought to a draw, but the Union forces succeeded in destroying the Confederate supply train. So this Texan invasion, like its predecessor in 1842, was forced to retreat. New Mexicans again celebrated their continued independence from the invading Lone Star State and its regional imperial aims, this time in its Confederate incarnation.

The leaders of Confederate Texas benefited from the fact that Union forces focused on turning back Lee's invasion of Pennsylvania and then on capturing the heart of the Confederacy in Virginia and Georgia. They did not have to reckon with the full might of the U.S. military. They did, however, have to face several Union incursions. They succeeded in repelling landing parties from an invading force of five ships that tried to capture Corpus Christi in August 1862, but were too weak to stop Union warships from entering the Sabine River on the border with Louisiana and destroying Confederate entrenchments near Beaumont the next month. In October, Union forces seized Galveston, by far the state's most important port. They held it until New Year's Day of 1863, when Confederate forces, their ranks swollen by veterans of the defeated New Mexico campaign, dislodged them in pitched fighting. Later in the war, Texas Confederates fought off another invasion of the Sabine River in September of 1863, but retreated from a large Union army that landed near the mouth of the Rio Grande that November.

The strong support for the Union by elements of Texas society posed more persistent challenges for the state's Confederates. In places with significant Union support, danger and tension bubbled just beneath the surface. "I am already as disgusted as I expected to be," wrote the twenty-one-year-old daughter of a wealthy Louisiana family that had sent her, with their slaves, to northeast Texas to be away from Union armies. "This part of the land . . . is a place where the people are just learning that there is a war going on, where Union feeling is rife, and where the principal amusement of loyal citizens is hanging" Confederate sympathizers, she complained to her parents. Texas Confederate leaders shared her fears. In Cooke County, sixty miles north of Fort Worth near the border with Oklahoma, widespread resistance to the Confederacy's draft

CIVIL WARS

prompted them to send state troops to arrest able-bodied men who had not joined Confederate ranks. A quick trial organized by Confederate colonel William Young led to the hanging of seven for treason. An angry mob demanded that more be killed, and fourteen more local men were hanged just outside the town of Gainesville. When Young and another prominent Confederate were assassinated, presumably by local Unionists, a second mob gathered and hanged nineteen more, bringing the total toll to a dramatic forty Texans lynched by other Texans.

Similar violence broke out in the Hill Country west of San Antonio. Few German residents wanted secession. But like Sam Houston, they also refrained from openly opposing the war, hoping to avoid conflict and bloodshed. In 1862, however, Germans living northwest of San Antonio formed a Union Loyal League and organized themselves into military companies. Confederate authorities feared, probably correctly, that they might use this organization to resist the draft, or even mount a rebellion of their own against Confederate authority. When the authorities sent soldiers to disband the companies and enforce the draft law, sixty Unionists, mostly Germans, fled toward Mexico. It was not to be: Confederate cavalry pursued them as deserters, rode into their camp on the Nueces River in August of 1862, and killed more than twenty of the surprised men in a quick and chaotic battle. More were executed afterward. Known German Unionists were assassinated throughout the rest of that summer and fall.

Texans opposed to the Confederacy who lived near the border with Mexico had greater resources to draw upon than did their counterparts in northern and central Texas. They could escape the Confederacy's grasp simply by going to Mexico. Nearly one thousand Tejanos from South Texas enlisted in the Union Army, by joining their ranks during Union incursions into the region or fleeing to New Mexico or to Mexico and then traveling by ship to the North to enlist. Many joined the Second Texas Cavalry, which fought alongside other U.S. forces as far away as Mississippi. Those who stayed close to Texas had a powerful ally in Juan Cortina, who welcomed Unionists into his ranks and happily armed them against his former foes, who were now fighting for the Confederacy. Tejano Unionists expressed admiration for "Old Abe, rail splitter," as one proclamation referred to U.S. president Abraham Lincoln. Some, who perhaps had seen fugitive slaves or even had them as family members, embraced racial equality. The "lower order" of Tejanos, complained a Brownsville pro-Confederate newspaper during the war, are "not only abolitionists but amalgamationists" willing to marry Blacks and "always assist a runaway slave to escape from his master."

The draft ensured that more Tejanos would join Confederate than Union ranks. The most prominent Tejano Confederate was the wealthy Laredo merchant Santos Benavides, who was a captain of a cavalry unit. He was promoted to colonel in 1863 as a reward for his service, which included finding a way around the effective Union blockade of Confederate ports like New Orleans. Benavides secured routes for cotton to be shipped across the Rio Grande and into Mexico, and from Mexican ports to world markets. Benavides walked a similar path as elite Tejanos like the Seguín and Navarro families had a generation before: slave-based cotton agriculture had been good to them, and they wanted to see it continue. Benavides and his compatriots found themselves fighting not only Black and white soldiers from the North, but also their Tejano neighbors. In December 1862, for example, just a few months after German Unionists were slaughtered on the banks of the Nueces, a force of two hundred Tejano Unionists led by a supporter of Cortina crossed back into Texas and captured Isidro Vela, the

Confederate judge of Zapata County. Vela had jailed and threatened Unionists before the election, ensuring that not a single vote for remaining in the Union was cast in Zapata County. The Unionists hanged him from a tree on his own ranch in front of his family, leaving a sign warning passers-by not to take down his rotting corpse. His hanging showed the depth of Tejano support for the Union. Here as elsewhere in Texas, the Civil War was not just between the North and the South, but also between Texans.

Confederate forces were not defeated and conquered in Texas. Indeed, they won the last battle of the Civil War, fought on May 13, 1865, outside of Brownsville, by combatants unaware that the war was effectively over. But more and more Confederate soldiers deserted once news of Robert E. Lee's surrender at Appomattox in April spread through the state. Texans who served in Lee's army and other Confederate units to the east began making their way back home. At the same time, Confederate soldiers from elsewhere who were stationed in Texas began abandoning their units. Many stole food and clothing on the way. Numerous Confederate officials left their posts, unsure as to whether they would be arrested or even executed for their service to the now-failed rebellion. "Confederate soldiers, without officers or orders, are coming in every hour, and there is nothing but plunder and sack going on," wrote an Austin resident in late May of 1865. "The citizens are as bad as the soldiers . . . everything in confusion . . . and there is no law." A few weeks later, a band of forty Confederate deserters broke into the state treasury in the capitol building, stuffing coins into hats, pockets, and bags before being chased off by other veterans who had organized a home guard to keep order.

Confederate commanders in Texas surrendered to U.S.

134 CIVIL WARS

forces in Galveston in early June. A few weeks later, on June 19, General Gordon E. Granger issued the proclamation that so overjoyed hundreds of thousands, including Preely Coleman, Jacob Branch, and their fellow emancipated slaves living in Texas. Reading the order out loud to crowds assembled in Galveston, Granger announced that "the people of Texas are informed that, in accordance with a proclamation from the Executive of the United States, all slaves are free." He then promised exactly the kind of equality that Confederates had gone to war to avoid: "This involves an absolute equality of personal rights and rights of property between former masters and slaves, and the connection heretofore existing between them becomes that between employer and hired labor."

Word of Granger's pronouncement spread slowly across Texas in the following months, along with an influx of Union soldiers. For some, daily life changed little: they still lived in the same homes and worked for the same white landowner, and faced violence if they defied his will. "Lots of Negroes were killed after freedom . . . shot down after they were trying to get away. You could see lots of Negroes hanging from trees in Sabine bottom right after freedom. They would catch them swimming across the Sabine River and shoot them," remembered one former slave decades later. For others, word of Granger's order brought instant change. "Hallelujah broke out," another told his interviewer, "soldiers, all of a sudden, was everywhere." Some freed people stayed close to home, hoping to make the most of their freedom where they already lived, while others packed up right away, moving to escape abusive masters or to head back east to try and find the spouses, parents, and children torn from them by the slave trade.

Nobody in Texas—Black, white, Confederate, Unionist, German, Tejano—knew exactly what terrors and hopes this new world would bring. But they knew that they had lived

CIVIL WARS 135

through the end of one chapter of history and the start of another. In August of 1866, the citizens of Comfort, fifty miles northwest of San Antonio, erected the state's first Civil War monument. Under the spreading live oaks in the town cemetery, they placed a granite monument honoring their friends and family members slaughtered by the Confederacy four years before. The monument stands to this day. "True to the Union," it reads in German.

The same year, freed people in Texas began a kind of living monument to emancipation. They gathered on June 19, the anniversary of General Granger's announcement, in Galveston and other towns, and soon enough across the entire state, for what they called Juneteenth. Most early gatherings featured a ceremonial reading of either Granger's proclamation or the Emancipation Proclamation from President Lincoln on which it was based. Former slaves testified to what they had endured, ministers preached sermons, and the crowds sang Christian hymns like "Free at Last" and "Go Down Moses" alongside secular songs like "John Brown" and "America." Black newspapers began printing the Emancipation Proclamation, often alongside portraits of Lincoln.

Juneteenth celebrations never lost their association with freedom from slavery. But over time they also became huge community parties and family reunions. In cities like Galveston and Austin, there were parades complete with marching bands, cowboys, fraternal lodge members in uniform, military veterans, women dressed as Lady Liberty, sometimes on floats, drawn by horse and mule, later automobiles. These gatherings took over public space in the hearts of cities. Dedicated space could be useful, too. In 1872, Black Houstonians raised money to buy a ten-acre tract they dubbed "Emancipation Park," which is now part of the city's park system. In the coming decades, Juneteenth became a major holiday for many Black

Texans. Railroad companies started running special discount fares to lure those who had moved out of state back home for a few days, and many white employers gave their Black workers the day off. The gatherings began to feature epic amounts of barbecue, auto races, beauty pageants, and baseball games.

They also spread beyond Texas. Towns in Coahuila where fugitive slaves and Indians had settled down began celebrating Juneteenth in the 1870s, calling it "Día de los Negros," or "Day of the Blacks." Later migrants brought the tradition to San Francisco, California, where Wesley Johnson, owner of a nightclub called the "Texas Club," led a parade mounted on a white horse, wearing a white cowboy hat to show his pride in being not only a free Black person but a Texan as well. The state government of Texas recognized it as a formal holiday in 1979, to be followed by nineteen other states in the next few decades. In 2021, the federal government of the United States made it one of eleven national holidays. What some Texans experienced as a bitter defeat—the destruction of the Confederacy—others brought to the nation as a celebration of a great triumph.

A BISON HUNT

11

A White Man's Country

The small group of Kiowas approached the magnificent ranch house one fall day in 1916. Its two stories rose high above the flat Panhandle plains, and its fine woodwork, tasteful paint, and crystal windows spoke of the owner's wealth and importance. Tonequoah, known to white people as George Hunt, led his friends Horse, Kiowa George, Luther Sahmount, Mokeen, Longhorn, Peattomah and her young baby Caroline, and perhaps a few others onto the property of Charles Goodnight. The white-bearded Goodnight (he had turned eighty earlier that year) was one of the most famous Texans, known across the state and indeed the country as an army scout, Indian fighter, and the rancher who blazed some of the earliest cattle trails from Texas to the north. By the time Tonequoah and his friends arrived, Goodnight had retired to a small ranch by the town that bore his name. There his employees maintained a herd of several hundred bison, an animal that Goodnight had exterminated in vast numbers in his youth yet worked to preserve in middle age.

Tonequoah and his friends must have found their trip to be deeply sad. They were, after all, traveling across territory that once belonged to them and their close Comanche allies, passing through ranches and towns and seeing railroad lines, barbed wire fences, homes, and fields where their parents' generation had once followed vast buffalo herds and tended to their own horses and mules. And they were visiting a man who was as responsible as any single individual for the fact that they lived in poverty on a few acres in southwestern Oklahoma. Goodnight fought Kiowas and Comanches with the Texas Rangers and Confederate forces, guiding them to important victories on the southern Plains in his youth. He selected Palo Duro Canyon, the site of a crushing defeat in 1874 that forced the Kiowas into confinement on a reservation, as the site of one of his ranches. He brought in professional hunters from Kansas to kill the bison that still lived in the canyon in order to make way for his cattle. They massacred as many as 15,000 in short order, a significant contribution to the slaughter that brought bison to the brink of extinction in the 1880s. Goodnight took lodge poles abandoned by departed Kiowas and Comanches to build his first living quarters. The Kiowas were going to visit a man who had stolen their homeland and literally their homes, and grown rich off doing so.

They were also continuing a partnership with Goodnight, maybe even something that could be called a friendship. Decades earlier, in 1887, a Kiowa delegation rode from their Oklahoma reservation to Palo Duro Canyon in search of a bison they needed in order to perform the Sun Dance, a sacred ceremony in which young men deny themselves food and then exhaust themselves through grueling dancing in order, as they understood it, to reconnect to the larger universe. Goodnight sold them one of the bison he held; they killed it and brought back the head and hide to their reservation, where they were again able to hold the Sun Dance. During the visit to Goodnight in 1916, the Kiowas again killed a bison, running it down on horseback and dispatching it in the old way with an arrow. The animal was cooked and served the next day to 125 guests. Two months later, Tonequoah and his friends returned. This time Goodnight brought in a film crew from Denver. They filmed the killing of another bison, making it a central chapter of their thirty-minute film *Old Texas*. The film tells the story of Goodnight's "discovery" of the canyon, his encounter with Plains Indians, their bison hunt and subsequent Sun Dance, and the passing of the Panhandle (and, by extension, Texas) from Indian to white hands.

Texans have found themselves drawn again and again to the story of the Kiowa bison hunts, made possible by the cooperation between Goodnight and the people he dispossessed. An astonishing 11,000 spectators came to watch the 1916 hunt. What did they make of this scene? Press accounts report that they admired the skill and nobility of Plains Indians on horseback, but not so much that they invited Kiowas and Comanches to return to the homeland from which they had been expelled by the spectators' parents and grandparents. The contrast between their automobiles, parked end to end to make the enclosure in which the animal was run down and killed, and the simpler technologies of bow, arrow, and lance filled them with pride in the accomplishments of modern Texas. As the Amarillo newspaper put it, "The Texas Panhandle halted from its daily routine of empire building and harked back to the days when buffalos grazed."

The scene of a handful of visiting Plains Indians hunting a bison in view of thousands of white spectators encapsulated one of the critical developments in Texas after the Civil

War: the removal or outright killing of almost all Indigenous people in the state. By the 1880s, just a generation after the Civil War, the Comanches, Kiowas, and Apaches had been defeated in battle and forced onto reservations in Oklahoma and New Mexico, where they joined Caddo, Anadarko, Waco, Tonkawa, and other previously expelled groups. Indian control of vast portions of land claimed by Texas was one barrier faced by white landowners in the 1870s. The other obstacle, at least for major landowners in eastern and central Texas, was the need for cheap labor in the wake of the independence of Black workers brought about by emancipation. Slavery was all about extracting uncompensated labor, which was most profitable on large farms growing cotton. What would replace the labor extorted by enslavement? There was no solution to this "problem" as dramatic as defeating Indians on the battlefield and expelling them from the state. However, by the 1880s, white landowners, essentially the farming counterparts of men like Charles Goodnight, regained much of their ability to command Black labor by rolling back voting rights and limiting Black economic independence. Within a generation of their bitter loss to the Union, white former Confederates again ruled Texas.

The destruction of slavery opened up new possibilities for Black Texans in every aspect of their lives. A young Lucy Carter saw this firsthand. Born into slavery back east, Lucy was brought by her owner to the Brazos River valley in 1863, when she was twelve, alongside her brothers and mother. With the coming of freedom, her mother married a man whose last name, Carter, she took and also gave to her children. The family lived together in Waco, where Lucy attended school and worked for wages. Her family, name, job, and education would have been impossible before emancipation. Some of her white neighbors

A WHITE MAN'S COUNTRY 141

had been transformed as well: a Confederate veteran named Albert Parsons moved to Waco at about the same time. Soon he renounced the cause of white supremacy, praised the enslaved woman who had "practically raised me, with great kindness and a mother's love," and began telling his Black neighbors that "they were the equal if not the superiors of the white people" in speeches and the pages of a newspaper he began editing. He and Lucy fell in love, shattered social convention in 1872 by marrying each other, and worked in labor and civil rights politics and journalism in Texas and then the Midwest, along with raising their two children.

Freedom in personal life—the opportunity to form families of their choosing without threat of forcible separation, the creation of churches free from the prying eyes of whites, and education—was the enduring achievement of emancipation in Texas and the entire South. Freed people also aspired to have political rights and economic opportunity, but in these realms they faced violent and rather successful resistance from former Confederates. In the late 1860s, the Republican-controlled U.S. Congress made swearing that one had never fought against the United States a precondition for holding office and protected political rights for emancipated slaves. The Freedmen's Bureau, a federal agency created to help former slaves assert their newly gained rights as citizens, had agents in fifty-nine districts in Texas. U.S. Army forces remained in Texas as in the rest of the former Confederacy, to ensure that order was preserved and the Freedmen's Bureau could do its job. From 1869 to 1873, the administration of Governor Edmund J. Davis, a white Democrat who had served as a state judge before the war and fought for the Union, ending the war as a brigadier general, supported this effort. Davis created a state police force that hired Black, white, and Hispanic officers and aggressively enforced the law, including the voting rights of freedmen. Defiant former Confederates despised the force as "the Governor's Hounds."

In this window of opportunity, Black Texans gained meaningful political power. Ten of ninety delegates elected to a constitutional convention in 1868 were Black. The state constitution created by this convention guaranteed the vote for all adult men regardless of race and provided for an ambitious public education system financed directly by tax revenue from the state government. The latter was a particularly important priority for freed people who remembered all too well the laws against even learning to read and write under which they had lived in slavery. A literate slave was a threat to the order of slavery, and educated free persons could assert themselves in a democratic society. Black church associations also founded Paul Quinn College in 1872 and Wiley College the following year to educate Black youth. These institutions came into being a decade before the University of Texas.

The legislature elected under the provisions of the state constitution included two Black senators (most notably, George Thompson Ruby of Galveston). It quickly ratified the new amendments to the U.S. Constitution: the Thirteenth (outlawing slavery), the Fourteenth (providing for citizenship and the equal protection of the laws), and the Fifteenth (forbidding racial discrimination in voting). Black men also filled many local offices, including as supervisor of Waco's public school system when Lucy Parsons still lived in Texas. And they voted at rates greatly exceeding the turnout of all voters in the twenty-first century, even in the face of intimidation and violence. Black Texans valued their freedom and fought for it through aggressive political action and institution-building.

Economic gains for freed people are harder to chart. Most freed people aspired to be independent farmers who owned their own land and therefore could produce most of what they needed by their own labor, and rely on and work only for themselves. (In that sense, they were very much like their white neighbors.) Some national Republicans suggested confiscating and redistributing the plantations of the Confederacy's leaders, a step that would have allowed for many more freed people to become landowners. But the U.S. Congress was unwilling to go so far, thus limiting Black landownership. Nonetheless, by 1880, 20 percent of Black farmers owned and worked their own land. This was a much smaller percentage compared with white farmers, the heavy majority of whom owned their own land, but a big step forward from slavery nonetheless. The rest either worked as farm laborers paid a cash wage, as sharecroppers (farmers who worked another's land and split the proceeds of the harvest with the landowner), or as wage workers in other kinds of jobs. In this regard, they were again not so different from white Texans, more than two-thirds of whom worked in agriculture in what was still an overwhelmingly rural state.

These gains for freed people, enough to raise their hopes that their children would be able to live with dignity and equality, were made in the face of considerable violence. As the Freedmen's Bureau agent in Houston wrote in 1867, "I find among the ex-confederate soldiers and younger part of the community a deep and violent hatred both in actions and words, and only the presence of a military force prevents them from many acts of violence." Another agent was more blunt: "To remove the troops is death to the freed people." These warnings proved to be well founded. White Texans unwilling to accept their Black neighbors as free people started torturing and murdering them. Men engaged in political organizing were targeted in particular, often by armed white mobs, some of which were organized by the white terrorist group the Ku Klux Klan. One historian has calculated that about 1 percent of the adult Black male population—approaching one thousand people—were killed by such violence in the late 1860s, a rate that looks more like war than peace. Leaving employment for better wages or a better share of the crop was also a frequent occasion for shooting or beating. Women and children could fall victim too. One planter shot a child whose mother had left his employment, and outside Waco two white doctors joined in the sexual mutilation of a Black boy. Teachers and ministers were beaten and shot, their eyes gouged out and limbs cut off, their schools and churches burned down. A furious Republican newspaperman referred to such examples when Texans complained about Indian raids. "For every ten killed on the Frontier," he wrote, "a hundred in other parts of the State are murdered in cold blood by ruffians as ruthless as the Comanche with his tomahawk and scalping-knife."

The violence and mobilization of white voters curtailed Black political power and economic independence. The former Confederate officer Richard Coke defeated Edmund J. Davis in the gubernatorial election of 1873, condemning the previous mixed-race legislature as a "government given over to tyranny." Coke's political coalition replaced the existing constitution with one that returned authority for funding schools to local jurisdictions (which were unable or unwilling to support them at the previously high levels). By the end of the 1870s, many northern Republican officeholders who had passed the Thirteenth, Fourteenth, and Fifteenth Amendments had retreated from the fight for political equality for Black southerners. Texas legislatures were subsequently dominated by white Democrats who made no apology for their past service in the Confederacy or their present advocacy of white supremacy. Black men remained eligible for voting, jury service, and other rights of citizenship on paper, but a moment of possibility in which basic equality seemed within reach had passed. In the late 1870s, after fifteen years of freedom at home, thousands of former slaves started fleeing the Lone Star State for Kansas and other destinations, where they hoped to find freedom, some peace of mind, and opportunity denied to them at home. George Thompson Ruby, who had himself departed for the relative safety of New Orleans, was among those encouraging people to leave Texas. Lucy and Albert Parsons moved to Chicago.

A much greater portion of the Native inhabitants of the state left in the same years, prompted by even more relentless and highly organized violence. The post-statehood population boom increased white demands for Indian lands. There were more and more Texans, and they were better and better armed. Native leaders recognized the mounting odds they faced. In 1854, Caddo, Tonkawa, and other Native leaders agreed to relocate to a reservation along the upper Brazos one hundred miles northwest of Fort Worth. They figured that the promised food rations and support for farming would secure their livelihood, and that the presence of federal Indian agent Robert Neighbors, whose integrity they trusted, would provide them with some protection against further white encroachment. They turned out to be wrong. Whites held the reservation's 2,000 inhabitants responsible for any Indian attacks on Texans, wherever they occurred and whether or not reservation inhabitants were involved. A newspaper from a nearby town proclaimed, "We regard the killing of Indians of whatever tribe to be morally right and that we will resist to the last extremity the infliction of any legal punishment on the perpetrators." Whites who murdered reservation residents went unpunished. In 1858, for example, a vigilante group murdered seven reservation residents (three of them women) who had left the reservation with the permission of the Indian agent, Neighbors, in order to hunt. Neighbors's protests convinced a judge to issue a warrant for the perpetrators' arrest, but the commander of the Texas Ranger unit charged with making the arrests refused to do so, believing that Indians did not deserve "the protection of the law." The next summer, a militia of several hundred white farmers from the region assembled and threatened to invade the reservation. Neighbors, convinced that he could not protect his charges, persuaded them to move across the Red River into Indian Territory (later Oklahoma), where they had a greater chance to live in peace. Their choices were to leave Texas, or die. "I have this day crossed all the Indians out of the heathen land of Texas," he wrote in despair to his wife. "If you want to hear a full description of our Exodus," he added, "read the Bible where the children of Israel crossed the Red Sea." The next day Robert Neighbors was assassinated by a fellow white Texan who despised his loyal service to Indians.

Of course, there were still free Indians in Texas able to resist removal with military force, Comanches the most powerful among them. It would take another fifteen years of hard fighting to force them onto reservations. Comanche, Kiowa, Arapaho, and Cheyenne warriors held off further white settlement during the Civil War, waging attacks that killed frontier families and fighting Texan forces to a standstill. The return of the U.S. military in full force to the southern Plains after the Civil War persuaded most of the still-independent bands to accept, in 1867, treaties that created substantial reservations in western Indian Territory, guaranteed their security against white encroachment, committed the government to the delivery of farming supplies and training, and allowed for some continued bison hunting both on and off the reservations. But

A WHITE MAN'S COUNTRY 147

some refused to sign the treaties, most notably Quanah Parker, the powerful son of a prominent chief and Cynthia Ann Parker, a white woman taken captive by Comanches as a girl of around age ten, in 1836, and assimilated into Comanche society. Quanah and others continued to live a life of freedom, hunting bison and defeating or evading the expeditions sent to force them onto the reservation. As the Comanche leader Ten Bears said to federal officials, "I was born on the prairie, where the wind blew free and there was nothing to break the light of the sun. I was born when there were no enclosures and everything drew a free breath. I want to die there and not within walls. I know every stream and every wood between the Rio Grande and the Arkansas . . . I lived like my fathers before me and like them I lived happily."

In the early 1870s, many hundreds of Plains Indians left their reservations and joined Parker. They were enraged by the failure of the U.S. government to protect them on their reservations and to deliver the promised economic support, and by the increasing slaughter of bison by white hunters. They struck at a hunters' camp in the Panhandle, but were repulsed by the well-armed men. The U.S. Army then sent a force of five thousand to drive all southern Plains people onto the reservations in Indian Territory. There was no climactic battle, but in late September of 1874, U.S. cavalry chased Parker and his allies into Palo Duro Canyon and managed to destroy winter provisions and kill almost all of their livestock. Deprived of food and mobility, Comanches and others trickled back to the reservations, finally joined in June 1875 by Quanah Parker and several hundred followers. Nearly two centuries of Comanche power were over.

White Texas celebrated the leaders of the wars against Indians as heroes. Lawrence "Sul" Ross, for example, who led the Texas Ranger unit that killed most of Cynthia Ann Parker's

Comanche family in 1860 and later served as a general in the Confederacy, was elected governor in 1886. He ran proudly on his reputation as the man who, as one paper put it, "WIPED OUT THE COMANCHE." Ross and his supporters believed that he had rescued Parker from her captives. That does not seem to have been her experience. Put on display in Fort Worth, she stared back at the crowds who came to see her, tears running down her face. Since her abduction in 1836 during an attack on a white outpost, she had lived with the Comanches. For all effective purposes, she had become Comanche. She went by the name Naduah, married a respected leader named Peta Nocona, and was raising three children, including Quanah, when Ross attacked. Returned to white society, she refused to speak English and tried several times to escape to her Comanche family in Indian Territory. In 1870, she gave in to despair, refused to eat, and soon died from the flu. Decades later, in 1910, her son Quanah succeeded in having her body removed from its grave in Texas and reburied in Oklahoma near his residence. Eventually, in the 1950s, both of their remains were reinterred in the same Oklahoma cemetery, giving mother and son a reunion in death that they were denied in life.

It is easy to exaggerate the extent to which Indians were removed from Texas. The idea that Natives are vanishing or already gone is frequently invoked by Americans who are not themselves Indigenous, probably because stereotypes of Indians are so strong that it can be hard to see them as participants in a modern world. I grew up hearing stories about the "extinct" Karankawa people. Karankawas had ceased to function as a sovereign, cohesive group by the 1850s, but individual Karankawas survived and passed along some of their language and culture. To outsiders, they were indistinguishable from the

A WHITE MAN'S COUNTRY 149

larger Mexican-descended population in South Texas. Recently, Karankawa descendants have found one another, networked, and are working to regain knowledge of their ancestral language, protect burial sites, and learn more about their own history. Similarly, about a thousand of the descendants of Indigenous people who lived in San Antonio missions organized themselves into the Tāp Pīlam Coahuiltecan Nation in the late twentieth century. This group also works for the protection of Native gravesites and human remains and seeks access to the Alamo chapel for religious ceremonies. The Tāp Pīlam Nation estimates that 100,000 who live in and around San Antonio are descended from the missions' Indian residents. Three tribes—the Alabama-Coushatta in East Texas, the Kickapoo Traditional Tribe of Texas, just outside of Del Rio, and the Ysleta del Sur Pueblo in El Paso—maintain reservations and conduct diplomatic relations with the federal and state governments to this day. Thousands of Native people from many different groups live in Dallas–Fort Worth and Houston. Many Indians—about 800,000 according to the U.S. census—still call Texas home.

Nevertheless, the onslaught against Native peoples after the Civil War mounted by the government and leaders of Texas was very successful in forcing Native people out of the state, to say nothing of killing them outright. By 1881, the only organized Indian nations left in Texas were the Alabama-Coushattas in the southeast and the Tiguas in West Texas. Less than 3 percent of today's Texan population is Native American, a sharp contrast both with the neighboring states of Oklahoma (13 percent) and New Mexico (11 percent), and with Texas itself before the campaigns led by men like Goodnight.

Maybe the removal of Indians from Texas explains why the story of the Kiowa hunts of Charles Goodnight's bison has been told and retold so many times, by so many different people. It circulated orally among the residents of the Panhandle, presumably for the same reasons that 11,000 of them showed up to watch one of the hunts. John Graves, born in Fort Worth in 1920, four years after the filming of one of the hunts, heard the story early in life and was seized by it. Graves, an author whose stories and essays brought Texas landscapes and histories to national audiences starting in the late 1950s, has written several versions of it, one of which was how I encountered the story. Larry McMurtry, whose epic novels of Texas and the West reached millions, also retold stories of the meeting between Goodnight and his former enemies several times. And N. Scott Momaday, a Kiowa poet, essayist, and novelist whose writings were hailed as one sign of an Indian cultural renaissance in the 1960s, was as drawn to the story as were his white counterparts. Their accounts fudged some of the details—often the Kiowas, for example, became Comanche—but continued the focus on the complicated relationship between Goodnight and his Indian former antagonists.

Why has this story, like the commemoration of Juneteenth that has only grown stronger over time, resonated for more than a century? It certainly encapsulates a basic factual truth about modern Texas, that the most powerful Indigenous groups now mostly live outside its bounds. But I think it goes beyond that: in the retellings, the tenor of the story became more and more ambivalent, not so much a marker and validation of white conquest and progress, as a haunting reminder of the existential toll that they took. In John Graves's story "The Last Running," the white rancher who provides a bison to Indians he had once met in combat is reduced to tears when they depart. Instead of celebrating the white conquest of Indians, at the story's end he sees a Texas without Indians as a loss. "Damn you for not ever getting to know anything worth knowing," he says to a younger white relative. "Damn me, too. We had a world, once."

12

Home on the Range

The words bring back countless childhood memories, and like so many others, I know the tune right away: "Oh give me a home where the buffalo roam, / Where the deer and the antelope play, / Where seldom is heard a discouraging word / And the skies are not cloudy all day. / Home, home on the Range." Americans have been singing "Home on the Range" for a century and a half, since huge cattle drives from Texas up to the Great Plains as far away as the Canadian provinces of Alberta and Saskatchewan filled western ranches with cattle and American bellies with steaks and hamburgers. My parents sang the song as schoolchildren, as did their parents. In 1945, American soldiers in France linked arms and belted it out when they heard that World War II had ended. They wanted to go home. And what was more American than the life of the open range that the song celebrated?

So many versions of "Home on the Range" were played

on the radio by the 1930s that there was an enormous, drawn-out lawsuit over who owned it. The royalties would make a person very rich. Lawyers ended up showing that the song was published as a poem in a small Kansas newspaper in 1876. The first recording of the song was made in 1908 by John Lomax, an English professor from West Texas who collected cowboy ballads and other folk music. It was sung to him by a saloon owner in San Antonio who had been a cook for cattle drives from Texas in the 1870s. (Lomax, alas, did not leave us with the man's name.) Lomax heard too many versions of the song in too many places to believe that anybody could claim to be its author. He felt that it was the "folk-national anthem of the United States," and especially of Texas, "kept alive for years and years only in the minds and hearts of the people." The song was their way of expressing the pride and joy they felt about the "bigness, the freedom . . . the wildness of the West."

The popularity of "Home on the Range" made up a small part of the fascination with cowboys that swept the United States after the Civil War and forever cemented the association of "Texan" and "cowboy." The image of the cowboy reflected the very real contribution that Texas made to the ways that Americans ate and thought of themselves in the late nineteenth century. It is such a strong image that you have to squint hard to see some of the reality behind it. But that reality is even more interesting and complicated than the myth.

Despite the worldwide fame of the Texas cowboy, only a small portion of Texans ever made a living running cattle. In 1880, for example, barely more than one of every hundred Texans described their work as "stock raiser" or "stock herder" (the terms closest to "rancher" and "cowboy" used by the federal government). There were at least twenty-five farmers or farmworkers for every person who could reasonably call them-

HOME ON THE RANGE 153

selves a cowboy. Indeed, in the years that the cowboy came to stand for Texas, the Lone Star State became the country's leading producer of cotton. More people cleaned homes and cooked meals for wealthier families than roped and branded cattle. Yet a person picking cotton or plowing a field, much less a woman scrubbing dishes or pushing a mop, has never screamed "Texas" in the way that a man on a horse with a lasso and a big hat still does.

The cowboy captured something deeply American—if also often very Texan—that went far beyond a question of numbers. Cowboys were celebrated as authentic and democratic, rather than crude. When "the English nobleman smelt Texas," wrote the novelist Owen Wister in 1895 in *Harper's Monthly*, "the slumbering Saxon awoke in him, and mindful of the tournament, mindful of the hunting-field, galloped howling after wild cattle, a born horseman, a perfect athlete." Cowboys stood at a distance from the more polite and refined society of urbanizing America made possible by factories, railroads, and the telegraph. They did not read magazines of the kind that published Wister's article. They did not read magazines at all. But people like Wister and Lomax, like countless other cultivated city people, admired them nonetheless. "The early cowpunchers," Wister said of Texas cowboys, "rapidly grew unlike all people but each other and the wild superstitious ancestors whose blood was in their veins. Their hair became long, and their glance rested with supreme penetration upon the stranger; they laughed seldom and their spirit was in the permanent attitude of war . . . indifferent to death, but disconcerted by a good woman." You could work behind a desk instead of on a horse and still admire the fact that "the old spirit burned alike in all, the unextinguished fire of adventure and independence."

These kinds of musings, which made cowboys, especially Texas cowboys, an image of Americanness across much of the

154 HOME ON THE RANGE

world, assumed the cowboy was white. Most Texas cowboys, like most Texans, were in fact white. But plenty of Black men worked as cowboys, too, putting to good use some of the cattle-herding skills they had learned as slaves. The camp cook turned saloon keeper who sang "Home on the Range" for John Lomax was a Black man. Men of Mexican descent were much more likely than any other group to work with livestock. They dominated the workforce in the border regions and could be found in West Texas and the Plains in large numbers as well. It is hard to know for sure, but probably a third of Texas cowboys in this period were either Black or of Mexican descent.

The specialized techniques and equipment used to raise cattle were also produced by the meetings of people of different origins. White and Black (both free and enslaved) residents of British North America worked with cattle from the early 1600s on, bringing their knowledge and skills into what was for them a new world. Cattle herding in the east, however, was done on foot or from horseback with the aid of dogs. Spanish herders used horses and ropes, developing a specialized technology (most important, a high saddle with a horn, to rope and hold cattle while mounted) and vocabulary to match. Americans enthusiastically adopted these roping techniques and equipment when they encountered Spanish, Mexican, and Native cattle raisers in Florida and the Gulf Coast all the way west to Texas. This explains why the words that we still use in the United States for ranching and ranchlands are mostly either Spanish or English versions of Spanish words—bronco, buckaroo, burro, mesa, canyon, rodeo, corral, lariat, lasso, and chaps, to name some examples. As Wister acknowledged, intent though he was on celebrating the Anglo nature of cowboys, "let it be remembered that the Mexican was the original cowboy."

There could be no cowboys without cows. By the 1870s,

the Texas longhorn emerged as a distinctive cattle breed, making profitable large-scale ranching take off and joining the cowboy as a symbol of Texan distinctiveness. Like the cowboys who tended them, longhorns were a unique creation of centuries of cultural fusion. There were no cattle of any sort in the Americas before the European explorations and conquests of the 1500s and 1600s. The Spanish were the great importers of livestock, including cattle, to the Americas. The cows they brought were themselves mixes of the two major lines of cattle created by domestications of the wild aurochs, a large plant-eating animal with long and broad horns that scientists think originally evolved in India. One line, dominant in Europe and the Middle East, produced abundant meat and milk, while the other, in South Asia, was less productive but more independent and better able to handle tropical climates. Because of exchanges with the Arab world, which had networks stretching east into Muslim kingdoms in India, Spanish cattle descended from both types. That is why they produced more meat and milk than the eastern line but were hardier and better adapted to the environment of Mexico than were other European breeds.

Like the horses brought alongside them, these cattle thrived in Mexico. Some were carefully tended on Spanish *ranchos* (the basis for the English word "ranch"), but they were independent enough for the managers of large estates such as the San Antonio missions to let them fend for themselves for months or even years at a time. In many places, cattle became completely wild, managed or owned by nobody. These cattle in particular had to defend themselves against predators, avoid dying from relentless summer heat or abrupt winter cold snaps, and go long periods without water.

So over hundreds of generations, cattle in the Mexican north evolved to look more like aurochs: tall and skinny with long, sharp horns that could kill predators, fiercer and smarter than their domestic cousins in eastern North America and Europe. Even cattle owned as property seemed halfway to wild animals. A British traveler visiting Texas in the 1840s was struck that "the 'domestic' cattle of the out-settlers . . . are nearly as wild as the native-born buffaloes of the land." He was scandalized that Texas cattle were "suffered to roam at large in the wilderness; are never housed, winter or summer; are driven up but once a year, in order that all the young ones may be branded with the owner's peculiar mark, and then set at liberty again to feed and increase after their own kind until another season is over." The word "maverick" was invented in Texas in the 1840s to mean an unbranded calf, in reference to the numerous cattle of Samuel Maverick, a veteran of the Texas Revolution and onetime mayor of San Antonio. Within a few generations, in another reflection of the global influence of Texas, it came to be used across the English-speaking world to mean a person or a point of view that was independent or unconventional.

Longhorns were worthless as milk cows and their meat was stringy. One observer wrote it tasted "like a boiled grand piano." But they could look after themselves and multiply, roaming the range as wild or semi-wild animals. When ready, a rancher could capture one and slaughter it for food, or process its skin to make leather and boil down its fat to sell as tallow, used in cooking, soap, and candle-making. Money may not grow on trees, but there was a time in Texas when it walked around on four hooves.

The distinctive circumstances of Texas and the United States after the Civil War allowed for longhorns to become the basis of a modern and large-scale cattle industry. With so many men away fighting in the Confederate Army, and access to the key port of New Orleans cut off by Union forces, cattle numbers grew and grew. By the war's end, there were between five

HOME ON THE RANGE

and ten cows in Texas for every man, woman, and child. A longhorn that could bring from $3 to $6 if sold in Texas would fetch $30 to $40 at a slaughterhouse in Chicago or elsewhere in the North. The trick was getting them there. Ranchers began driving their cattle from Texas ranches up to railheads like Abilene and Dodge City in Kansas, where they would be loaded onto trains and shipped east. The Texans charted trails that maximized access to water and shelter and minimized contact with farmers and Indian reservations. The Chisholm Trail, stretching from Kingsville in South Texas north nearly nine hundred miles to Abilene, set the model, joined by others like the Great Western and Goodnight Loving. The trails shifted west over time, avoiding expanding farm settlements and reaching newly established railroads and railyards. They carried with them not just men, horses, and cattle, but also the speech, clothing, and irresistible style of Texas to huge swaths of the middle of the country. Teddy Blue Abbott, whose memoir of cowboy life became famous in the twentieth century, remembered that "the Texas cowboy's mode of speech and dress and actions set the style for all the range country."

The drives north were epic journeys that became a part of the lore of Texas even while under way. Each took three to five months and involved several thousand head of cattle. On these trails, longhorns proved their advantages. Conventional cattle might mature more quickly and produce more beef and milk, but "if put on the road with the active, wiry Texas steers, and compelled to travel the same distance," one magazine writer noted, "they almost invariably break down, and those that got through arrived at their destination weak in body, and low in flesh." Collectively these drives moved a staggering number of cattle; perhaps ten million left Texas from 1865 to 1890. One scholar reckons this is "the largest short-term geographical shift of domestic herd animals in the history of the world."

Texas longhorns also stocked the ranches of the American and Canadian Wests. One day on a drive in Nebraska, Abbott rode up a small hill by the Platte River and looked over his outfit's herd. "I could see seven herds behind us. I knew there were eight herds ahead of us, and I could see the dust from thirteen more of them on the other side of the river . . . All the cattle in the world seemed to be coming up out of Texas." If Texas had first come to world notoriety as a place that attracted migrants from across the United States and Europe, its new claim to fame was as a place that sent millions of cows to the rest of the continent. No place on earth was more associated with cows and cowboys.

Behind this abundance stood thousands of cowboys and their labor. The work was demanding but had its rewards. Cowboys were paid $25 to $40 a month in the 1880s and usually provided with simple but hearty food. Lodging under the stars on a trail drive, or in a simple bunkhouse if they tended to a herd that remained on a ranch, was generally included. This was good money for manual work, like being a plumber or an oil rig worker today. And they earned it by performing such varied and demanding tasks as camping out for months on end, standing watch over the herd at night and early in the morning, trailing a herd and thus eating the dust of thousands of animals all day, riding down strays, lassoing and branding calves, fixing broken fences, and occasionally shooting predators like wolves and mountain lions. Cowboys on major ranches like the King or XIT could make a lifetime of the work, laboring for a ranch as long as they were able, and often raising their sons to do the same. Most who joined the drives north quit after one or two times, many to try to settle down as a rancher with their own herd.

It was hard, sometimes dangerous work that could take your life from drowning in a river, being run over by stamped-

HOME ON THE RANGE

ing cattle, or getting shot by a would-be rustler. But it had its rewards, too, which went beyond money. Ben Kinchlow, born into slavery in Wharton in East Texas, worked for decades on South Texas ranches after emancipation. As an old man in his eighties, he still remembered cowboy life with great fondness. It brought him decent wages and food and the opportunity to do skilled work that earned the respect of his fellow cowboys. Kinchlow was hardened by his life working outside, but not so hardened that he forgot the beautiful sights he saw. "You could just see the lightnin' all over the steers' horns and your horse's ears and mane too," he recalled. "It would dangle all up and down his mane." No wonder, as an observer in East Texas wrote in the 1840s, "The young men that follow this 'Cow-Boy' life, not withstanding its hardships and exposures, generally become attached to it."

All of this cattle ranching changed the landscape of Texas just as much as it did the culture of the United States. Slowly but surely, cattle made most of the Texas countryside look different. Mesquite—a small tree or a large bush, depending on how you look at it, with narrow, drooping, olive-green leaves and thorns up to three inches long—is a good example. We know from archaeological digs and reading Cabeza de Vaca's accounts that mesquite has been in parts of Texas for thousands of years. One story that circulated in nineteenth-century Texas holds that "when Jesus Christ arose and ascended to Heaven, He passed over the country adjacent to the Rio Grande and that in his flight heavenward, He dropped the 'crown of thorns' and from it sprouted all of the mesquite and cactus on the border."

Whatever the role of Jesus Christ in the origins of mesquite, its range grew in lockstep with the expansion of cattle grazing, first around the missions of San Antonio and the ranches of the Rio Grande valley, then by the 1880s across central Texas and the Panhandle. Cattle were one agent of spread. Not only did they eat the tree's bean pods and thereby pass the seeds through their dietary tracts, but heavy grazing of grasslands left the bare soil that allowed mesquite and prickly pear cactus to grow more easily. Before white settlement, wildland fires had killed young mesquite and stimulated the regrowth of prairie grasses. By the 1880s, however, ranchers put out these fires to protect their fenceposts and buildings, unknowingly reducing one force that had kept grass growing in most rangelands. In much of West Texas, the grasslands that dominated the landscape in the middle of the century changed into deserts dominated by mesquite and creosote bushes by 1900. Soil washed down arroyos or was blown into dunes. There was at least one change of note in the animal life. At some point in the nineteenth century—it is hard to know exactly when—armadillos came into South Texas from Mexico, part of a long and slow journey north that has brought them into North Carolina, Indiana, and Georgia in the twenty-first century. A landscape with the distinctive light green of mesquite swaying in the wind, with prickly pears underfoot and an armadillo or two hiding in the grass seems like a timeless image of Texas. That is what I think of when I think of home. Yet like so much else that we associate with the state, this image bears the stamp of the dramatic changes of the nineteenth century.

The cattle drives that transformed the country and made Texan cattle culture so famous did not last long. The writers Owen Wister and John Lomax may have admired the cowboy because he stood apart from lives spent behind a desk or on a factory floor, but ranching was a modern business. In the early 1880s, successful ranchers like Charles Goodnight began to reinvest some of their considerable profits in barbed wire fencing, improved cattle herds such as the Hereford, and wells. The scale of their operations attracted British and Scottish capital. The fences they built closed off the open range, eventually making impossible the long-distance drives that had made Goodnight's reputation in the first place. Expanding rail networks across the southern Plains soon enough meant that cattle rode rather than walked to midwestern slaughterhouses.

Perhaps the clearest sign that ranching had changed was that in 1883 hundreds of Panhandle cowboys went on strike. They had the same complaints that people have in any other declining industry: too little money for too much work, with smaller and smaller chances to go into business for themselves. A few of the ranches raised wages slightly, while more simply fired the strikers. Unable to shut down the big ranches and force their owners to negotiate, the strikers failed.

As longhorns faded in economic importance and cowboys became more and more like other manual laborers, they only became stronger as symbols of a pure and noble history, with Texas lying at its heart. As ranchers replaced longhorns with calmer, fatter, and tastier breeds, Texans began celebrating the mean and tough animals. One cowboy—we do not know who—wrote the song "The Last Longhorn" in the late 1800s to mourn the passing of the longhorn as a symbol of how a cruder yet admirable past was giving way to a richer but less noble and somehow less Texan future. In this sad song, a dying longhorn declares: "I care not to linger / When all my friends are dead. / These Jerseys and these Holsteins, / They are no friends of mine; / They belong to the nobility / Who live across the brine." The song ends on a similar note of sorrow. "The cowboys and the longhorns / Who partnered in Eighty-Four / Have gone to their last round-up / Over on the other shore."

But not quite. In 1916, during the halftime of a football

game against archrival Texas A&M University, graduates of the University of Texas dragged a somewhat orange and very frightened longhorn onto midfield. "Behold him!" bellowed alumnus Tom Buffington to the huge crowd. "The Longhorn of Texas, emblematic as he stands of the fighting spirit of progress . . . As the great longhorn was free to roam the wilderness of Texas, so must the University be free to roam the world of thought, unhampered and unafraid." The steer was named "Bevo" and became an instant celebrity. (A&M students found him useful as well, sneaking into the stockyard where he was kept and branding him with 13–0, the score of their victory in the previous year's football showdown.) Bevo's habit of charging and trying to impale spectators made him poorly fit to remain on campus. He was removed to a ranch west of Austin, and several years later fattened and served as barbecue to the football team. Texans propelled themselves into the future by consuming their past.

13

Taming the Frontier

"In writing the history of a State, it is too often the case that a superficial view is taken of the factors that contributed to its development," wrote a Texas minister in the early twentieth century. "The soldier and the statesman are sure—but seldom is mention made of the educational and formative influences of the pulpit, the religious press, Christian education, and the Christian home." The author, the president of the Texas Methodist Historical Association, was referring to the remarkable success of Christian churches in the decades after the Civil War. They succeeded in attracting members, erecting thousands of houses of worship, changing the behavior and daily lives of their members, and shaping culture and politics far beyond their walls. Ministers were neither unchallenged nor alone in remaking culture and institutions in these years. Schools, universities, fraternal organizations, and newspapers also blossomed. Their leaders sometimes fought with Christian ministers, even ridiculing and attacking them. Alongside the elections and fighting that returned government into the hands of former Confederates and the wars with Indigenous nations that cleared the way for the cattle kingdoms of the Great Plains, these slower cultural changes in the countryside, small towns, and the state's emerging cities marked a new era for Texas. In its own distinctive way, it became a hotbed of culture, ideas, and civic institutions.

The Texas of these decades was by any measure an isolating, violent, and rough place for most of its inhabitants. San Antonio had long-standing and tight-knit communities, the founding wave of Anglo-American settlers formed close connections with one another, and German, Czech, and other European migrants were particularly likely to move in extended family and hometown groups that provided social support and economic security. Yet most of the state's rapidly swelling population came with only their immediate families and lived relatively far from one another. There were few churches, schools, or other social organizations in which these settlers could make friends, find romantic partners, or learn about the larger world. Farm wife Amelia Barr, impressed though she was by how the "flowery prairie rolled away magnificently to the far-off horizon," was haunted by the prospect of living her life in such a "lonely desolate place."

Violence was commonplace. In addition to the organized political and racial violence against Republicans, African Americans, people of Mexican descent, and Natives that took place in these decades, assaults, murders, and fights over all sorts of disputes were commonplace. The southern culture of most Texans made it legitimate, even admirable, for men to use violence to defend themselves, their property, their families, and their "honor"—a broad term that encompassed a person's reputation and public standing. It also made many men feel entitled to the bodies of women, who often found themselves vulnerable to sexual predation. The infusion of guns and veterans after the Civil War, the continued influx of new residents, and the poor functioning of the criminal justice system in most communities fueled more violence. In the 1870s a number of Texas locales, especially Lampasas and DeWitt Counties, became known nationally for violent "feuds" between families that lasted years, even decades. John Wesley Hardin gained notoriety for killing dozens of men in these years. His autobiography, published in 1896, a year after his death, only cemented his reputation as a quick-drawing gunman. "A bullet to the front of the head," he wrote, "demonstrates good marksmanship. A bullet to the back of the head demonstrates good judgement." Hardin's national celebrity testified to how much Texan culture glorified violence. The best statistics that researchers have generated suggest a murder rate around thirty times that of the United States in the 2020s, about 250 per 100,000 inhabitants. "We can scarcely conceive," wrote one shocked northern observer after reading accounts of Texas violence, "how it is possible to live and be happy in a country where every man's hand seems to be raised against his neighbor; where the law is disregarded from the inefficiency of the central government to enforce its execution, where each member is the sentinel of his own safety, and where the shedding of blood, and even of life, is held to be a mere bagatelle."

Over time, however, the isolation, violence, and general roughness of Texas society softened, gradually making way for a life with more social ties, self-restraint, and even refinement. Cultural and intellectual changes are hard to quantify because they have so much to do with beliefs and feelings. But there are some numbers that suggest something of the scope of this transformation. The decade of the Civil War was hard on churches and schools. Even taking into account the congregations and schoolrooms that newly freed slaves soon established, in 1870 there were fewer than seven hundred church buildings for an overwhelmingly Christian state population of more than 800,000. "I am afraid the way from Texas to Heaven has never been blazed out," opined one writer. Over the next two decades, the number of churches grew at about three times the rate of the population, soon surpassing the ratio seen in other southern states. The churches themselves were more substantial structures and their ministers much better paid. Congregations in towns and cities supported their own full-time ministers, while smaller assemblies were served by preachers who rode from church to church, often ministering in addition to their regular employment.

Formal education saw similar growth, even if Texas schools did not become as comparatively well developed as the state's churches. Low population densities made it hard to establish schools close enough to a critical mass of children, a factor that was made all the more difficult to overcome when different schools were run for Black and white children. Most families preferred for teenagers to work in the fields than attend distant schools. And you needed teachers to run schools, but there were few ways to train or recruit them. So Texas left the 1860s with the lowest rates of schools, teachers, and enrolled students of any state in the entire country. But this gradually began to improve. The number of schools and teachers nearly tripled from the early 1870s to 1885. In primary education, unlike religion, there was an enormous difference in the experiences of white and Black Texans. By 1900, 94 percent of white men were literate, but barely half of Black men were; almost half of white children were enrolled in school, but barely a third of Black kids were. The shadow of slavery (which made it illegal for the enslaved to learn to read and write), segregation in education, and the comparative poverty of the Black population (which led teenagers to leave school for the fields or other workplaces) all still took their tolls.

It is difficult for modern readers, maybe even religiously observant ones, to appreciate just how important Christianity and church communities were to the lives of nineteenth-century Texans. To hear that you were a child of God, loved and deserving of respect, was to gain a standing that your ragged clothing, rough farmstead, and meager possessions could not give you. Sermons and hymns reminded churchgoers that a better world was waiting for them, beyond the endless hard work, disease, and violence of this one. "O they tell me of a home far beyond the skies," begins the hymn "An Unclouded Day," written in the 1880s and sung often enough nearly a century later for a young Willie Nelson to put it on one of his albums. "O they tell me of a home far away; O they tell me of a home where no storm clouds rise; O they tell me of an uncloudy day."

The dominant forms of Christianity, especially the Methodism and Baptism that were the most popular among both Blacks and whites, held that true religion was a matter of individual belief, and even direct communication between individuals and God. They also validated and reinforced the ties that bound people to one another. This was the theme of "Blest Be the Tie That Binds," an eighteenth-century hymn from England that became one of the most frequently sung in Texas.

> Blest be the tie that binds
> our hearts in Christian love;
> the fellowship of kindred minds
> is like to that above.
> Before our Father's throne

we pour our ardent prayers;
our fears, our hopes, our aims are one,
our comforts and our cares.
We share our mutual woes,
our mutual burdens bear,
and often for each other flows
the sympathizing tear.

Believers would be reunited in heaven with spouses, children, and siblings torn from them by war, diseases, or the slave trade. In this world, their marriages were holy and demanded respect. And the ethic of love and respect for others at the center of Christian doctrine could be a powerful incentive to refrain from the violence and fighting so commonplace in this rough society. Christians were supposed to forgive, not retaliate; as the Lord's Prayer says, "Forgive us our trespasses, as we forgive those who trespass against us." The social consequences of this impulse were widely discussed. As a Dallas writer put it in an article entitled simply "Believe God," the aim of Christian doctrine is "to restrain and correct our evil propensities." One Ellis County man who confessed his sins at a Baptist church in front of his neighbors was typical in experiencing his conversion not just as a matter of him and God, but him and his neighbors as well. "When I opened my eyes the congregation appeared transfigured. I loved everybody." Religion promised individual salvation and righteousness, but was also key to social harmony. "The gospel of Christ," boasted a Dallas pastor, "throws around you a stronger and more efficient protection than can be given by law or musket."

In addition to refraining from violence, one of the primary ways that Christians could live better with one another, and in the eyes of God, was to avoid alcohol. So believed the ministers of most Protestant denominations. Cumberland Presbyterians, Baptists, and Methodists expected one another to avoid consuming alcohol at all. Drunkenness was one of the most common sins confessed at church meetings, a fact that speaks to both the ubiquity of alcohol and the growing opposition to its abuse. Ministers consistently advocated temperance, the avoidance of alcohol and drunkenness, which they believed would reduce all kinds of social problems, especially violence. By 1871, temperance societies formed a statewide association and began publishing the *Temperance Family Visitor*. Ministers played key roles in these organizations, and many churches hosted meetings devoted to the advocacy of temperance. The focus of temperance crusades on restraining violence and misbehavior by men may account for some of the disproportionate appeal that Protestant denominations held for women. By the twentieth century, nearly 60 percent of white Methodist, Baptist, and Church of Christ denominations were female, with Black congregations seeing even higher rates.

Efforts to regulate gun ownership emerged from the same commitment to restraint and peacefulness as did temperance. Although supporters of gun control never became as organized or powerful as temperance advocates, they made Texas a national leader in the regulation of weapons in the 1870s. Texas constitutions from the days of the republic onward incorporated language about protecting the right to bear arms, but legislators also sought to limit who bore arms and how, restricting trading guns with Indians and the ability of slaves to carry weapons. Appalled by "thoughtless youths and others who bear them for show or other purposes," legislatures in the 1860s considered placing a steep tax on firearms carried in public. They could not agree on an amount, but settled on a measure banning the firing of guns in urban areas and the carrying of guns on private property without the permission of the landowner. In practice the latter measure limited the firearms rights of poor white and Black Texans, since few owned their own land. Measures passed in the 1870s, when Black Republicans and white Unionists controlled the statehouse, went further in limiting where and when weapons of many sorts could be carried. One law banned the possession of "any pistol, dirk, dagger, sung-shot, sword-cane, spear, brass knuckles, bowie knife, or any other kind of knife" in most public places. Law enforcement officers claimed that the measure, passed in 1871, was one cause of the sharp decline in violent crime from the 1870s on. The legislature repeatedly changed penalties for carrying sanctioned weapons over time, but the 1871 law remained on the books until the 1990s, making Texas a national leader in gun control. This was another reflection of the effort by Texans to tame their most destructive impulses.

The formation of a statewide temperance organization was another sign of the gradual development of larger-scale religious and educational institutions. Church life remained rooted in individual congregations, but denominations developed a social and educational infrastructure to better carry out their work. Larger Protestant denominations caught up with the smaller but better-established Catholic Church by creating regional bureaucracies that provided training and support for the ministers and materials for church services and Sunday schools. The Baptist General Convention of Texas, an organization of white Baptist congregations and ministers, consolidated itself in the 1880s. B. H. Carroll, the pastor of Waco's First Baptist Church, made himself the state's most influential minister by virtue of his spellbinding sermons, publications on Christian doctrine and history, and Baptist institution-building. In 1886, Carroll became chair of the board of Baylor University (where he also taught). Baylor merged with Waco University, putting it on solid enough footing to offer undergraduate education, train ministers, and in the coming decades begin training medical professionals. The Agricultural and Mechanical College of Texas (later Texas A&M), the state's first STEM-oriented institution, opened its doors in College Station in 1876, with a counterpart for the education of Black students and training of Black teachers in Prairie View. They were soon joined by the University of Texas in Austin and a medical school in Galveston in 1883. Together with Southwestern University, Austin College, and AddRan Male and Female College (later Texas Christian University), the opening of these schools meant that Texas, formerly dependent on the migration of educated people from elsewhere, could now train its own professional class.

Organized religion and public education were not the only tools Texans had for understanding the world. The Patrons of Husbandry, known commonly as the Grange, brought farmers together to discuss how to best practice agriculture. They not only learned about fertilizers, crop rotations, and new varieties of plants that might yield more or better resist drought and insects in their particular environmental conditions, but also discussed policy matters such as monopolies, the regulation of railroads, and banking reforms. The first Grange chapter was formed in Salado in the summer of 1873. Two years later, more than a thousand lodges brought together 40,000 members across the state. The focus of Freemasonry, a fraternal order with secret internal rituals but a public focus, was broader, aimed at fostering the virtues of reason and self-governance (as opposed to relying on religious authority backed by the authoritarian governments in Europe where Freemasonry originated). Masons supported education, to the extent that lodges ran informal schools, and raised money to support orphans, widows, and the aged. The Texas branch of the Masonic fraternity also expanded in these years, drawing on better educated and wealthy men for its members, who numbered around

18,000 by 1880. A host of smaller voluntary organizations, such as the Sons of Hermann or the Gran Círculo de Obreros Mexicanos, provided burial insurance and legal aid to members and also supported libraries, adult education in history and culture, and festivals celebrating German and Mexican holidays.

Music and food bore similar marks of the maturation of Texas society. Tastes and sounds brought by new neighbors could stimulate the imagination. Tejanos began playing the accordion and polka tunes favored by Czechs and Germans, adding goatskin drums to the singing of northern Mexican ranch songs and ballads. This laid the groundwork for the music known as "conjunto" that became more widespread in the twentieth century. With a beat that sounded like a biergarten band in central Europe and lyrics about Mexican country life, conjunto was a child of Texas. In the same years, German immigrant William Gebhardt became enamored with the taste of Mexican food. He began to experiment with drying and grinding chilis (rather than eating them only when in season), at first for his own restaurants in San Antonio and New Braunfels, and then for wider sale. The result was Gebhardt's chili powder, which grew into a national business, and the publication of one of the first English-language Mexican food cookbooks.

Texan culture is thought of as one of doing, not thinking, one of emotions and instincts rather than ideas and arguments. But the denseness of these social networks, the rich set of overlapping institutions, the constant exposure to different and even conflicting ideas about God, the world, and society, leave no doubt that Texas culture of the late nineteenth century was indeed intellectual. Cities including Waco and Dallas hosted key nodes in these networks of ideas and culture, such as prominent congregations, universities, and newspapers; Waco was known as the "Athens of Texas" for this reason. But to a degree that is hard for many contemporary city-dwellers who learn about the world through the internet or publications from New York to understand, intellectual life remained locally rooted. A town like Auburn, forty miles south of Fort Worth, was typical in boasting only several hundred residents but supporting a Masonic lodge, four churches, a post office, and a school. Small-town residents "are in such close touch with the world," wrote one Methodist preacher to another, "that they are no longer the 'ignorant country folk' of a decade back." In his town, residents "know what the world is doing." A Lutheran counterpart agreed, observing, "Texas has been looked on as rather an uncivilized country, in which wild cowboys and lawlessness reign supreme." But because of "Christianity and its handmaid, general education," he continued, "social and political life everywhere is made better."

A heavy majority of Texans were Christian and the largest organizations were churches. Yet ministers and churches had very little power over elections and policies. They found this out in 1887, when Protestant ministers pushed a constitutional amendment to ban the sale of alcohol and were overwhelmingly defeated at the polls. Many thousands of churchgoing voters who saw drunkenness as a sin nonetheless voted against this measure. Anti-clericalism—opposition to religious organizations and leaders wielding political power—characterized the branches of Christianity most observed in Texas. "Ah my fellow-citizens," thundered Senator Richard Coke to a crowd of 5,000 gathered in a Waco park in 1885, "whenever your preachers go into politics, scourge them back!" Criticizing B. H. Carroll by name, Coke repeatedly drew cheers from Waco's citizens not just for his opposition to banning the sale of alcohol, but also for his attack on the whole idea that ministers should have anything to do with what laws politicians passed. "The worst sign of the times that I can perceive," he said, "is to be found in the delivery of stump speeches on the holy Sabbath day from God's pulpit." Coke was by any reasonable measure a very, very conservative leader. He had fought for the Confederacy, led white Democrats back to power over an interracial coalition of Texas Republicans, and cut state expenditures in his two terms as governor in order to keep taxes low. The fact that he drew such a sharp line between religion and politics, and was supported by so many when he did so publicly in the heart of the state's Baptist establishment, shows just how strong Texans' anti-clericalism was. Indeed, the state constitution ratified in 1876 banned state money from going to "any sectarian school," teachers were forbidden from praying or reading the Bible in school, and ministers could not hold public office. One governor in the 1870s refused to declare a public day of prayer for the recovery of President James Garfield as he lay dying, on the grounds that doing so violated the separation of church and state.

In some ways, this was not so different from the rest of the United States, especially in the South, where at the time religious involvement in politics was associated with the northern abolitionists whom most white southerners faulted for starting sectional conflict and ultimately the Civil War. ("The religious principle of New England and Ohio makes their politics," said one of Coke's allies, and "we have seen plenty of that in the war.") The memory of living under Mexican rule, which mandated adherence to Catholicism, was a Texas twist to this widely shared anti-clericalism. Leaders like Coke mentioned religious coercion and its ugly legacies, offering lurid depictions of ignorance and violence in medieval Europe as proof that freedom and the separation of church and state went hand in hand.

TAMING THE FRONTIER 175

Religious pluralism—the belief that not all needed to practice the same religion, or indeed any religion—further limited the political power of Christian ministers. The twenty-eight state representatives elected in 1870 who claimed "no religion" were the largest single group in the legislature, outnumbering Methodists (fourteen), Baptists (ten), and Episcopalians (seven). One legislator identified himself as a deist, another as a spiritualist, and four simply as "liberal."

The state's Jewish community came into its own in these decades. Several thousand Jewish residents, mostly German in background and practicing Reform Judaism, assembled congregations in scores of towns and cities. They became numerous and organized enough to hire formally credentialed rabbis, maintain their own burial plots, and erect their own buildings. The one hundred or so Jewish families living in Waco were able to hold bar mitzvahs, throw parties on Purim, and erect a handsome temple. When a visiting Jewish leader from England came to Waco in the early twentieth century, he was impressed not only that the rabbi of Temple Rodef Shalom had been trained to the Torah in eastern Europe, but also that he was invited to address such gatherings as the "Possum and Tater Club," where he delivered a speech entitled "The Moral Effect of the Possum" to several hundred of the leading citizens of the capital of Texas Baptists. In this congregation as in the state's other Jewish communities, members managed both to practice their own distinctive religion and culture and to take part in a larger Texas society.

Texas, one newspaper editor wrote, "is an exceedingly cosmopolitan state, made so by its very immensity. Tolerance is indigenous there because of that exalted idea of person or individual freedom which finds its highest type and its most exalted expression in range, latitude, and boundlessness." "When

176 TAMING THE FRONTIER

a man in Texas," he continued, "begins to prescribe certain metes and bounds wherein his neighbor shall walk and conduct himself, he is either lassoed or scalped."

Religion was central to cultural and intellectual life, but it was not the only source of cultural authority or insight into the world. "Freethinking"—a European tradition that rejected adherence to organized religion or other creeds in favor of a devotion to what its followers considered to be reason—was particularly strong in German Hill Country towns, but found adherents across the state. Some freethinkers went so far as to see organized religion as a con game. A Dallas freethinker stated that "Hell and heaven are the inventions of human leeches called priests and preachers, who live upon the blood they suck from terrified ignorance." In a similar spirit, Waco's J. D. Shaw, expelled from his Methodist pulpit in 1882, formed the "Religious and Benevolent Association," which organized lectures and discussions aimed to "satisfy the growing demand of our most liberal and independent thinkers on the moral, intellectual, and social questions of the day." Shaw provoked the anger of the Baptist establishment to the degree that he was criticized personally and at length in numerous sermons. But "Liberal Hall," his organization's Waco headquarters, stood as a kind of secular church and a physical rebuke to Christian orthodoxy. Shaw himself sat on Waco's city council and served as an officer in a Confederate veteran's organization, proving that you did not have to conform to dominant Christian ways to enjoy social prominence.

There were, however, limits to this culture of debate and criticism. The world of the church, university, and schoolhouse never replaced the violent, coarse side of Texas culture. In fact the two went together, as William Cowper Brann discovered. Brann, a newspaperman who wrote and edited for numerous Texas newspapers, launched a monthly paper, *The*

Iconoclast, from Waco in the 1890s. One hundred thousand readers from all over Texas, the United States, and the English-speaking world beyond subscribed, making Brann wealthy and influential. *The Iconoclast*'s readership dwarfed the circulation of *The Baptist Standard,* the voice of the Baptist establishment published across town. Brann's readers admired him for insisting that rationality and freedom of thought, not social convention and inherited religion, should guide modern people. His friends and frequent correspondents included the civil rights crusader Frederick Douglass, poet Walt Whitman, and socialist Eugene Debs. Brann ridiculed Baylor University as a "great storm-center of misinformation" whose students "are chiefly forks-of-the-creek yaps" who "wear the same undershirt the year round [and] take but two baths in their lifetime—one when they are born, the other when they are baptized." He gleefully accused its president and other leaders of covering up the rape of Antonia Texeira, a young woman from Brazil studying to become a missionary while lodging in the president's home. Baylor's defenders struck back: a student group kidnapped Brann in 1897, and a few days later, after his release, a Baptist judge beat him with a cane on the street in front of *The Iconoclast*'s offices. The next month, in retaliation, Brann's friend, a county judge, shot and killed the editor of Waco's daily paper and his brother on the city's main street. The following April, fate caught up with Brann. An enraged Baylor University supporter shot him in the back as he walked down the street. Brann turned, drew his own weapon, and emptied six bullets into his assailant before he collapsed. Both men bled to death on the street in front of horrified onlookers. For better or for worse, Texans fought and died for their ideas.

14

The People's Party

Part of the mythos of Texas is that it is conservative. Texans, the assumption goes, and especially white Texans, and even more so rural white Texans, believe in unregulated capitalism and celebrate male bravado and prowess. They have for a long time, the myth continues, and there is no end in sight. After all, Texas was a slave state, part of the Confederacy, practiced formal racial segregation until the Civil Rights Movement stopped it, and as of the publication of this book has not elected a Democrat to statewide office for thirty years. If you want to find labor unions, leftist politicians, and people who experiment with gender roles, try California or New York.

The People's Party (or Populist Party) of Texas and the farmers' organizations from which it emerged contradict this myth. In the 1880s and 1890s, hundreds of thousands of farmers and their families—mostly white people born in Texas and nearby southern states, but also considerable numbers of African American, Bohemian, German, and Hispanic Texans—supported a third party that was all about reforming capitalism, that opened up new roles for women, and that at times practiced interracial cooperation and solidarity. In the 1890s, Populists won twenty-two seats in the Texas House of Representatives and two in the state senate. They earned as much as 44 percent of the statewide vote (peaking in the gubernatorial contest of 1896) and made credible runs for national congressional seats. The threat to the monopoly on power of the Democratic Party was serious enough to prompt leading Democrats to address the key issues of railroad regulation and the banking system. (And later, it made Democratic leaders see the appeal of stricter and more codified racial segregation, to prevent another serious challenge to their single-party rule.) Populism was strong across the South, in much of the Midwest and Mountain states, and even in places on the West Coast. Nationally, it is the most successful third-party movement since the solidification of the Republican Party in the 1850s. Its key institutions and ideas and many of its leading figures came from Texas. Though ultimately defeated as a political movement, Populism changed the institutions, policies, and politics of Texas and the United States.

"Secure to our people freedom from the onerous and shameful abuses that the industrial classes are now suffering at the hands of arrogant capitalists and powerful corporations," thundered the Grand State Farmers' Alliance in its 1886 meeting at Cleburne, a farm town thirty miles south of Fort Worth. Founded in 1877 in the Hill Country town of Lampasas, the Alliance sought to improve the economic security of farm families by aiding in their self-education about such practical matters as accounting, bookkeeping, crop yields, and interest rates, but also in more intellectual fare like the histories and politics of the United States, Europe, Latin America, and Asia, with an emphasis on the role of farming and farmers. In this regard, it was clearly a part of the intellectual and cultural awakening of the 1870s and 1880s. The organization's work was wildly popular. By the end of the 1880s, it had 225,000 members statewide—more than 10 percent of the population—and 1.2 million nationwide. Alliance leader Charles Macune, from Cameron, predicted that the organization would become "the most powerful and complete educator of modern times." He had reason to brag. In addition to education, the Farmers' Alliance also fostered economic cooperation. County Alliance chapters bargained with merchants for lower prices in exchange for Alliance members' business, and many began to open farm supply stores and mills for cotton and grain of their own, hoping to keep more of the wealth produced by farming in the hands of farmers rather than with merchants and banks.

These efforts at economic cooperation raised political questions. Farmers needed loans for their spring plantings and household essentials until the fall harvest, so it made sense to concern themselves with how money and credit were created. Most were dependent on railroads to get their harvest to markets, so they discussed whether state governments should regulate railroad companies (especially since the companies had benefited from government funding and land grants) or let them set their own prices. Some Alliance members and leaders opposed any move into politics, believing it most effective for farmers to defend their interests only by education and cooperation, and fearing that partisan competition would bring rivalry and division. Others saw developing populist policies and running candidates to implement them as the logical next step for the Farmers' Alliance. In 1891, these Texas Alliance

THE PEOPLE'S PARTY   181

members met in Dallas and founded the People's Party, which began competing for office the following year.

It is hard to make the Populist platform fit neatly into current ideas of what is liberal or conservative. Populists seem left-wing in their condemnation of corporations and concentrated wealth, which they felt were strangling democracy. "Corporations are wielding dread influences in national and state politics," proclaimed the Texas party's first platform, and "the United States senate has become a den of millionaires, who are infinitely a more terrible menace to free government than the dreaded house of lords of Great Britain." For Populists, wealth rightly belonged to those whose work produced it, and its theft by the rich threatened democracy itself. As the party's national platform declared in 1892, "The fruits of the toil of millions are boldly stolen to build up colossal fortunes for a few, unprecedented in the history of mankind; and the possessors of these, in turn, despise the republic and endanger liberty." In this vein, Populists supported the right of wage workers to form unions, and laws limiting work to eight hours a day. The call for railroads and telegraphs to be regulated, and if necessary owned by the national government, struck many Texans as a call for Socialism.

On the other hand, the purpose of this regulation was to allow Americans to live proudly and independently as owners and operators of farms and other small businesses. So the desired outcome was in one sense an intensely capitalist society, in which property was owned by individuals and goods and services were exchanged in markets they freely joined. The party's denunciation of excessive government expenditures and the ownership of land by foreigners seems to anticipate later conservative ideas. So does the widely shared sense in Populist circles, or at least among white Populists, that common people had been better off in the past, that bankers in far-off cities had somehow robbed the common working people of their birthright. They wanted America to be great again.

Populists focused, sometimes to the point of obsession, on currency policy, how money was produced and regulated. This has been harder for later observers to characterize or even understand. Monetary policy may seem arcane, but it was a pressing concern at the time: a limited supply of money and dramatic economic growth across the country after the Civil War made it difficult to get loans and meant that farmers who had to go into debt to buy land and seeds to plant did so on very disadvantageous terms. This was particularly true in the South, where the banking system had been wrecked by the Civil War and emancipation. Increasingly, farmers in Texas and elsewhere had to rely on local merchants for advances of food, clothing, equipment, and seed stock. The merchants insisted on higher prices for credit than for cash, and charged astonishing interest rates, sometimes over 200 percent annually! Farmers with no choice had to sign agreements called liens on their next harvest, granting the merchant first access to the money from the sale of their crops. Merchants generally insisted that indebted farmers plant cotton, and that it be sold immediately after harvest (when prices declined because the crops ripened all at the same time). The high interest rates, lowered cotton prices, and deflation caused by limited money supply meant that many farm families who went into debt could never repay it. Such families had lost their independence and were effectively trapped working for their lenders, even if they continued to own their own land. Others ended up selling their land or simply abandoning it and moving to escape crushing debt. By 1890, almost half of Texas farmers (and a heavy majority of Black farmers) worked land owned by others, a figure that only continued to increase. No wonder that farmers referred to such merchants as "the furnishing man," or simply "the man."

To address these problems, Populists wanted to dramatically expand the amount of currency in circulation, in order to make it easier for farmers and other producers to secure loans and invest in their businesses. A call for the government to put more money into circulation by linking money to silver (of which there was a rapidly expanding supply) instead of gold (which had a relatively fixed supply) became a staple of Populist platforms. A more elaborate proposal to democratize the finance system, called the subtreasury plan, became increasingly popular in agrarian circles in the early 1890s. The brainchild of Texas Farmers' Alliance leader Charles Macune, the subtreasury plan provided for the federal government to issue greenback dollars to farmers who deposited crops in government-owned warehouses. This currency would be "full legal tender for all debts, public and private," and would thus mean that farmers could avoid going into debt to merchants, banks, and mortgage companies. The more crops the country produced, the more money would be in circulation, and the more profits would end up in the pockets of those who actually produced wealth.

The subtreasury was a complicated proposal, so much so that I find it difficult to explain to my students more than a century later. It provoked angry denunciations from mainstream party officials and leading bankers, who insisted that money was not "real" unless it could be exchanged for a precious metal like gold. They were also angered that mere farmers would dare to weigh in on such complicated matters. "Men with unkempt and matted hair, men with long beards matted together with filth from their noses, men reeking with lice," as one newspaper described a Populist convention, "men whose feet stank, and the odor from under whose arms would have knocked down a bull." Yet the subtreasury plan demonstrates that no matter how hardscrabble the lives of most Populists were, their economic thinking was very sophisticated. Indeed, later in the twentieth century, long after Populism per se had been defeated, academic economists came to accept the idea of "fiat currency," or that money is in fact created by societies and has no "real" value outside of that context. How many Americans today actually understand how the Federal Reserve works to regulate the money supply, or could even name the head of the Federal Reserve? Although they were derided for being backward-looking, simple "hicks" or "hayseeds," Texas Populists were deeply informed about the economy of their day and forward-looking in their efforts to change it.

Perhaps this is because they had witnessed such dramatic social changes in their own lifetimes. In the time since the Civil War, Texas had developed more integrated markets, a vastly larger railroad system, and urban economies in real cities. San Antonio had been the only place that could claim to be truly urban when Texas joined the United States. Galveston's bustling port made it the state's largest city by 1870. The boom in the following decades was spectacular. In 1878, for example, more railroad track was laid in Texas than in the rest of the country combined, expediting a statewide population explosion from 818,000 in 1870 to more than three million in 1900. By 1890, Dallas, Fort Worth, and Houston joined Galveston and San Antonio in exceeding 20,000 people each. These were still very small places when compared with New York (2.6 million) or Chicago (1.1 million), but residents and visitors could see some of the features of modern cities. Electrical networks brought light to streetlamps and powered streetcar systems. Telephones, first installed by the publisher of the *Galveston News* to connect his home and office, could be found in these cities and larger towns as well.

THE PEOPLE'S PARTY 185

Yet even as the twentieth century approached, the state remained overwhelmingly rural. The vast majority of people, 84 percent, lived in the countryside, where almost all worked in agriculture. The most important industries—flour milling and lumber production—were tied closely to the countryside, where most of the state's dramatic population growth went. The number of farms increased from 61,000 in 1870 to 228,000 in 1890. Therefore, the Populist efforts to make the agricultural economy fairer for farmers affected the lives of almost all Texans.

By the 1890s, about one in every five Texans was Black. They asked themselves what promise or threat this energetic movement held for them. On one hand, the factors that created Populism hurt Black farmers even more: they had less money and were less likely to own land than the rest of the population, and were therefore even more dependent on lenders. But white farmers, who in Texas were mostly former Confederates and even slaveowners, balked at working alongside their Black neighbors. The Farmers' Alliance refused to accept Black farmers as members, so Black organizers founded the Colored Farmers' National Alliance and Cooperative Union later in 1886. The union published its own newspaper, sponsored lecturers to advance the education of farmers, and engaged in cooperative economic efforts. White Populists were more open to Black participation than the Farmers' Alliance: Black activists were present at the founding convention of the Texas People's Party in Dallas in 1891. They spoke in meetings, voted on measures, and were addressed respectfully by white delegates. Two Black attendees were elected to the new party's seventeen-member state committee.

Black Populists worked energetically and effectively to drum up support for the new party, and to advocate for the distinctive needs of Black Texans within it. John B. Rayner, a

Calvert schoolteacher, and Melvin Wade, a Dallas carpenter, became the two best-known Black Texas Populists, and among the most active and sought-after Populist speakers across the state. In one of his best-known speeches, Wade openly compared the economic conditions of both white and Black farmers to the exploitation of slavery, encouraging his interracial audiences to see that they had the same interests and the same enemies. If you take Black Populists like Rayner and Wade together with their counterparts across the South as a whole, then Black Populism was the largest political mobilization of African Americans until the Civil Rights Movement six decades later.

White Populists listened to these leaders if for no other reason than the fact that they had to if they wanted to win elections. Rayner, Wade, and others successfully pushed white Populist legislators to support Black demands for equal funding for schools and to oppose a bill requiring separate railroad waiting rooms for Blacks and whites. White Populists also voted to allow Black citizens to hold a memorial for the abolitionist and civil rights crusader Frederick Douglass, who died in 1895, in the chamber of the Texas House of Representatives. Leading white Populists publicly committed themselves to supporting Black political rights, as when "Stump" Ashby told his fellow white delegates, "We want to do good to every citizen of the country, and he [the Black man] is a citizen just as much as we are."

Yet there were sharp limits to what inclusivity meant to white agrarians. Many white Populists articulated a strong sense of innate white supremacy in their writings, like other white supremacists pointing to Darwinian biology as proof of their supposedly greater "fitness." White Populist officeholders seated Blacks on juries in some counties, while in others they criticized Democrats for courting Black voters. Populist guberna-

THE PEOPLE'S PARTY 187

torial candidate Jerome Kearby was much more reluctant to condemn lynching than was the Democratic governor James Hogg. And more generally, white Populists were very afraid that being depicted as too sympathetic toward African Americans, particularly as willing to tolerate social intimacy with them, would doom their chances for success with the overwhelmingly white electorate.

Populists were more clearly egalitarian when it came to questions of gender. More freedom for women was part of the bright future for which they hoped. "If independence of thought and action is good for the development of man," wrote a woman correspondent under the pen name "Ann Other" to a Dallas agrarian newspaper, "why would it not be for women?" Most men active in the movement agreed. At the close of the nineteenth century, women were barred from the professions, could not vote or serve on juries, were legally dependent on their fathers or husbands in economic matters such as selling property or opening a bank account, and could not vote or hold positions in most Christian denominations. But in the People's Party and its allied agrarian organizations, there was a more progressive attitude and infrastructure. Women could attend meetings, speak, vote, and hold office on the same terms as men. Many served as lecturers, secretaries, and treasurers for chapters of the Farmers' Alliance. Male and female authors alike in the Populist press addressed the need for expanded opportunities for women. Bettie Gay, who took over the management of her family's farm outside of Columbus after her husband's death in 1880, was among the most prolific. Not only did she join most other Populists in supporting voting rights for women, but she also believed more generally that the Populist movement would "redeem woman from her enslaved condition." This would happen through the security for farming brought by cooperatives and a flexible currency, but also by changes in married life such as fair divorce laws, the removal of the word "obey" from women's marriage vows, and equal sharing of housework. No wonder that the novelist Hamlin Garland, a close observer of agrarians, believed that "No other movement in history—not even the anti-slavery cause—appealed to women" as much as Populism.

The complicated religious cultures of Texas left their mark on Populism. Most Populists, like most Texans, were evangelical Protestants. It was no accident that the party's camp meetings looked like Christian revivals. Families came in wagons from miles around, with picnic dinners in tow. Children played with one another while adults listened to speakers on a temporary stage with canvas covering (often borrowed from a church). Most campaign songs, backed by string and brass bands, were adaptations of hymns, as when "All Hail the Power of Jesus' Name" became "All Hail the Power of Working Men." Populists called one another "brother" and "sister" and spoke of their message as a "gospel." Many Populist orators and candidates, including a former president of Baylor University, were ministers or former ministers, to the extent that the *Dallas Morning News* referred to the "popular belief that more than two-thirds of the populist orators have at some time or another been connected with the ministry." These Populists were particularly likely to rebuke conservative ministers who held that the purpose of Christianity was to reconcile believers with God in preparation for the afterlife. "Christ did not come," said a white minister from Austin, "to prepare men for another world, but to teach them how to live rightly in this . . . if we do not christianize human relations in business, trade, and industry, substituting the law of association and fraternal justice for the infernal principle of competition, our civilization will go down in ruin, we will go down with it and we will deserve our fate." The Populist organizer and stump speaker Melvin Wade

THE PEOPLE'S PARTY   189

similarly took aim at apolitical Black ministers, once telling an audience, "I love the church and believe in Jesus Christ, but the darkies run too much to church. We're allus singin' 'Give me Jesus' . . . Well the white man owns the world and the n*****s own Jesus. Let us sing, 'Give me Jesus and a share of everything else.'"

Nevertheless, Protestantism did not have a monopoly on Populist thought or political style. A great number of leading Populists were quite skeptical of conventional Christianity, especially the claim of Jesus Christ's unique divinity, to the extent that they had to fend off charges of atheism or hostility to Christianity. Some, like John Rayner, left the ministry, convinced that free thought and science, rather than Christian orthodoxy, were the right tools to understand and improve the world.

As a political party, Populism crashed and burned by 1900. The party was not strong enough to replace either Democrats or Republicans. Its best route to power was to ally with reform-minded elements of one of the two major parties. But some Populists refused to make alliances with Democrats, viewing such partnerships as a betrayal of the commitment to real economic freedom and a compromise with opponents who lied, cheated, and sometimes killed to maintain their positions of power. When the national Democratic Party nominated the young and charismatic Nebraska senator William Jennings Bryan, who endorsed many Populist measures, as its presidential candidate in 1896, Texas Populists split over whether to follow suit.

This disarray was joined by massive fraud and violence organized at the polls by the Democratic establishment. "Not a negro voted," bragged the judge of Robertson County, where John B. Rayner lived, because "I went down to the polls and took my six-shooter." In Grimes County, sixty miles north of Houston, electoral violence after 1896 looked a lot like a coup.

The "White Man's Union," founded by Democrats who had been defeated over several elections by a coalition of white Populists and Black voters, assassinated Black leaders and wounded the white Populist sheriff Garrett Scott, who had hired Black deputies and helped equalize funding for schools. As his injury turned gangrenous, armed members of the White Man's Union occupied the county courthouse and kept Scott pinned down in the jail across the street. On the edge of death, he was evacuated by a National Guard unit and left the county. Leading white Populist families and as much as a third of the county's Black citizens followed him in fleeing the county. Populist nominees for office withdrew their candidacies, fearing for their lives. This was the kind of onslaught that ensured that Populism as a viable statewide party contending for power died before 1900.

What would Texas have looked like had the Populists continued as a party, fielding candidates, sponsoring newspapers, developing policies, and making its case to the electorate? That is the greatest "might have been" of modern Texas. Had their policies been enacted and worked at least to a degree, more Texans would have owned their own land (and perhaps remained on farms and in small towns). Cooperative businesses, trade unions, and social organizations would have left a much larger stamp on economics and social life, as they did later in Germany and Nordic countries with strong cooperative movements. The Black fifth of the population would have continued to enjoy more political rights, like voting, and tangible benefits of power such as well-funded schools, that a white supremacist Democratic Party denied them with discriminatory laws and horrific mob violence.

In fact, despite its end as an organized movement, Popu-

THE PEOPLE'S PARTY 191

lism proved to be hugely influential, in Texas and beyond. The Democrat James Hogg, twice elected governor in the 1890s, implemented key aspects of the party's platform. He created a Railroad Commission to control railroad prices, forced railroad companies to honestly account for their value, pushed landowning corporations to sell some of their holdings to settlers, passed the second state-level anti-monopoly law in the country, and expanded state funding for higher education. These measures created regulatory agencies and laws that would become critical players in Texas in its more urban and industrial twentieth-century economy. Like the Populists to whose platform he was so sympathetic, Hogg appealed to Black voters, proposing strong laws against lynching. In the next few decades, better-heeled and more urban reformers in both the main parties adopted Populist policies, creating a national income tax, the direct election of U.S. senators, support for farmers, direct democracy measures including referendums on legislation, voting rights for women, and federal regulation of the supply of money. All of these measures were backed by the Populist Party or had been widely espoused by this creative political movement deeply rooted in Texas and its culture.

15

Fighting for Democracy

One bright winter morning in 1919, José Tomás "J. T." Canales walked up to the state capitol building, which loomed over Austin. This was normal, since he was in his fifth term as a state representative from Cameron County, on the Mexican border at the state's southern tip, and the legislature was in session. What was less routine was how he walked—with his wife, his friend and fellow representative Sam Johnson, and other trusted colleagues surrounding him so as to make him a more difficult target for assassination. Years later, Canales wrote that his work that legislative session "nearly cost my life."

Canales feared murder not from an angry constituent or deranged stalker, but rather from the Texas Rangers. The Rangers were a legendary force dating back to the days of Austin's colony, famous for their physical prowess, wiliness, and use of extreme violence against the enemies of Texas. Canales was worried about a specific Ranger, Frank Hamer. Hamer would

FIGHTING FOR DEMOCRACY

not achieve national fame until 1934, when he tracked down the outlaws Clyde Barrow and Bonnie Parker to their Louisiana hideout and initiated the battle that cost the legendary couple their lives. But the reputation that the six-foot-three-inch, 230-pound Ranger had as the "Angel of Death" was already well established when he began threatening Canales. In late 1918, Hamer accosted the lawmaker in South Texas, telling him, "if you don't stop that [criticizing the Rangers] you are going to get hurt." Once Canales returned to Austin, Hamer followed him through the streets, trying to scare Canales into dropping his proposal to reduce the number of Rangers, require those hired to have two years of experience and proof of a law-abiding past, to post a large bond guaranteeing their good conduct, and to make them liable to civil suits for abuse of their authority. The proposals, very similar in outline to recommendations to limit police violence a century later, would have brought dramatic change to the Rangers and perhaps to policing more generally.

Years of violence by the Rangers, mostly against Hispanic people in the border regions of Texas, prompted Canales to file his bill. From 1915 to the time of his confrontations with Hamer in late 1918, Rangers routinely executed suspects rather than turning them over to authorities for charges and trials. In addition, they illegally confiscated weapons, expelled people from their homes and ranches, tortured them by hanging and pistol-whipping, and in one case rounded up fifteen men and boys in a village, lined them up against a bluff, and mowed them down. The efforts of local leaders like Canales were not enough to stop them; neither was the condemnation of U.S. Army officers, one of whom threatened to put the border region under martial law to control the Rangers and stop their orgy of violence.

The Rangers did not act alone in perpetrating violence.

194 FIGHTING FOR DEMOCRACY

Instead, they were joined and cheered on by many private citizens, from farmers to big ranchers to lawyers and politicians. That is one reason why the toll of border violence in the 1910s alone was so high—hundreds, quite possibly thousands, died. Decapitated bodies floated down the Rio Grande, people were too afraid to bury their own family members lest they become targets themselves, and bodies were burned and defiled with beer bottles. Prominent Anglo Texans cheered on the rampage, as when a newspaper editor wrote that "there is a serious surplus population . . . that needs eliminating." People of Mexican descent like Canales were not the only targets of mass violence. The kind of organized white mobs, often associated with the Democratic Party, that had done so much to repress coalitions of Black voters and white Populists continued in force into the twentieth century. Between 1900 and 1920, white mobs in Texas lynched 178 Black men, women, and children that we know of, and surely many more that we do not.

The bill that Canales introduced in 1919 prompted legislative hearings that lasted for several weeks, generating dramatic confrontations with Ranger leaders and discussions of violence by mobs and state authorities that grabbed headlines. The hearings were the last, best chance for state authorities to rein in this violence. They did not take it. Canales's bill was gutted of its most meaningful measures and there were no serious consequences for Rangers or others who had perpetrated such violence. Canales escaped assassination, but when his term ended in 1920, he returned to Brownsville and never again sought elected office.

His defeat was the end of a period of at least some meaningful democracy for Blacks and Hispanics that had been opened by the Union victory in the Civil War. His showdown with the Rangers took place in the midst of two longer national struggles—a political fight over whether women should still be excluded from voting because they were women, and an actual war, the First World War. These larger conflicts were decisively settled in their own time, or so it seemed: Black and Mexican Texans were deprived of most of their political rights as citizens of the United States, and in most places subjected to systematic segregation; white women gained the vote; and Texas threw its weight behind the war effort. Those defeated, like Canales, did not so much abandon the fight as retreat and wait for another day. It would be a long wait.

The borderlands society of the early twentieth century differed greatly from the rest of the state. In Texas at large, people of Mexican descent made up a little more than 5 percent of the population. Almost everybody else was white (75 percent) or Black (20 percent). But in the border regions, especially in the huge triangle from Laredo east to Corpus Christi then south to Brownsville, Mexican Texan people remained in the majority. Spanish was the most commonly used language, and Anglos who moved in became bilingual. Sometimes they converted to Catholicism, and they often married local women. The Mexican peso was used as often as the U.S. dollar. Although the most powerful business and political figures were white, Mexican Americans voted, served on juries, held elective offices, and owned land in ways that very, very few of them or their Black counterparts did in the rest of the state or, indeed, anywhere in the entire country.

When the railroad network in Texas penetrated this borderland in the early 1900s, it made the region attractive for white farmers for the first time because it facilitated the infrastructure of market agriculture. Real estate developers aggressively marketed border regions, especially the Rio Grande valley at the state's southern tip, as lands of plenty to outsiders in

Texas and the Midwest. New arrivals flooded the area by the tens of thousands, founding new towns and nearly doubling the valley's population from 1905 to 1910. The boom in land titles benefited some landowners, but hurt many more. Property titles dating from the Spanish period remained extremely complicated and poorly documented. Multiple heirs claimed ownership, ran stock, and lived on undivided properties. These arrangements were ripe fruit to be picked by those familiar with modern legal mechanisms such as forcing the partition of an undivided tract by purchasing one heir's interest or claiming land by paying overdue back taxes. The growing value of land also tempted some to resort to the simple expedient of occupying a desired tract and violently dislodging previous occupants. "I told him to pack up his doll rags and piss on the fire, and he was gone," said one land developer of a Mexican American rancher.

In 1915 and 1916, many of these dispossessed families decided not to play the victim and struck back, joining a guerrilla army that mounted a series of attacks on ranches, irrigation works, railroads, and newly arrived farm families, particularly those who had abused laborers and called for Mexican Americans to be stripped of voting rights. A deputy sheriff uncovered an incendiary manifesto called the Plan de San Diego (named after the Texas town, not the California city). It called for a "liberating army of all races" to overthrow U.S. rule in Texas, Colorado, New Mexico, Arizona, and California. This plan only makes sense if you take into account that a revolution to return land and power to the dispossessed in Mexico had broken out in 1911 and succeeded in driving the country's dictator into exile. Rebels in South Texas spoiling for a fight with whites who had taken their land were inspired by the example, and for a time enjoyed weapons and support from a revolutionary commander across the river in Mexico.

FIGHTING FOR DEMOCRACY 197

Mexican Americans who had seen the broader world feared from the beginning that the rebellion had no chance and would only make things worse. They were right. Rebels enjoyed some spectacular successes, such as attacks on ranch headquarters and the derailing of the train out of Brownsville, but were crushed by the U.S. Army and soon lost their refuge in northeastern Mexico. The revolt served as a great excuse for those who wanted to drive remaining ethnic Mexican landowners from their homes or simply kill them, a task that the Rangers and private-sector vigilantes took to with a savage fury. One day in January 1918, for example, Rangers came to a small West Texas village town called Porvenir, a month after an attack on the Brite Ranch that cost three bystanders their lives. Although there was no evidence linking the Porvenir residents to the raid, the Rangers separated fifteen men and older boys from their families, marched them a short distance, lined them up against a low rise, and gunned them down.

Some of the Rangers' victims joined or supported the uprising, but most were like the Porvenir residents, guilty only of being Mexican, living where they had lived for generations. "We have reason to believe that our liberty and even our very lives are menaced," pleaded Hispanic residents of Kingsville in a petition to President Woodrow Wilson. "One or more of us may have incurred the displeasure of someone, and it seems only necessary for that someone to whisper our names to an officer, to have us imprisoned and killed."

By the 1920s, South Texas emerged as one of the nation's most prosperous agricultural regions; Cameron County's abundant cotton and vegetables made it the single highest-producing county in the nation. But Tejanos shared in very little of this bounty. "The lands which mainly belonged to Mexicans pass to the hands" of whites, lamented Laredo newspaper *La Crónica*.

"The old proprietors work as laborers on the same lands that used to belong to them."

Border violence was intentional: aimed to secure land and control labor for white citizens. The white mobs that so often tortured and murdered Black citizens in central and East Texas shared a desire to assert their dominance over victims and the communities from which they came. In the late nineteenth and early twentieth centuries, these killings increasingly took on a different form from either previous anti-Black violence or mob violence directed at white or Hispanic targets. In horrific events that historians call "spectacle lynchings," mobs would seize victims and hold them until large crowds of men, women, and children assembled, often drawn by newspaper stories that essentially advertised the imminent lynching. The point here was not only to take a life with no legal justification, but to create a public spectacle by doing so in a cruel, ritualistic way that amplified the terror of the killing and advertised the impunity of the murderers.

In May 1916, for example, a white crowd kidnapped a seventeen-year-old farmworker, Jesse Washington, from Waco's courthouse, parading him through the streets while beating and stabbing him. Washington, who was probably mentally disabled, had been accused of the murder (and, it was implied, rape) of a middle-aged white woman. Onlookers threw bricks and hit Washington with shovel blades, leaving him covered in blood. Some leaders of the mob sliced off an ear, then his testicles, while others prepared a bonfire by the side of city hall and threw him on it. Then they hung him from a chain thrown over a tree limb, and sliced off his fingers when he tried to pull on the chain. The crowd of 15,000 to 20,000 roared as the mob's leaders pulled Washington's now lifeless body off of the fire where it could more easily be seen, and lowered it back again to burn some more. A photographer took pictures of the torture, Washington's body, and the crowd. Nobody tried to conceal their identities and many posed with the mutilated, charred corpse. Attendees took parts of Washington's bones, some of his teeth, severed fingers, and genitals as souvenirs. Next, a man on horseback lassoed the corpse, dragged it around Waco's central square, then all the way to the nearby town of Robinson, following a route I once used regularly to visit my family's farm. There they put it in a sack and hung it from a utility pole along the main drag. Attendees and bystanders, or just people who heard or read about the killing, bought postcards with pictures of Washington's body in different stages of dismemberment and mailed them to family and friends.

The cruelty and sadism of Jesse Washington's ordeal can still shock more than a century later. If there were any comfort to be found, perhaps it would lie in thinking that surely the white leaders of Waco and its numerous Christian institutions condemned the torture, that the mob's leaders were brought to justice, and that Texans were so appalled that nothing like this ever happened again. In fact, however, the police chief and the mayor watched the spectacle from the latter's office (where a photographer had stashed his bulky equipment), nobody was ever charged with a crime, and mobs would enact similar torture again and again.

To be sure, some did their best to fight against such atrocities. The Black civil rights organization the National Association for the Advancement of Colored People (NAACP), only seven years old at the time, hired the women's suffrage advocate Elisabeth Freeman to investigate. She interviewed multiple participants and witnesses and acquired photographs that the NAACP then used to publish "The Waco Horror," a special run of its magazine that was sent to all congressmen, the members of President Woodrow Wilson's cabinet, and to newspapers across the United States. Because of this effort, Washington's lynching was covered and condemned internationally. Waco, once known as the "Athens of Texas," was now shorthand for the horrors of lynching. "There is not enough manhood in Waco," wrote one New York editor, to "cause one [person] to rise up in defense of the law." "Now we stand before the world," admitted the *Houston Chronicle* of the state's reputation, "involved in one of the most revolting tragedies of modern times; a tragedy for which sheer barbarism has seldom been paralleled in American history."

Freeman and other NAACP members went on speaking tours to raise donations to support the NAACP and its antilynching campaign. Within a few years, Texas boasted thirty-one local chapters and more than 7,000 members, a greater number than any other state. NAACP members were not alone in contesting racial violence. The Laredo journalist Jovita Idar, who ran in J. T. Canales's circles, covered anti-Mexican violence in the pages of her family's paper *La Crónica* and other outlets. She and her brothers were instrumental in gathering delegates from dozens of Texas towns together to form the "Gran Liga Mexicanista" to mobilize against violence and land loss. It proved difficult to sustain the organization in the midst of the upheaval of the 1910s, and the effort disintegrated in May of 1916 when Laredo's district attorney and Texas Rangers shuttered her paper and watched while a mob expelled her collaborators into Mexico.

Mob violence and state repression were intended to keep Black and Hispanic Texans from voting and organizing. But the leaders of the state's Democratic Party sought more systematic solutions, remembering that Black voters and white Populists had defied violence to assert their right to vote in great numbers. In 1902 and 1903, Democratic leaders implemented a poll tax (a tax that had to be paid nine months before an election to permit a person to vote) and allowed counties to run all-white primary elections to select a party's candidates for the general election. Since the Democratic Party was the only game in town, this had the effect of mandating an all-white electorate without running up against the Fifteenth Amendment's ban on an outright racial criteria for voting. A new system of city governance put into place in Galveston in 1901 similarly distanced local government from democratic elections. Pointing to the need to rebuild after a hurricane virtually destroyed the city, the port city's business leaders designed a system where the governor would appoint commissioners to run the city, rather than vest power in the hands of a city council and mayor elected by the populace. Court challenges eventually converted the so-called Galveston Plan into a system where commissioners were elected, but the fact that the system got rid of a city council elected from specific districts made it another way that white Democrats could monopolize political offices. The system spread to five hundred cities across Texas and the United States by 1920.

The intended results of these measures to disfranchise nonwhite voters were fast and clear. In the 1890s, about 80 percent of eligible voters actually went to the polls to cast a ballot. In 1904, the first year the poll tax was in force, this rate dropped to about 35 percent, and dropped again to under 25 percent in 1906. In other words, for every three Texans who voted when Republicans, Democrats, and Populists were viable parties in the late nineteenth century, now fewer than one did. African Americans experienced the largest drop, but white voting also plummeted. Very few Mexican Americans outside of border enclaves voted; along some of the border, political organizations, generally led by Anglos, paid poll taxes in bulk for Mexican American voters in exchange for bribes, small gifts, and occasional appointments to local positions. The disfranchisement measures changed who held public office along with the voting pool. Politicians who embraced populistic policy proposals were sometimes elected to offices—James "Farmer Jim" Ferguson won election as governor twice in the 1910s, for example—but failed to implement coherent reforms because so many who would have backed them could no longer vote. There were no Black members of the state legislature between 1898, when Colorado County's Robert Lloyd Smith departed, and 1966, when Barbara Jordan won election to the Texas Senate in my hometown of Houston. Canales's departure in 1920 left all legislative seats and all statewide offices in the hands of Anglos. A systematic, legalized white supremacy, backed by the real threat of brutal violence, ruled Texas politics.

White Democrats were not shy about using their monopoly on political power. They implemented the "Jim Crow" system of legal segregation. New laws in the 1910s required that Black and white passengers wait in different rooms at train stations. City ordinances mandating residential segregation and different bathrooms and water fountains followed this example. Shopkeepers and managers put up signs that read "no Negros" or "no dogs or Mexicans." Public cultural events like concerts and movies could admit Black patrons, but only if they sat in an area reserved for them, generally a balcony or the back seats. The University of Texas and Texas A&M, like white private universities, refused to admit Black students altogether. The days of serious consideration for equal funding for public elementary and high school students were as distant as the era of Black Texans serving on juries or as constables.

The Mexican American population fell under similar but less comprehensive restrictions. Where they were a minority, including in new farm towns sprouting along the railroad in J. T. Canales's South Texas, they were placed in separate schools from the white population and excluded from some neighborhoods and jury service. In parts of West and South Texas where Mexicans and Mexican Americans remained a majority, they continued to enjoy social freedoms and interacted with whites outside the strictures of Jim Crow, serving on juries and holding offices in local government. Wealthier Mexican Americans like Canales could usually enjoy a measure of freedom, living on the white side of town if they wanted, or even sending their children to UT Austin or Texas A&M. But this small minority of a minority knew that Mexican Americans, like Black Texans, lived in a world somebody else owned.

16

Homefronts

In the spring of 1918, women across Texas began planting gardens, first scattering seeds of lettuce, mustard, and collards, herbs like dill and parsley, and peas, then moving to tomatoes, cucumbers, corn, melons, and squash as it grew warmer. This was the usual pattern—kitchen gardens had always been the province of women, even in farm families where men normally did the heavy field work, and many town and city housewives continued the tradition as a cheap and even rewarding way of feeding their families. But this year, the context was different. The United States was at war against Germany and its allies in Europe, and the nation's leaders were urging the planting of "victory gardens" to ensure that the country had enough food even with millions of men in uniform overseas. Even many well-heeled women married to lawyers and brokers joined in, some of them because the Texas Equal Suffrage Association (TESA) and other organizations urged them to do so. TESA and its president, Minnie Fisher Cunningham, embraced the roles that women could play on the homefront in this war, advising supporters of voting rights for women to show how critical they were to the perpetuation of society. They wanted the United States to win abroad, and women to win at home.

It did not take long for the wisdom of this approach to become apparent: by the end of 1918, white women were voting in Texas state elections, had decisively shaped its gubernatorial election, and made the University of North Texas professor Annie Lee Blanton the first woman to hold statewide office, as state superintendent of public education. The entry of the United States into the Great War—which later, after an even more destructive and wide-reaching conflict, we started calling World War I—gave women like Cunningham the chance to leverage traditional women's work like gardening into new political and professional opportunities. As an early example of what scholars would later call "total war," the conflict went beyond a small slice of professional military men to touch virtually all aspects of life, from gender roles to race relations, employment, and culture. Cunningham and the "land army" of women gardeners were particularly successful in using the war to advance their goals, but they were hardly alone in trying to do so.

The U.S. involvement in World War I was relatively brief, lasting only from declaring war on April 16, 1917, to the armistice that ended the conflict on November 11, 1918. Yet these nineteen months saw mobilizations and institutions created that would prove to be long-lasting. The war effort extended the reach of the federal government into daily life in a way that had little precedent other than the Civil War. The governor appointed prominent citizens to a State Council of Defense, which coordinated the work of 240 county councils and a stupendous 15,000 local community councils. These organizations worked on security, public health, recruiting soldiers, supporting the war efforts by way of publicity and the subscription of war bonds, and economic efforts such as resolving labor disputes and planting victory gardens. There were, in short, few aspects of life that the war effort did not reach, even for those not among the nearly 200,000 Texans drafted or enlisted into the military. More than 5,000 Texan soldiers and nurses lost their lives, many from the flu pandemic of 1918 rather than from combat itself. The economic footprint of the mobilization was larger than these numbers suggest. The military found that forts like Bliss in El Paso and Ringgold in Rio Grande City, which had served as staging grounds for combat against Indian nations and Mexico in the nineteenth century, could be easily adapted to train the huge influx of soldiers. Texas was particularly important for the young practice of military aviation. Nine of the twenty-eight pilot training airfields built by the military across the country were constructed in Texas, including the Kelly and Brooks airfields in San Antonio and Love Field in Dallas. These installations paved the way for the emergence of commercial aviation in the 1920s, with regular flights that carried mail, cargo, and eventually passengers.

This broad-reaching mobilization presented both threats and opportunities for different segments of society. Minnie Fisher Cunningham was typical in women's suffrage circles in seeing the war as a game-changer. The extensive role of women in Populist mobilizations had raised the question of whether women should have the vote in the 1890s. Women who thought that they should created the Texas Equal Rights Association in 1893. But that organization quickly fizzled, as did a similar group founded in 1903 with chapters in three cities. Cunningham and her colleagues revitalized this moribund movement in 1912, founding chapters of the TESA in Galveston, San Antonio, Houston, and Dallas. By 1916, the organization boasted eighty local chapters composed of white middle-class and wealthier women, with a headquarters in downtown Galveston.

Suffragists chafed against the exclusion of women from professional and civic opportunities and their subordination to men across different realms of Texas life. Cunningham, one of the handful of women in the state with a pharmacy degree, resented the lack of professional opportunities and the much lower pay than her male colleagues she received while working. The Laredo feminist Jovita Idar was publicly blunt about the need for women to break the chains that bound them. "The obrera [female worker] recognizes her rights, proudly raises her head and joins the struggle," she wrote in 1911. "The time of her degradation is over, she is no longer a slave sold for some coins, she is no longer a servant, but the equal of a man." But most suffragists avoided such open criticism, instead presenting votes for women as a way to support their own pursuits in traditional roles as loyal mothers, wives, and agents of civilization in an increasingly complicated economic system. When commercial dairies sold tainted or expired milk, for example, Cunningham observed that "women could bring their knitting to . . . court and stare at jurors when milkmen were on trial, but they had no voice in the selection of judges nor in the choice of municipal officers who were responsible for conditions."

Backed by their own efforts and supportive men, such as leaders of Texas unions and newspapermen like Jovita Idar's brothers Nicasio and Clemente, suffragists mobilized for the war in an effort to convince more male political leaders of the practical virtues of ending the exclusion of women from voting. Part of their strategy was to point to groups of men with the vote as dangerous, and to hold out female voting as a check to this threat. Suffragists pointed out that "enemy alien" men from Germany and its allied countries were allowed to vote even if they had only filed preliminary citizenship applications. Loyal American women could more than make up for this if only they were given the vote. One white southern suffrage association went further, arguing that southern states should enfranchise white women to avoid a restoration of the voting rights the Jim Crow system had effectively taken away from Black men. Cunningham and the other leaders of the TESA did their best to avoid this question, neither showing support for the disfranchisement of Black voters nor criticizing it. TESA formally affiliated with the explicitly anti-Black voting organization but did nothing to support it. At the same time, when they received an application for membership from a Black women's club, TESA leaders delayed acting until the next statewide convention, by which point national suffrage advocates had secured, in 1919, the passage of a constitutional amendment stating that "the right of citizens of the United States to vote shall not be denied or abridged by the United States or by any State on account of sex." They thus avoided having to state publicly whether they thought Black women deserved the vote. Cunningham herself seems to have been more respectful of African Americans in her private life than her public actions might suggest; she declined to join the United Daughters of the Confederacy and wrote directly about the horrors of slavery in family letters despite the fact that her father had owned at least seventy-two human beings. Yet in Texas as in the rest of the South, the coming of "votes for women" fought for and celebrated by Minnie Fisher Cunningham and her colleagues really meant "votes for white women."

Women like Cunningham found that the war altered the social and political environment in ways that opened up opportunities for them. So did some men. Mexican American leaders like J. T. Canales and Clemente Idar thought that supporting the war would gain greater rights for Mexican Americans. They gave speeches urging the purchase of war bonds and registration for the draft. The roughly 5,000 Mexican Americans from Texas who served were integrated into the army as a whole, unlike African Americans, who were confined to segregated units that were often limited to construction and manual labor. So these soldiers encountered a wider range of American citizens than they ever had before, living and sometimes fighting side by side with not only Anglos, but other Americans with similar deep ties to other countries and identities. J. Luz Sáenz, a South Texas schoolteacher whose letters were widely published in the Spanish-language press, wrote of conversations with Polish immigrant soldiers and Native Americans from Oklahoma. At a time when Mexican Americans faced violence and political repression (topics that Luz also wrote about), these experiences suggested that they might be able to find something better by claiming their rights as citizens of the United States.

Black leaders saw a similar opportunity for wartime service. The last great national military mobilization, the Civil War, resulted in the enlistment of several hundred thousand Black soldiers and the destruction of the institution of slavery. This was a precedent that held out enormous hope. But it had to be balanced against the more recent precedent of a national government that stood by while states like Texas disfranchised their Black populations and did little to nothing to prevent gruesome mob violence. Black newspapers, like their Spanish-language counterparts, extolled the heroism of their community's soldiers and held it out as a model of assertiveness in peacetime. It is time "to rectify the wrongs done us" by "bloody, savage vampires of the white race," proclaimed the *Galveston New Idea.* In Houston, returning Black soldiers tore down signs banning African Americans from waiting and dining rooms and took seats reserved for whites in streetcars. In Waxahachie, a young man named Ely Green invoked the war to urge fellow Black bystanders to stop white deputy sheriffs who had kidnapped three Black schoolteachers and intended to rape them. "You are going to fight for Democracy," he shouted to draftees in the assembled crowd. "This is where you should start, at your own doorstep, to defend your own women. If you haven't got guts enough to fight, you don't need no Democracy." Green succeeded in foiling the abduction and then enlisted in the army to get himself safely out of town. He was not alone. As one impressed but nervous military intelligence officer reported to his superiors, returning Black soldiers organized groups to "maintain and strengthen the social equality between the races as established in France" and to oppose "any white effort . . . to re-establish white ascendancy."

Leaders such as Green, Luz, and Cunningham made the war into an opportunity for the advancement of their interests. Others experienced the war as a threat to their greatest hopes and dreams. This was perhaps the most obvious with the state's German population. German communities remained distinct from the rest of Texas, from the timber and stone buildings and gothic churches of the Hill Country, the sauerkraut on their plates, the German language most still spoke at home and in public alike, the use of German in the Hill Country's public schools, and the several dozen German-language newspapers, to the politics marked more by freethinking than Christianity. The mobilization of millions of Americans to fight Germany put this cultural distinctiveness under siege. National authorities viewed the country's cultural diversity as a big weakness going into the war. About one of every three Americans was either an immigrant or the child of an immigrant parent or parents, and a third of these—about 10 percent of the country—had family ties to Germany or one of its allies. "There are citizens of the United States, I blush to admit," warned President Woodrow Wilson, "born under other flags but welcomed under our generous naturalization laws, who have poured the poison of disloyalty into the very arteries of our national life." "Such creatures of passion, disloyalty, and anarchy must be crushed out," he concluded, and "the hand of our power should be closed over them at once."

It was pretty easy for Texas Germans to see this "hand of power" at work. A law in 1917 requiring foreign-language newspapers to file translations of war coverage with the postal service imposed serious expenses on small German-language papers, some of which dropped war coverage altogether. Papers that had supported Germany early in the war changed their editorial stance or remained silent on the question. It was hardly enough to satisfy those who saw German culture in Texas as a tool of the enemy. Caldwell County's Council of Defense advocated the passage of a law banning the circulation of German-language newspapers and magazines. No such law was passed, but nonetheless half of the state's German papers went out of business over the course of the war. The state also suppressed the use of the German language in daily life. Governor William Hobby vetoed financing for the German Department at the University of Texas and fired its chair. The legislature passed a measure making English the exclusive language of instruction and banning all training in foreign languages until high school. The English-only policy was intended to help students become "real citizens imbued with a love of our country and its institutions." Authorities also targeted private institutions such as churches and religious schools. Fayette County leaders warned a German Lutheran congregation that its use of "the enemy language" was "opening the door wide to German propaganda, friction, disorder, and disloyalty," and that continuing to use the language would "provoke a storm of indignation which once unleashed cannot easily be checked in its fury." Such calls helped to incite violence against German Texans. Although this never reached anything like the scope and brutality of anti-Mexican and anti-Black violence, German farmers and ministers were publicly beaten, whipped, tarred and feathered, and threatened with death in 1917 and 1918.

German Texans got the message loud and clear. Many stopped speaking German in public, kept any critical opinions about the war that they might have had to themselves, and in general minimized public displays of German distinctiveness. They changed the name of the San Antonio neighborhood "Kaiser William" to "King William," referred to frankfurters as hot dogs, sauerkraut as liberty cabbage, and sometimes changed last names like "Braun" or "Müller" to "Brown" and "Miller." World War I ended up giving a huge shove to Germans down the path of absorption into a general kind of American whiteness. As one German newspaper lamented, many German Texans had become so fearful that they "would deny the Holy Ghost if He were to approach them in German garb or with a Teutonic accent."

Leftists suffered similar persecution. Texas and Oklahoma were, along with heavily German Wisconsin, the bastions of support for the Socialist Party in the 1910s. *The Rebel,* one of the most influential Socialist newspapers, was published out of Hallettsville, Texas, by Irish immigrant Thomas "Red Tom" Hickey. Hickey and his circles sounded a lot like Populists in their laments about the loss of family farms, and were as likely to invoke Thomas Jefferson and Jesus Christ as Karl Marx to justify their criticism of income inequality and the rich. "The

HOMEFRONTS

great appear great to us only because we are on our knees," proclaimed the paper's masthead. "Let us arise." National legislation outlawed criticism of the war. Hickey, like most Socialists, opposed the U.S. entry into the war. Texas Rangers stormed Hickey's farm outside Hallettsville and held him hostage for two days on grounds of disloyalty. When he condemned this action in the next issue of *The Rebel*, the postmaster general in Washington, D.C., whom Hickey had criticized in print for replacing tenant farmers with prisoners on his 4,000-acre Texas cotton farm, banned the publication from the mail, effectively killing it. The Farmers' and Laborers' Protective Association (FLPA), an interracial union of tenant farmers, sharecroppers, and small farmers, met a similar fate. A federal spy reported internal discussions about whether the group should oppose the draft. The government used this report to charge fifty-three FLPA members with treason. Several officers were convicted and sent to prison.

You did not have to have connections to Germany or be a leftist to believe that it was unfair to be forced to kill and possibly be killed across the Atlantic. Refusal to cooperate with the draft worried federal officials, who at one point calculated that there was almost one "slacker" for every three men inducted into the military. "Slackers" could be found across the state, but were particularly numerous in rural East Texas and in counties along the border with Mexico. The rural South and Midwest were the most reluctant to go to war, and representatives from these areas accounted for most congressional opposition to the war. In parts of Texas, reluctance to support the war was heightened by the fact that draft boards generally exempted large landowners and employers, leaving the fighting and dying to poor men who worked on others' land. In South Texas, the Texas Rangers violently arrested and beat those whom they accused of fomenting opposition to the war and the draft (including a Mexican American constable in Duval County), evoking memories of the bloodletting of 1915 and 1916.

The bloodiest conflict of the homefront, not just in Texas, but the entire country, took place in Houston in 1917. What became known as the "Houston Riot" was set up by the deployment of more than six hundred members of the all-Black 24th Infantry in late July of 1917. They were sent to watch over the construction of a National Guard training camp in a city where white civilians and police enforced segregation and the daily subordination of Black people, often with violence. A month after the soldiers' arrival, white city police officers beat and shot a soldier who came to the aid of a Black woman whose house they had entered and whom they had beaten. The pent-up frustrations with segregation exploded when rumors that a white mob was approaching swept through the infantry encampment. Sergeant Vida Henry led more than a hundred Black soldiers in a march toward downtown. Along the way they shot several policemen, including the one involved in the beating that set the revolt into motion, and ended up killing fifteen (some of whom were innocent bystanders). That night they dispersed and trickled back into camp. Henry, terrified of what might be done to him, shot himself in the head. City authorities imposed martial law and a curfew, and the army moved the soldiers out of the city, soon trying them in a mass court-martial. One hundred and ten soldiers were found guilty, nineteen of whom were hanged and sixty-three of whom were sentenced to life in prison. More than a century later, in response to requests from the condemned men's descendants, the U.S. Army vacated their convictions and acknowledged the violence directed against them and Black Houstonians.

Just one in twenty Texans served in the military during the First World War. Yet such matters as who voted, whether the loyalty of Hispanic and Black soldiers would be reciprocated, whether Germans would remain a distinctive people, were deeply shaped by the war. The hopes and fears that this far-off conflict brought out endured long after Germany's surrender. In different ways, Minnie Fisher Cunningham, José Luz Sáenz, Texas Germans, Tom Hickey, and Ely Green found their Texas changed by the war, if not necessarily enough or in ways that they hoped for.

A GUSHER

17
After Spindletop

The soldiers—more than a thousand of them—descended from railroad cars, unloading their rifles and horses. They first seized the key East Texas railroad junction of Kilgore, then moved north to Longview and fanned out across fields and towns covering some 2,800 square miles. Officers announced that martial law had been imposed. Those who violated the orders of soldiers were to be arrested and held in jail without trial. Some of the local populace welcomed them, waving and cheering; others looked away or just stared.

It was August of 1931, and the cause for the deployment of the National Guard was different from any before. No foreign army had invaded, and there was no strike or riot or rebellion. Instead, it was oil—far, far too much oil, about 900,000 barrels (thirty-seven million gallons!) a day pumped from 1,200 oil wells. The soldiers seized the seventeen pipelines, all privately owned, and monitored the five rail connections that had brought so much oil from the East Texas oil field, known

AFTER SPINDLETOP 217

widely as the "Black Giant." Under their watchful eyes, no more oil would be pumped or transported to Beaumont and Houston for processing and storage.

People had known about Texas oil for centuries, if not longer. East Texas Indians used blobs of petroleum that floated on local springs as lubricants, and Spanish explorers in the 1500s sealed leaks in their watercraft with clumps of oil they found washed up on the Gulf Coast. A minister traveling through East Texas in 1862 was astonished to find locals illuminating revival meetings "by setting fire to slabs of the raw material dug from the asphalt beds and piled on scaffolds built for the purpose." East Texas and Louisiana sailors knew of a stretch not far from Sabine Pass where an oil slick stilled the waves, and found refuge there during rough weather. In the 1890s, enough oil was found around Corsicana to create a small set of drilling and refining businesses, even if Texas remained unimportant to the national oil industry centered in Pennsylvania and Ohio. By 1931, petroleum had become one of the world's most valuable commodities—it had long since replaced whale oil as a source of light, could be used in place of coal to generate heat for homes and businesses and electricity for manufacturing, was processed into gasoline and diesel to power cars and tractors, and was the key fuel for ships and aircraft both military and civilian. And Texas was one of the most important sites of oil production, not just in the United States but in the world. The Black Giant alone could meet more than a third of U.S. oil demand at the time.

Those who discovered, pumped, transported, and processed oil could become fantastically wealthy. John D. Rockefeller, whose very name had become synonymous with great wealth and high living, made his fortune in the 1870s by way of the Standard Oil Company, with its monopolistic control over the oil industry that embodied everything many Americans

218   AFTER SPINDLETOP

concluded was wrong with big business. But there was plenty of wealth to be shared. "Roughnecks" and "roustabouts," the men who did the hard and dirty (very, very dirty) work of building derricks, attaching pipes and drill bits, and channeling the often gushing petroleum they hit far below the surface, could make a very comfortable living from their work in the oil fields, much more so than by chopping cotton, loading ships, fixing cars, or working on an assembly line. Texans, wrote one journalist, "are sitting on top of the world's greatest single source of wealth and its greatest single source of power."

So the Black Giant, at the time the largest oil field in the world and still the largest ever developed in the continental United States, should have been a blessing. Then why were hundreds of soldiers there to shut it down? The short answer is abundance—the oil field produced so much that unrestricted pumping was driving prices down, from 95 cents a barrel at the start of 1931 to 14 cents (in some places in Texas less than 3 cents) by August, when Governor Ross Sterling declared martial law to control production. Low prices were great for consumers but were destroying the oil industry, especially smaller businesses owned by Texans rather than people from the Northeast. More than six hundred of these businesses, known as independents, drilled a majority of the wells on the Black Giant. They could not make a profit at these rock-bottom prices, but the only way for each small company to repay the debt they had taken on in order to build derricks, buy pipe, and hire workers was to drill as much oil as possible. Any individual operator who drilled less would simply go bankrupt faster, and the companies were unable to strike a deal with one another. So together they were bankrupting themselves and bringing more economic chaos to a state already staggering from the Great Depression. Governor Sterling's declaration of martial law was an effort to impose a solution to the problem of too much oil.

The power of petroleum on such stark display in 1931 marked a new era of Texas history. Oil made Texas a factor in the daily lives of anybody, wherever they were, who drove an automobile, boarded a plane, or lived through a war. That is pretty much everybody on planet earth. It also added on to the state's outsized reputation: Texas became associated with advances in geology and chemistry, industrial production, and huge cities like Houston and Dallas. Roughnecks dripping in oil and new-money millionaires with enormous cars, ranches, and private planes joined cowboys and longhorns as images of the state.

If there was a single beginning to these changes, it came thirty years before the National Guard seized control of the Black Giant, in January 1901 at Spindletop. There on a mound just south of Beaumont, men drilling down seven hundred feet saw drilling mud boiling up out of the hole. Then the drill pipe began to move up, smashing the top of the derrick and breaking into three- and four-foot lengths that rained down on the workers. The well died down momentarily, and the workers returned to the derrick floor to begin cleaning up the mess. Then they heard an explosion like a cannon shot and saw oil bubbling up slowly, then faster and faster. Soon it shot up into an uncontrollable geyser six inches thick and 180 feet high. "Practically everybody came from town" to watch, remembered Al Hamill. The black geyser roared for nine days until it was capped, coating all of Beaumont's buildings in crude oil. It settled down into a steady production of 100,000 barrels a day, a thousand times greater than what had been considered a good well.

Even if nothing else rivaled the drama of Spindletop, it set the pattern for later Texas oil fields. Significant strikes in similar salt dome geological formations near the Gulf Coast took place in 1902, 1903, 1905, and 1908. Oil fields of similar size were brought online farther inland in the 1910s, and by the 1920s, North Texas, the Panhandle, the Permian Basin, and South and southwest Texas joined the east as major sites of oil production. By 1928, Texas produced about a fifth of the world supply of oil; by 1940, the state's production determined the price of unrefined oil not only in the United States, but in the world; by 1950, oil had been discovered and produced in 80 percent of Texas counties.

The burgeoning petroleum industry fed a new Texas society of industrial manufacturing, technological expertise, large corporations, a host of smaller services and businesses, and banking. Significant discoveries rapidly transformed places like Beaumont and Wichita Falls from small towns to small cities— the latter exploded from a population of 8,000 in 1910 to 40,000 in 1920 after nearby oil fields were brought online. Fort Worth, Dallas, and Houston emerged as the key centers for oil companies, where supplies, refining and shipping facilities, financing, and technical expertise from geologists and engineers were combined. Oil put Houston on a particularly steep rise. The city's ship channel, completed in 1914, combined access to shipping lanes with greater protection from storms, and soon drew numerous refineries. By 1930, some forty oil companies had set up shop in Houston, helping to make it the largest city in the state. Before oil, the only large corporations in Texas were railroad companies and a few enormous ranches and timber operations. Now Texas had Texaco, Exxon, Mobil, Gulf, and Sun, to name major oil companies that owed their origins to Spindletop alone.

Like the ranching of previous generations, oil also pro-

AFTER SPINDLETOP   221

duced its own culture and folklore. "Wildcat" was used as far back as the early nineteenth century to mean a risky business proposal, but by Spindletop the amazing word "wildcatter" had taken on the more specific meaning of somebody who drilled for oil without corporate backing in a place where it was not known to exist in significant quantities. Texas wildcatters Patillo Higgins, whose dogged insistence that southeast Texas held massive amounts of petroleum had led to Spindletop, and Columbus Marion ("Daddy") Joiner, who first tapped the Black Giant, joined roustabouts and roughnecks as heroes of what one author called "the romance of American petroleum and gas." Texas wildcatters embodied the best of the American character, maintained the journalist A. R. Crum. "In reality Columbus was a wildcatter. He went out with his rude tools and dug up a new continent." "In oil," continued Crum, "more than in any other line of human endeavor does the world owe a debt of gratitude to the discoverer, the wildcatter who seeks out the new places in which to ply his hazardous trade." Texas oil was never just a business; it also became a metaphor for the exuberance, tenacity, and fierce determination that impressed and sometimes appalled those who looked at the Lone Star State from afar. "When your oil starts to flowin' baby, please don't close your door," sang Houston's rhythm and blues singer Eddie Vinson in "Oil Man Blues," a hugely popular song with sexual innuendo that kept it off the radio.

There was no doubt that oil created boomtowns, great fortunes, solid paychecks, and the ballads that went along with them. It also brought chaos and destruction. "Whenever you punch a hole so deep into the ground that oil pops out," observed one East Texas newspaper editor in 1931, "Hades comes out with it. And the more oil the more Hades." Oil boomtowns were hellish. When Beaumont went from 6,000 to 50,000 residents within a month of Spindletop, raw sewage surged from outhouses and the air reeked from the hydrogen sulfide gas vented by oil drilling. The gas stripped paint off houses and sulfur poisoned the groundwater. Here as in later boomtowns, the unfathomable quantity of oil posed even greater risks. It took years for the infrastructure of tanks and pipelines to catch up to drilling, and in the meantime operators stored oil like it was water, in open, hastily constructed reservoirs. Lightning strikes, passing trains, or careless smokers could turn these lakes into enormous fires, some so powerful that the ground quaked and spattered scalding oil for miles. In the oil fields themselves, gas that escaped from drill heads could make men dizzy, blind, unconscious—and if they weren't careful, dead.

There was social chaos too, with oil towns, like the lawless mining towns of the nineteenth century, quickly becoming legendary for public drunkenness, fighting, and prostitution. Within a few years of Spindletop, eighteen bars and four hundred prostitutes sold their wares in one small section of Beaumont known as "Hell's Half Acre." Easy money drove prices for food, water, and other daily goods through the roof. Wives who followed their husbands to these places found themselves particularly discontented with the rough living conditions. "Listen to the wives complain," went country musician Slim Willet's popular "El Paso Gas": "Most of 'em say, if they ever get away, they'll never be back again." For some, the destruction and changes were not worth it. "Is there enough money in the world to pay us for the things we are losing?" an old man in East Texas demanded to know from a visiting journalist. Oil made some rich, but brought danger, squalor, and disorder along with it.

The impact on Texas society of all the changes brought on by the oil boom can be overstated. It is easy to forget, for example,

AFTER SPINDLETOP

that cotton sales generated more revenue than oil until 1930; in that year, 60 percent of the population was rural and the 40 percent of men working in agriculture greatly outnumbered the less than 3 percent who toiled on derricks and in refineries. Oil was an indispensable part of bringing many modern dimensions of life into being, but it added to the older, agrarian Texas rather than replacing it. Indeed, in important ways the new world of oil was shaped by that older world. One example is the racial segregation codified at the turn of the century. Some Black farmers who owned mineral rights profited from oil fields, but the companies that drilled for and extracted oil almost entirely excluded Black people from working in the oil fields. "Now, they won't allow no n****r to do oil work," remembered a white Spindletop roughneck. "They can drive a truck and go through there with a little lumber and anything like that . . . but you can't get out and take the brake and drill for oil. We just won't stand for it." White workers "rounded up" Black men trying to work at Spindletop and "scared them pretty bad and that's about all the trouble they ever had." Black men made up only 0.5 percent of employees in oil exploration and 3 percent in refining, even as late as 1940. The exclusion of African Americans from employment in the professional, white-collar side of oil production was just as complete. So Black workers in Texas got only table scraps from the emerging industry that created so much wealth for whites.

The knowledge that Texas oil explorers used to find oil also came from agrarian Texas, as much as it did from university science departments or corporate headquarters. The shock of Spindletop was not just that so much oil had been discovered; it was that rednecks with strange theories about the earth saw what professional geologists and Standard Oil had missed. Patillo Higgins, a born-again Christian with limited formal education, smelled sulfur and knew of places on the low mound where gas bubbled up through springs. There must be a huge reservoir of oil underneath, he figured. Higgins trusted his own senses, even after numerous wells of several hundred feet failed to hit oil. A geologist working for the state of Texas was unconvinced, denouncing "idle dreams or insane notions of irresponsible parties" that made them think there was oil in Beaumont. Higgins's reasoning was far from the craziest idea; in East Texas as elsewhere, people claimed to be able to find oil with divining rods, sticks they said would twitch and sway back and forth in their hands when brought near oil deposits. "Doodlebugs" used bizarre contraptions to light up or vibrate in the presence of black gold, and "oil seers" claimed to feel shocks or have visions that could be used to locate the precious substance. Not surprisingly, geologists and oil executives dismissed such claims out of hand. One Yale University professor denounced them as "an offense to reason and common sense, an art abhorrent to the laws of nature, and deserving universal reprobation." U.S. geological survey scientists and executives from Standard Oil agreed that there was no reason to think there were large oil deposits in East Texas. The pattern was repeated with the Black Giant, when Daddy Joiner, a seventy-year-old man who learned to write while copying the book of Genesis under his sister's watchful eyes, struck oil in Rusk County in 1930 with flimsy, used equipment, after a geologist working for the company that later became the behemoth Texaco laughed in his face and vowed to "drink every barrel of oil you get out of that hole." It was not until late in the 1930s, a generation after Spindletop, that formally trained geologists working for oil companies were able to find oil in Texas more reliably than country boys like Joiner and Higgins.

The policies and politics of the Populist crusade against monopoly and big business in the 1890s served as another boost for wildcatters and independent oilmen. Standard Oil had managed to assert dominance over the U.S. oil industry, controlling 90 percent of the nation's oil by the time of Spindletop. It might well have made Texas another province in its empire. But Texans used state government and their own ingenuity to prevent this. In 1894, before Texas was a consequential producer of oil, Governor James Hogg protected Texas oil consumers by putting into motion the court-ordered breakup of a marketing and shipping division of Standard, which at the time controlled 99 percent of oil sales in the state. "Shall Texas, or the Trusts, control?" Hogg demanded to know, at one point going so far as to try to extradite John D. Rockefeller and other Standard executives from New York and Florida. State antitrust laws written previously to protect farmers from the power of railroads limited the ability of companies that stored or transported petroleum to produce or refine it, a strategy that economists call "vertical integration" that lay at the heart of Standard Oil's monopolistic strategy. Texas governance also produced some of the first regulations limiting the environmental harm from drilling. A law in 1899 mandated the plugging of abandoned drillholes, prohibited simply letting natural gas vent indefinitely, and limited the burning of gas in drilling fields.

So rather than monopoly, the Texas oil industry was characterized by a rising group of homegrown companies like Texaco and Gulf, and a host of small operations funded by friends, neighbors, and sweat equity. The sheer volume of oil produced, refined, and shipped by these companies served as a major cause for the reduction of Standard Oil's share of national oil refining from 90 percent to 63 percent in the decade after Spindletop. The Populist streak of Texas changed the national oil industry forever in big ways.

Clearly the Texas oil industry had its own problems, or it would have been able to stop the chaos that led to the National Guard's seizure of the East Texas oil field in 1931. Texas oilmen congratulated themselves on how well they had resisted the rule of big business. Now some of them were themselves big businesses. Gulf Oil, for example, operated the world's largest petroleum refinery and was emulating Standard Oil's total control of oil products from exploration to sale at the gas pump. Small oil business owners were more than a little suspicious that Governor Sterling had been president of the Humble Oil Company, the general in charge of the National Guard an attorney who worked for Texaco, and one of his chief aides an official of Gulf Oil. When he closed the oil field, was Sterling trying to save Texas, or his own money? Was a homegrown Rockefeller who wore boots and a hat and talked like a Texan any better than the original? Soon enough, federal courts struck down the declaration of martial law on the grounds that no law gave the governor the power to regulate a business in this way. Within a few years, an agreement between Texas, Oklahoma (where the governor had also seized oil fields), and other oil-producing states brought some stability to production, supply, and prices. Dealing with the spectacular, sometimes horrible plenty that oil brought was a more difficult challenge, one that in an age of oil-derived plastic waste and climate change we still have yet to meet.

The Sounds of the Larger World

18

Automobiles and Burning Crosses

In 1927, Texans, and a good share of the reading public beyond the state, were captivated by a murder trial. The accused, Frank Norris, and his victim, Dexter Chipps, had argued over politics several times. One day Chipps showed up at Norris's office, and the two men began quarreling again. Chipps challenged Norris to a fight, and the latter responded by pulling a pistol from his desk drawer and firing three rounds into his visitor.

The killing would have been enough to make the papers anywhere, but what made it a sensation was that Frank Norris was the most prominent minister in Texas, and maybe the most important southern fundamentalist of the first half of the twentieth century. Norris rose to national fame from an impoverished childhood in Hubbard (a small town thirty miles northeast of Waco) as the son of an abusive and alcoholic father. The

"Texas Tornado," as he came to be known, survived numerous beatings and at least one shooting, finding God at a Baptist revival meeting in his teenage years. He became a pastor at age twenty, graduated from Baylor and then a seminary in Kentucky, and went on to become editor of the *Baptist Standard*. In 1909, he assumed the leadership of Fort Worth's First Baptist Church, a position he held until his death forty-four years later. Under his leadership, First Baptist built an auditorium that seated 5,000, called attention to itself with a revolving electric sign and spotlight, and sponsored radio shows, a weekly newspaper called *The Fundamentalist*, concerts, sports teams, bands, and comprehensive social activities for children and families.

Norris's public fame rested not only on his success as a Christian minister, but also in his insistence that Christians had to attack modern sins if they wanted to be true to the Bible, which was the literal word of God (hence the term "fundamentalist"). Norris railed against political corruption, drinking, gambling, the teaching of the scientific theory of evolution, and "flappers" (young women with short hair and skirts). At the same time that he condemned much of the modern world, calling on his flock to return to the virtuous life of a purer and more righteous past, he took full advantage of modern technologies (radio, electricity, cheap newsprint, and commercial air travel) and organizations like consolidated denominational associations and universities in order to raise money and spread his message. The Texas Tornado was one of a kind, but his simultaneous rejection of the modern world and skillful use of its tools and technologies was a paradox that characterized a great deal of Texas in the 1920s.

The victory of Prohibition in Texas politics was the clearest sign of the rise of what would later be called the "religious right"—

AUTOMOBILES AND BURNING CROSSES 229

conservative Christians like Norris who engaged in politics on the explicit basis of their faith and the organizational platforms of their churches. Those opposed to the drinking of alcohol, almost all of whom were Anglo Protestants, had succeeded in passing "local option" laws in the 1870s and 1880s, under which municipalities, counties, and city neighborhoods could forbid the sale of alcohol. By 1895, just over a fifth of Texas counties were "dry" and another third included dry jurisdictions. But across Texas, there was a more liberal sensibility, as voters repeatedly defeated statewide measures to ban alcohol, and prominent elected officials and ministers maintained the importance of separating religion from politics.

A renewed push for Prohibition took place in the 1910s. In substance, the arguments on both sides were the same as they had been for a generation. "Dries," or advocates for "dissolving the alliance now existing between King Alcohol and our great commonwealth," as a Prohibition platform described the movement, pointed to the economic damage of drinking— "the absolute waste . . . expended by the people of Texas for alcoholic beverages, hurtful and not helpful to their consumers . . . burdensome taxes to meet the cost of State and local judicial and constabulary expenditures, and maintenance of prisoners, paupers and lunatics chargeable to its agency." They also argued that drinking was a threat to morality, "the lion in the pathway of the onward march of the Christian religion in its supreme struggle to uplift humanity, save men and women from sin and evangelize the world." The "wets," on the other hand, blasted a statewide ban on the sale of alcohol as "an unwarranted interference with the personal happiness and liberties of the people" that "inevitably leads to a union of Church and State."

The belief in the separation of church and state invoked by the wets had kept Prohibition at bay by convincing many devout evangelical Christians that their personal opposition to drinking should not become the law. In 1911, Texas voters again rejected a measure for statewide prohibition. Yet the tide was turning: as time went on, more and more white Christians, led by their ministers, abandoned this anti-clerical tradition. The battle was first waged within denominations. Through the 1890s, Methodist and Baptist statewide conventions rejected proposals to weigh in on policy matters such as Prohibition. "The more closely we keep ourselves to the one work of testifying to all men repentance toward God and faith toward our Lord Jesus Christ," proclaimed the Methodist Church in 1894, "the better we shall promote the highest good of our country." Advocates of political Christianity saw it differently; for them, the demands of their religion should spill over into public life. "Every Christian ought to be a politician to the extent of taking an active interest in every public or political question that touches the morals or the material prosperity of the people," said Pat Neff at a Baptist conference in 1909, striking a note that would lead him to the governor's mansion in 1921 and later to the presidency of Baylor University.

Texas exported this brand of politicized Christianity beyond its borders. Frank Norris became pastor of a second church, Detroit's Temple Baptist Church, and flew between there and Fort Worth. Similarly, thirty-year-old "Fighting Bob" Shuler moved from the pulpit of the largest Methodist church in Paris (Texas, not France), to Los Angeles in 1920. There he built a huge congregation of 5,000 and became a key player in city politics with his condemnations of gambling, the teaching of evolution, and specific judges and elected officials who he felt tolerated immorality.

Within the state, leaders including Neff and Norris gained ascendancy congregation by congregation and came to occupy the pulpits of the largest and wealthiest congregations, control of key media outlets like the *Baptist Standard,* and the presidencies of universities, such as Baylor. The victory of political Christianity was never complete even within the white evangelical circles of Texas. Dissidents remained in Methodist and Baptist pulpits, and Christians who believed that their churches should remain focused on the next life and refrain from the temptation of worldly power swelled the ranks of Disciples of Christ congregations. In the 1890s, the latter church's Texas leader, the Reverend James William Lowber, dramatically expanded congregations in Fort Worth, Galveston, and Austin and served as chancellor of the Disciples of Christ–sponsored Add-Ran Christian University (later Texas Christian University). A humbler, less political strain of Christianity endured.

Lowber was the exception that proved the rule. Political Christians began asserting themselves in Texas electoral politics, backing such candidates as the ardent Prohibitionist and devout Methodist Morris Sheppard, who won election to the U.S. Senate in 1913. There he championed national Prohibition. In 1918 and 1919, the Texas legislature and voters passed a statewide ban and backed a national constitutional amendment that banned the production and sale of alcoholic beverages. It had been a long, hard war, lasting for decades on many fronts—the editorial pages of Baptist and Methodist newspapers, local elections, faculty meetings at Baylor and Southern Methodist University, Senate contests, and statewide votes. In a new era of far-reaching media, Prohibitionists had exploited them in what would become models of political campaigns, and they had won, across Texas and the United States. And the media-savvy, political brand of Christianity that stood behind that victory would far outlast the policy of banning the sale of alcohol. Sheppard's key role nationally was another sign that, as with Populism a generation before, and open-range cattle ranching another generation before that, Texas had left its distinctive mark on national politics and culture.

Prohibition was a familiar topic in Texas politics. The rebirth of the Ku Klux Klan reflected the profound cultural and social changes of the 1910s and '20s. The Klan was an import from Georgia, where in 1915 a few dozen men burned a cross near a large monument to Confederate leaders. They announced the resurrection of a secret society originally formed in the South in the 1860s with the purpose of subordinating the newly emancipated Black population by any means necessary, including violence. The original Klan had gone defunct as a result of federal arrests and the return of many ex-Confederates to power; the new organization spread quickly, however, not just in the former Confederacy but across the country, gaining more than three million members within a decade. Texas was one of its strongholds, along with Indiana, Oklahoma, and Oregon.

This "Second Klan," as it is known to scholars, again preached the gospel of white supremacy and organized itself as a secret society with masks, hoods, and its own elaborate rituals and hierarchy. Local chapters were "klaverns," their leaders were "grand cyclops," and recruiters were "kleagles." This Klan reinforced the subordination of Black people under the Jim Crow system. One of its first prominent acts in Texas came on April 1, 1921, with the kidnapping of Alex Johnson, who worked as an elevator operator in the Adolphus Hotel in downtown Dallas. Klansmen took Johnson to the roadside outside of town, beat and threatened to hang him, then let him go after burning "KKK" on his forehead with acid, because he allegedly had sex with a white woman. Klansmen continued to harass, torture, and sometimes murder Black Texans, but

AUTOMOBILES AND BURNING CROSSES   233

this second Klan had the wider goal of fighting back a host of changes in sexuality, culture, and education that its members associated with Jews, Catholics, and modern life more generally. The Dallas dentist Hiram Evans, who was elected as the organization's national leader, or "Imperial Wizard," in 1922, warned of "the moral breakdown that has been going on for two decades . . . all our traditional moral standards went by the boards or were so disregarded that they ceased to be binding. The sacredness of our Sabbath, of our homes, of chastity, and finally even of our right to teach our own children in our own schools fundamental facts and truths were torn away from us. Those who maintained the old standards did so only in the face of constant ridicule." Changing gender roles and especially the open expression of sexuality rankled Klan members, who associated this shift with sinful city living and evil modern technologies. "The coming of the automobile, the licentious screen . . . have multiplied many times the evil snares for womanhood in the land," warned the Presbyterian minister C. H. Storey of Corsicana in a Sunday speech sponsored by the local Klan.

Even Texans repelled by the Klan recognized that major cultural changes were under way. In the small-scale society of agrarian Texas, dances, concerts, and dating were enmeshed into the fabric of local society. You knew the musicians or brought your own fiddle or guitar, and your parents and maybe the minister of the church you went to were there, checking on you as you checked out a possible romantic partner. Larger revival meetings and market days in towns or cities stretched this fabric by bringing the chance for fun or love (or just sex) with those outside your usual circles, but daily socializing and culture remained deeply localistic.

Urban life, mass media, and the automobile opened holes in this social fabric. The number of town and city dwellers in Texas grew at a faster rate than the overall population, so that by the end of the 1920s more than 40 percent of all Texans lived in towns and cities of more than 2,500, including three cities of more than 200,000 (Houston, Dallas, and San Antonio). These places boasted entertainment and music districts such as Dallas's Deep Ellum that were destinations for music, dancing, and drinking. Although Prohibition resulted in the closure of major breweries, it did not stop drinking or drunkenness. Texans could slake their thirst with bootleg whiskey made in some of the countless small distilleries ("stills") that popped up in discrete places on farms, or with tequila smuggled from Mexico.

The automobile changed life in the countryside even more than did the rise of cities, allowing for rural residents to make day or just evening trips that were previously long and grueling. By 1929 there was one car in the state for every 4.3 Texans, on average more than one per household, in excess of the national rate despite the state's comparatively greater poverty. At first, automobile ownership outpaced road construction, which was relegated to counties and resulted in odd routes, widely different surface qualities, and a lack of integration into a coherent whole. Advocates of better roads persuaded four counties to build and maintain a larger gravel-covered roadway between Austin and San Antonio in 1914. In the 1920s, the state government entered the road-building business, using a small tax on gasoline to finance a highway system that approached 20,000 miles by 1930, allowing for the much easier movement of goods and people. As a child, I remember crossing into Louisiana, New Mexico, or Oklahoma and immediately noticing that the roads were narrower and rougher. We Texans have loved our cars and roads for more than a century.

In the 1920s, you did not have to leave the home to be reached by the outside world. Radio first came to Texas at the University of Texas and Texas A&M as part of technological

AUTOMOBILES AND BURNING CROSSES 235

instruction in physics labs in the 1910s. Early broadcasts of weather forecasts and crop reports were soon joined by music, football games, sermons, and news reports. The nation's second broadcast license was awarded to a Dallas radio station in 1921, and by the end of the following year there were twenty-five commercial stations in operation. Radio helped to consolidate and popularize new forms of music. Boogie-woogie was a good example. A distinctive genre of blues with a rolling bass adapted to a piano-forward form, it was incubated by Black musicians in lumber and turpentine camps in the piney woods of northeast Texas. It was loud, centered on a repeating rhythm rather than a melody, and easy to dance to. One observer thought he could hear "the rhythms of the steam locomotive and the moan of their whistles" in the music. The style was further advanced in the club districts of Dallas and Houston, taken by Texan expats with them to New Orleans, Kansas City, and Chicago, and cut for records and played on the radio by the end of the decade.

Boogie-woogie was just the kind of thing that infuriated the moral sensibilities of C. H. Storey and Hiram Evans. Its churning rhythm is something of a metaphor for the let's-have-some-fun culture of 1920s Texas, pounding on in a sinuous drumbeat in defiance of churches, the Klan, and the law. Couples divorced at more than twice the rate of the 1910s by the end of the 1920s, and the average family size dropped dramatically from 4.6 to 3.5 people over the course of the decade. It was illegal to produce alcohol, yet a tenant farmer erected a 130-gallon still on a farm owned by Senator Morris Sheppard, the architect of national Prohibition. Matters like sex and drugs do not leave the same kind of tracks in documents as elections and speeches, but the fabric of life seems to have changed in defiance of the terribly strict law and religious authorities.

The Reverend Storey surely despised boogie-woogie, yet

he was part of the world that made it possible. His speech was delivered at the Palace Theater, an irony that underscores the fact that the reborn Klan bore the markings of the very modern world it rejected. Klansmen were inspired by Thomas Dixon's 1905 novel *The Clansman* and the 1915 movie version of *The Birth of a Nation,* which depicted the time after the Civil War as a chaotic period in which Black men presided over massive political corruption and abused white women. They structured their organization like a direct-marketing business, with Kleagles and Cyclops earning cash for every new member they signed up. Much of their impact came from using mass media—the Klansmen who terrorized Alex Johnson, for example, made sure to bring along a reporter from the *Dallas Daily Times-Herald.* For a time the organization was wildly successful, boasting as many as 150,000 members and the effective control of the city governments of Dallas, Fort Worth, and Wichita Falls by 1923. While small shopkeepers, wage laborers, and housewives made up the bulk of Klan membership, it also succeeded in recruiting doctors, lawyers, ministers, government employees, officeholders, and corporate leaders. In Dallas, for example, the Klan's membership included a newspaper reporter, high-ranking executives of the power company, the chair of the county's Democratic Party, a bank president and future mayor, the county tax assessor, and the chief of police.

Some of the Klan's targets had so little power that they were not in a position to openly combat the organization. Deprived of the vote and subject to terrorism and violence, African Americans began leaving Texas and the South more generally for Chicago, Detroit, Los Angeles, and other cities where they were enfranchised and able to live life free from the daily humiliations and traumas of Jim Crow. The numbers were at first not huge—by 1930, for example, 15,000 African Americans

AUTOMOBILES AND BURNING CROSSES   237

born in Texas had relocated to California, and a little more than 5,000 to Chicago. But they added up. By 1930, about 13 percent of Black people born in Texas had left. This Texas stream of the "Great Migration," the term scholars use for the movement of seven million Black people out of the former Confederacy to the West and North starting in the 1910s, contributed to the decline in the relative share of the Black population in Texas. Before the Civil War, Black people made up almost a third of the state's population. By 1940, their share had fallen to 14 percent, the lowest of any former Confederate state.

Leaders of the state's small Jewish community were understandably hostile to and afraid of an organization that blamed Jews for a great share of supposed vices like jazz and political corruption, and that encouraged citizens to boycott their businesses. "When Klansmen trade only with Klansmen," advised one Texas Klan chapter, "then the days of the Jews' success in business will be numbered and the Invisible Empire can drive them from the shores of our own America." Mollifying the Klan and avoiding its wrath seemed to most Jewish leaders the most sensible path.

Other white Texans who despised the Klan for its secretiveness and violence were in a much more secure position to act on their feelings, and to capitalize on the widespread resentment of the organization. "Do you want a republic like our forefathers founded or an empire ruled by an imperial gizzard?" demanded the former governor "Pa" Ferguson. Ferguson, whose first stint as governor ended in 1917 with his impeachment and removal from office for corruption, became one of the Klan's most scathing critics. He was joined by Dan Moody, the district attorney for the region encompassing Austin, and a host of local figures including Fort Worth mayor H. C. Meacham, a friend to Dexter Chipps, the man shot by the Reverend Frank Norris. But the Klan remained strong in the face of such criticisms, winning a U.S. Senate seat for a member in 1922, and backing Felix D. Robertson of Dallas for governor in 1924. Robertson, proclaiming that "America and Texas have forgotten God" and ought to return to the "rugged cross of Christianity," seemed poised for victory in the Democratic primary. But then "Ma" Ferguson, wife of the former governor (precluded from running by his previous impeachment), entered the race. She presented herself as a humble farm woman loyal to her husband, who described her candidacy as "two governors for the price of one." She trounced Robertson, earning the support of suffragists like Minnie Fisher Cunningham, who held their noses and braced for more corruption but felt that they had to oppose the violent and secretive Klan. When Ferguson assumed office in 1924, she was, along with Wyoming's new governor, the first woman elected to such a position. It was hardly the era of clean politics and good governance that activists like Cunningham had hoped for, but it was a milestone nonetheless.

Dan Moody won the office of state attorney general in the same election, and despite many disagreements, he and Ferguson pursued the Klan with vigor. They were joined by George Dealey, the publisher of the *Dallas Morning News*, who railed against the Klan as a dangerous and ignorant mob. Ferguson wanted to ban mask-wearing, publish Klan membership rosters, and strip churches used for Klan meetings of their tax-exempt status. The legislature met her halfway, banning the wearing of a mask or disguise in public. Several years later, because of a growing backlash to the organization, the Klan candidate lost the U.S. Senate seat that the organization had previously won. Klan numbers went into free fall, down to just a few thousand by the decade's end. Somebody burned down

AUTOMOBILES AND BURNING CROSSES 239

the Klan auditorium in Fort Worth. Chapters in Dallas, Houston, San Antonio, and Fort Worth went broke, and Klansmen watched as the electric cross that lit up the night sky from Houston's Klan building was removed because they could no longer pay the bills.

Yet a rejection of the Klan did not mean a rejection of its platform, and particularly of its defense of white supremacy. "The opponents of the Klan demonstrated that in their group were negro-haters who could vie with any the Klan might marshal," argued a white journalist after Ma Ferguson's victory. Even those who railed against the Klan publicly, like Moody and the Fergusons, shared most of its racist and antisemitic beliefs and vowed to uphold segregation. "The Lone Star people accept unquestionably the color of a man's skin as an altogether divine method of demarcation," the journalist further argued, "and the thought of regular social intercourse with members of such an indigenously inferior race as the negro is as intolerable as the idea of the earth's sphericity was to the intelligentsia of the middle ages."

Frank Norris's career was another sign that the attitudes and work of the Klan long outlived the organization itself. At his trial, the jury exonerated him of murder by reason of self-defense, despite the fact that he shot an unarmed man in cold blood. So Norris remained in his pulpit, preaching of the ills of the modern world, with decades more of fame and prosperity ahead of him.

LEADBELLY AND JOHN LOMAX

19

Looking to the Past in Hard Times

In 1936, Texas threw itself one hell of a party. On Saturday, January 6, a giant parade snaked through the streets of Dallas. "Dallas welcomes the world," read a huge sign on the first float, which was led by Texas Rangers on horseback, carrying the Spanish, French, Mexican, Lone Star, Confederate, and U.S. flags in a succinct summary of centuries of Texas history. Hundreds of thousands of spectators lined the sidewalks for miles as military planes flew overhead, cheering for Governor James Allred and countless other dignitaries. The throngs approached Fair Park, the traditional site of the Texas State Fair, now transformed by a massive building and landscaping project into the site of the Texas Centennial Central Exposition, a world's fair designed to mark the hundredth anniversary of Texas independence. Daniel Roper, the U.S. secretary of commerce, sent a telegraphic signal to activate gigantic shears

LOOKING TO THE PAST IN HARD TIMES 241

that snipped the ribbon at the main entrance. The crowd roared and poured into the fairgrounds. There the people mingled among the fifty exhibition halls, illuminated at night by floodlights that accentuated the sleek vertical lines of their art deco design, and by a few dozen spotlights from the Hall of State, the exhibition's central building. More than six million people visited in the six and a half months that it was open.

The exposition was intended to be great entertainment, to entice locals and travelers from around the world to linger and trade their money for games, cheap trinkets, fried food, and, in carnival style, even a peep show. But its organizers, whose ranks included leading political figures and businessmen from Dallas and across the state, had bigger plans in mind than just boosting tourism for a few months. They wanted to show off Texas to the whole country as a place Americans should know about, respect, and visit. The exposition, as one newspaper aptly put it, was "calculated to display the blend of wild west tradition and modern cosmopolitanism that is the Texas of today." The "modern cosmopolitanism" could be seen in numerous places: displays of new model cars mounted by Chrysler, General Motors, and Ford; an on-site radio studio sponsored by Gulf Oil that could broadcast live programming; air-conditioning (a new and very welcome experience in an often sweltering climate); and General Electric's "House of Magic," which displayed the "domestic life of the future served by electricity" in the wondrous form of electric refrigerators, ovens, and automatic doors.

The "wild west tradition" was produced just as dramatically. Murals, dioramas, exhibits, and performances marked the hundred years that had passed since Texas won its independence from Mexico. Pioneers, cowboys, Rangers, and oilmen were the heroic Texan figures most often portrayed. The central drama of the story was the Texas Revolution of 1836.

The massacres of rebelling Texans at the Alamo and Goliad, and their victory later at San Jacinto, were depicted as the foundational experiences of the story, reflecting an exceptional toughness unique to Texas that put it on the path to its contemporary greatness. As the folklorist J. Frank Dobie said when the Centennial took place, the Alamo lies "at the core of Texas history, whether being celebrated by a centennial or told over in tenant shacks by men who have never opened a history book." Those who fell there are "the dead who gave us life."

The histories told at the Centennial Exposition did not deny the deep southernness of Texas, which could be seen in the embrace of the state's service to the Confederacy. But they did frame its past as fundamentally one of the western frontier, where white settlers contended with Indians, Mexicans, and a harsh if beautiful landscape. As Cullen Thomas, the Centennial Commission chair, put it in almost mythological terms, the foundations of the Lone Star State's modern greatness were laid by "the plain pioneer men and women who first trekked the unpeopled wilds, with axe and plow and rifle and spelling book and Bible." Chasing cattle and drilling oil wells, not chopping cotton, was quintessentially Texan.

The Dallas gathering, and the smaller Frontier Centennial Exposition organized in Fort Worth by the oilman and renowned western art collector Amon Carter, were the centerpieces of sustained campaigns to convince Texans to care about their past. Working with the Texas Highway Department, the Centennial Commission oversaw the erection of more than 750 roadside historical markers across the state between 1936 and 1939. Most of these markers celebrated early Anglo settlers, frontier battles, and the Texas Revolution. The graves of the revolution's veterans were marked. The remains of seventy-six "distinguished Texans"—those who fought in the Texas Revolution, signed the Declaration of Independence, had settled

LOOKING TO THE PAST IN HARD TIMES 243

in Stephen F. Austin's original colony, or were killed in prominent Indian attacks—were dug up and reburied in the State Cemetery in Austin. Beyond roadside markers and gravestones, four hundred other buildings and monuments were built. Most notable among them were the San Jacinto monument and the Alamo cenotaph, both of which I visited on family vacations and school trips in my childhood, and both of which remain major attractions for tourists and field trips nearly ninety years after their erection. Exhibition funds helped to establish museums at the universities that later became Texas Tech, the University of Texas at El Paso, Sul Ross State University, and West Texas A&M University. The Centennial Commission also distributed an enormous quantity of teaching materials to educators, from elementary school to college instructors. These history lessons were intended to prompt students "to know Texas better, to love Texas more and to serve Texas with single-hearted zeal."

This massive effort did not come out of thin air. Instead, it was the intensification of a deepening turn to the past, one that in previous decades had become visible in different ways in almost all segments of Texas society. In 1905, the Daughters of the Republic of Texas, a preservation and education society founded in the 1870s by female descendants of the founding generation of the Republic of Texas, became the custodians of the Alamo. The chapel of the old Spanish mission had been owned by the state since 1883. But the government had let it languish, holding no ceremony on the fiftieth anniversary of Texas independence in the crumbling chapel or anywhere else. The "Long Barracks," where much of the fighting during the siege in 1836 actually took place, was used as a warehouse by a commercial company. Clara Driscoll and Adina de Zavala, leaders of the Daughters, saved the barracks from being leveled and replaced with a hotel. The two women then fought viciously over how the site should be managed, but their aggressive actions in the name of Texas history assured that it would not be given over to private development.

The founding in 1909 of the Texas Folklore Society, devoted to the study and preservation of the stories and legends told by ordinary Texans, was another reflection of the heightened interest in the past. The 1920s saw John Mason Brewer, a Black military veteran from Goliad who had become a professor at Huston-Tillotson University in Austin, begin to collect and publish Black folktales. At the same time, a critical mass of painters known as the Dallas Nine emerged. These artists, most notably Jerry Bywaters and Alexandre Hogue, achieved national prominence with their depictions of the landscapes of the Southwest. Their paintings drew on Impressionism and the work of Mexican muralists in their naturalistic representation of southwestern landscapes. Collectively these artists celebrated the region's rugged beauty—more of the vegetation and topography of West Texas than the plains or piney woods—but also captured the devastation of droughts in haunting portrayals of farm buildings and dying livestock engulfed by wind-blown soil. By the time of the Centennial, Texans were becoming more immersed in their history and some of the complex legacies that it brought.

It was a tough time to throw a birthday party for the state. The crash of the stock market in New York in October 1929 raised the specter of a larger economic collapse. At first it was easy to dismiss the loss of nearly 40 percent of the value of the nation's stock as a remote problem for national banks and investors, but not for ordinary businesses and farms in places like Texas. Texans should worry about "Jim Rural" and "Joe Normal," as one smalltown newspaper editor put it, since, as another paper

LOOKING TO THE PAST IN HARD TIMES   245

observed, "the changes in stock prices are purely an affair of and for stock speculators."

The state did not escape the crisis of the ensuing Great Depression for long. The agricultural economy was decimated, with prices for cotton, corn, and cattle falling by half. Wages for cotton picking fell by almost two-thirds, and some 90 percent of Black farm laborers could not find work by 1935. To make matters worse, a long and brutal drought accompanied by mounting dust storms, known as the Dust Bowl, hit the southern Plains, including the Texas Panhandle. "Black blizzards," enormous dust storms that blotted out the sun with soil lifted thousands of feet above the earth's surface, seemed as much like divine wrath as natural events. "Though it was mid afternoon, the sky was darker than midnight," reported the *Perrytown Pipeline* of a storm in 1935. "Visibility was reduced to zero; even your hand in front of your face was impossible to see. Some thought the world had come to an end. For more than 10 minutes, no one could see anything." Seven times that year, Amarillo experienced blackout conditions, once for eleven straight hours. More than a third of farmers in the Panhandle counties hit hardest by the Dust Bowl abandoned their farms, moving to Texas cities or west to California.

Things were somewhat better in towns and cities, in part because of employment opportunities provided by the continued growth of the oil and gas industry. But even there, times were tough. The basic infrastructure of economic life buckled and sometimes collapsed, as when more than a hundred banks failed statewide by the end of 1931, in many cases taking with them their customers' life savings. Panicked depositors at the remaining banks rushed to withdraw their money, threatening to ruin the entire financial system and prompting the governor to order all banks closed on Texas Independence Day (March 2) of 1933. Four days later, U.S. president Franklin

Roosevelt took a similar action nationwide. By that point, a quarter of Houston workers were already unemployed. San Antonio's west side, where housing discrimination and poverty forced most Mexican American residents to live, was described by one federal observer as "one of the foulest slum districts in the world," with many residents living in floorless shacks without plumbing, electricity, or sewage connections. The infant mortality rate of the city's Hispanic population was more than 14 percent. These were probably the state's worst urban conditions, but the Depression made life difficult everywhere. The chambers of commerce of at least three cities decided to establish gardening programs, providing the unemployed with seed and access to land in the hopes that they could grow the food that they could no longer afford to buy.

This suffering brought upheaval in numerous workplaces. Strikes peaked in 1935, when more than 150,000 working days were lost to labor unrest. The largest confrontation between employers and workers took place in San Antonio in 1938, when nearly 12,000 pecan shellers, mostly Mexican American women, walked off the job in search of a rollback of wage cuts. Strikers persisted for three months despite mass arrests by the city's police force, directed by city leaders alarmed at the militancy of a strike initially led by the Communist organizer Emma Tenayuca. The police action, later judged by a governor's commission to violate the right of free assembly, was not enough to stop workers from winning substantial raises. San Antonio's strikers were more successful than labor organizers at Dallas's Ford automobile plant—fifty of whom were kidnapped and beaten in the fall of 1937 in a temporarily successful effort to prevent unionization—or repeated efforts to organize unions of agricultural workers in South Texas.

LOOKING TO THE PAST IN HARD TIMES 247

The Centennial exhibit did not address this poverty and conflict. For some, the extended birthday celebration offered an escape from these challenges, while others may have found its depictions of pioneer striving to offer a message of hope in their midst. The heroes of the stories told in the exhibition's publications, murals, and classroom lessons were Anglos. Mexicans and Indians appeared as enemies of Texas. Only one Black person, Bill Goyens of Nacogdoches, was acknowledged in a Centennial property, with an inaccurate headstone that identified the East Texas businessman and negotiator of treaties with Cherokees as a former slave rather than a free Black person. But Texans who were not white seized this moment of historical myth-making to tell their own stories, presenting their own epic histories as part of the fabric of Texas.

You did not have to leave the Dallas fairgrounds to see these counter-histories. "The Hall of Negro Life" was part of the exhibit. Dedicated on June 19—Juneteenth—the 10,000-square-foot pavilion hosted exhibits on business and industry, art, industrial life, agriculture, health, and education. An outdoor amphitheater that could fit several thousand spectators and a foyer allowed for the showcasing of music, dance, and art, most prominently four large murals by the painter Aaron Douglas. The building and its exhibits and programming were organized by the Dallas businessman and civil rights activist A. Maceo Smith. Unlike the other exhibits, the Hall of Negro Life did not receive state funding. This was punishment for Smith's support of a Black colleague who dared to run for a vacant judgeship in Dallas in 1935 in an effort doomed to failure by the disenfranchisement of Black voters. Smith and his colleagues launched a campaign to sell bonds to Black Texans in support of the festival, an effort that helped to ensure that a slice of the federal funding for the fair was designated to support the Hall of Negro Life.

248 LOOKING TO THE PAST IN HARD TIMES

Like the rest of the exhibit, the Hall of Negro Life told a story about the past in order to make a claim about the kind of society Texas should be in the future. The four paintings by Aaron Douglas that loomed over visitors when they entered the foyer told a history of Black people in the United States, from enslavement on the west coast of Africa to their roles in modern Texas. The images did not shy from suffering and exploitation. The first one, "Into Bondage," portrayed men and women in a tropical forest with their wrists chained, filing in a line toward sailing ships waiting offshore. But the emphasis was on persistence and progress rather than oppression. The other painting that survived, "Aspiration," pointed to a modern future for Black people. Upraised hands with chains at the bottom of the image evoked slavery, but the three figures looked up and ahead to a modern city, with skyscrapers and smokestacks. The two men and one woman were drawn with tools of modern education and industry—a book, a globe, a compass, and a carpenter's square (held together in a way that evoked the Masons), and a laboratory beaker. Modern education would take Black Texans into a better future, lit up by a glowing Lone Star at the base of the city that evoked both Texas and the North Star that guided so many of the enslaved to freedom in the North.

Smith and his colleagues chafed at the second-class treatment the Hall received from the exposition's leadership, including cruder fire extinguishers than the other buildings and landscaping that marked their exhibit off from the others. Yet it was an extraordinary success, the most prominent venue that Black people anywhere in the United States had ever had to tell their own histories. The Hall presented Black Texans as an indispensable part of the creation of modern Texas, not just as laborers in cotton fields but as inventors, craftsmen, educators, artists, and musicians. The claims of this history on the present were made explicit in the pamphlet "What the Negro has done for the United States and Texas," distributed to all of the Hall's visitors. Written by W. E. B. Du Bois, the civil rights pioneer and the country's most important Black historian and intellectual, the pamphlet finished its explication of Texas history with the argument that the state could enjoy "enduring prosperity" if it guaranteed "justice and freedom and understanding among men."

Fair officials estimated that about 400,000 people, slightly more than half of them white, entered the Hall over the course of the fair. Not all of them liked it. "Many of the white people came in expecting to see on display some agricultural products . . . and 'Black Mammy' pictures," recalled one of the exhibit's organizers. "No! No! N*****s did not do this," a staff member heard a white woman visiting from Corsicana exclaim. The Hall of Negro Life was shuttered and bulldozed the following year, the only major exposition building destroyed so soon after the festival.

The Mexican American response to the Centennial Exposition and its Anglo-centric history followed similar lines, though it was not nearly as publicly prominent as the Hall of Negro Life. In 1934, leaders of LULAC, the League of United Latin American Citizens, a civil rights group for Mexican Americans that coalesced in the 1920s, formed a committee to develop the organization's plan for engaging with the larger Centennial. Its main accomplishment was commissioning and publishing a history of Texas Mexicans who fought for the Texas Revolution in 1836. *Viva Tejas: The Story of the Mexican-Born Patriots of the Republic of Texas* insisted that Anglos had not won independence for Texas alone, and thus implicitly called for a multiracial democracy. Numerous short stories, poems, and historical sketches that appeared in the organization's magazine over the course of the 1930s explored wide-ranging topics in the history of Texans of Mexican descent. Many of the authors were women, most prominently Jovita González, a South Texan who earned a graduate degree in folklore and became president of the Texas Folklore Society in the early 1930s. González and her colleagues presented stories that captured the challenges of living as an oppressed minority group subjected to disrespect and, frequently, outright violence, but that also offered sly critiques of the political corruption and lack of respect for women that characterized some of Tejano culture and even male LULAC leaders. History was as much about the present and future as it was about the past.

Perhaps the single most important person involved in the immersion of Texas in its own history in the 1930s was John Lomax. Raised on a Bosque County farm where his family arrived by covered wagon in 1869, Lomax was fascinated by the epic cattle drives that took place during his childhood. In the early 1900s, after studying and working in administrative positions at the University of Texas, he began to write down the music and lyrics of songs sung by unlettered Texans. He was one of the founders of the Texas Folklore Society, and his work was so highly regarded by others that he was elected president of the American Folklore Society. Lomax was a prosperous, educated white man who worked as a university administrator and banker but never lost his deep admiration and fascination with the struggles and creativity of ordinary folks. He could talk to professors, politicians, business executives, waitresses, workers, and convicts with the same intense charisma. Although Lomax was not himself a musician, it is thanks to him that today we know the words and music to such classics as "Home on the Range" and "Git Along, Little Dogies."

LOOKING TO THE PAST IN HARD TIMES   251

One of Lomax's most important publications came out the year of the Centennial. *Negro Folk Songs as Sung by Leadbelly* was the product of a remarkable collaboration. Lomax's informant and collaborator was the musical prodigy Huddie Ledbetter, who came to be known by his nickname "Lead Belly." Like Lomax, Ledbetter grew up as a hardscrabble farm boy, and he came to some prominence in the Dallas music scene as a teenage guitar player in Deep Ellum bars and dance halls. Lead Belly had a much harder life than Lomax, and he radiated a combination of artistic genius and grittiness that fascinated his white interlocutor. Lead Belly was first imprisoned, for murder, in the late 1910s, before being pardoned in 1925 by Governor Pat Neff, who had been left deeply impressed by Lead Belly and his music on visits to penitentiaries. John Lomax met him in 1933 in Louisiana's Angola prison. Lead Belly had been sent there after a later conviction for assault. Lomax, who had lost his job at the University of Texas and all of his money in the stock market crash, came looking for songs composed "before the spread of machine civilization."

The two men began a collaboration that brought both fame and economic security. Lead Belly served as Lomax's driver and guide, helping the white folklorist to identify and record the songs of Black and other musicians in Texas and beyond. Lomax recorded and published the work of Lead Belly and other folk musicians, preserving and popularizing a body of work that became foundational for later music dubbed "Blues," "Rock and Roll," and "Folk." I remember the songs "In the Pines," "Goodnight Irene," and "Midnight Special" from my own childhood, and countless millions have listened to versions of these tunes that Lead Belly and Lomax captured.

The vision of life in these and other songs was certainly darker than that offered at the Centennial Exposition. If there were heroes in these songs, they weren't people who started revolutions, won great battles, or settled thousands in a wilderness. As in Jovita González's stories, the characters in Lead Belly's and Lomax's songs survived life—poverty, relentless work, unfaithful lovers, fights, stabbings, shootings, and the inevitable prison bosses. Generations before Outlaw Country and Gangsta Rap glorified rough men who broke the law and tangled with the police, Lead Belly's anthems featured convicts and cruel field bosses. They were a cultural reflection of the heavy reliance on incarceration in Texas, which by the end of the twentieth century would have one of the highest imprisonment rates on earth.

By the time Lead Belly and Lomax met, the state had rationalized its penal system, in large part in response to criticisms of mob violence and the use of convicts as a workforce put out for hire. As was the case elsewhere in the nation, in Texas executions had been conducted by county governments, usually in the form of public hangings on courthouse squares. In 1923, however, the legislature centralized the procedure. Now the death penalty would be carried out behind closed doors in an electric chair operated at the state penitentiary at Huntsville. The architects of this change thought of it as "more modern and humane," particularly because the old way of state killing looked uncomfortably like lynching, with a white crowd gathered to exult in the death pains of a Black man being hanged. Governor Neff, who condemned lynching as "a sad commentary on our civilization" and several times dispatched Texas Rangers to prevent them, welcomed the measure as another sign of Texas coming of age as a modern and enlightened society.

Lead Belly and many others who found themselves in the clutches of the state's penal system saw the matter otherwise. "Some folks say it's a sin," he sang to Neff when the governor

LOOKING TO THE PAST IN HARD TIMES   253

visited the Imperial penitentiary farm west of Houston. "Got too many women and too many men. / . . . in da pen." Daily life inside the modern prison system had clear markers of the practices of slavery and Jim Crow. Inmates who balked at working in the prison fields were whipped, and sometimes took to self-mutilation to avoid the punishing, even deadly pace of work. The electric chair was dubbed "old Sparky," a name that conveyed humor and the celebration of death rather than the sober sense of duty and the impartial administration of the law that Governor Neff believed he was implementing. Of the first thirteen men executed under the new system, twelve were Black and one Hispanic. In 1931, the prison system started putting on a rodeo in Huntsville. Crowds of tens of thousands roared with approval and maybe blood lust as they watched untrained prisoners trying to ride bulls, rope cattle, and the like, often getting gored and trampled in the process. As millions celebrated the wide open spaces of Texas and the freedom promised by its amazing history, others knew all too well that the shadows cast by the old worlds of slave masters and lynch mobs still darkened the land.

LAID TO REST

20

The Good War

On a rainy February day in 1949, Private Felix Longoria was laid to rest in Arlington National Cemetery. Felled by a Japanese soldier in the Philippines in the closing days of World War II nearly four years earlier, Longoria's body took years to be recovered and sent back to the United States. His parents, his widow Beatrice, and their daughter were joined by elected officials and the uniformed soldiers who lowered the casket, folded the American flag that had adorned it, and fired a ceremonial three volleys in his honor.

Longoria was one of more than 750,000 Texans to serve in the Second World War, which the United States entered at the end of 1941 after the devastating surprise attack on Pearl Harbor, where Japanese bombers sunk most of the American Pacific fleet in Hawaii. Twenty-two thousand Texans joined Longoria in giving their lives to the war, thousands of miles away from home in Europe or the Pacific. The contribution of Texas to the American military was notable for the service of

12,000 women in the Women's Army Corps, the most of any state, and for the 14,000 officers who came from Texas A&M, more than from all the federal service academies combined. Ovetta Culp Hobby (from Houston) served as director of the Women's Army Corps, and Audie Murphy (from Greenville) became the war's most decorated American soldier. The full assimilation of German Americans was visible in Chester Nimitz (from Fredericksburg) in his role as commander of the U.S. Pacific Fleet, which forced Japan to surrender in September 1945, and Dwight Eisenhower (born in Denison) in his role as supreme commander of Allied forces in Europe.

Service abroad and losing loved ones like Longoria forever changed the lives of hundreds of thousands of Texans. But the changes brought by nearly four years of war ran deeper, touching nearly all aspects of life. By the time soldiers started coming home, hundreds of thousands of Texans worked in new jobs, lived in cities and suburbs rather than on the farms and small towns of their childhood, and were more likely to have neighbors and friends who had just recently become Texans. Like other Americans, they made more money, went to more movies and football games, and were generally wealthier than they had been before the war. Despite the stress of family separation and the constant fear of losing a son, husband, or brother on the battlefield, Texas emerged from the war better off, more powerful, poised for dramatic internal changes just as it became a huge political and economic force on the national landscape. Though none of it was fought on Texan soil, the war was a watershed event in the state's history.

It is easy to think of wars as happening on battlefields and being fought only by soldiers, but industrial warfare in the twentieth century required a huge infrastructure to recruit, train, equip, feed, and move armies. The work of millions of civilians in American factories, fields, labs, and ports allowed the United States to arm its Soviet, Chinese, and British allies and to nurture the forces that defeated their opponents and occupied Berlin, Rome, and Tokyo by September of 1945. No place was a more important part of this infrastructure than Texas. A total of 1.2 million soldiers and 200,000 airmen (and some women) were trained on fifteen army bases and forty airfields in the Lone Star State. The Naval Air Station in Corpus Christi, commissioned nine months before Pearl Harbor, became the largest naval training facility in the world, graduating 35,000 pilots over the course of the war, including future president George H. W. Bush and astronaut John Glenn. Texas as a whole became what one historian has called "the largest military training ground in the world." As the war continued, Texas also became the host of twenty-four camps holding prisoners of war (mostly German) and civilians with ties to Axis powers.

The industrial infrastructure of the state was just as important. Workers built ships for the navy and merchant marines in shipyards in Corpus Christi, Galveston, Houston, Beaumont, and Port Arthur, and aircraft in Garland, Grand Prairie, and Fort Worth. Fourteen ordnance factories (most notably, Pantex outside of Amarillo and Lone Star Ammunition Plant west of Texarkana) manufactured bombs, artillery shells, dynamite, and bullets. The petrochemical industry that took raw oil and turned it into synthetic rubber and fuel for military vehicles, ships, and aircraft grew rapidly along the coast between the Louisiana border and Corpus Christi. By 1945 this coastal strip had the largest concentration of petrochemical production in the world. The oil industry itself developed relatively slowly in these years, as the collapse of European markets limited the demand for petroleum and kept Texas oil fields producing well below capacity. Fear of German submarines sinking tanker ships that brought oil from Texas to the Northeast, however, led the federal government to build "Big Inch," a pipeline twenty-four inches in diameter, from Longview to New York and Philadelphia, and "Little Big Inch," a twenty-inch-diameter pipeline, from Houston to New Jersey. The pipelines, each in excess of 1,400 miles long, together carried 600,000 barrels of petroleum and petroleum products every day.

All of this breakneck economic growth to meet wartime demand meant that the infrastructure for a sustained boom in oil, petrochemicals, and manufacturing was in place by the end of the war. Numbers are one way of capturing the fundamental changes in the daily lives of millions. When the federal government conducted a census in 1950, for the first time more Texans (60 percent) lived in cities and large towns than in the countryside. Jobs paid by the hour tripled during the war. At the same time, farm employment, sharecropping, and owner-operated businesses all stagnated or even declined with the mechanization of agriculture. Much of the basic contours of life today—living in a city or suburb, going to work for a large company—became the norm during the war.

A similar change happened in politics: more complexity and choice. The stranglehold that the all-white Democratic Party put on Texas in the early twentieth century had not entirely eliminated competition at the polls, as the disputes over pro- and anti-Klan candidates, or between the Fergusons and their enemies, indicate. The Depression, the rise of a liberal national Democratic Party willing to expand the powers of the federal government under Franklin D. Roosevelt, and the Second World War allowed for candidates with starkly different ideas to contend for power for the first time since the 1890s.

The overwhelming majority of Black and Mexican American citizens remained locked out of formal political power, and the state remained a one-party system. But Texans who could vote had real choices in these years, and Blacks and Hispanics began to rattle the cage of Jim Crow.

The career of Lyndon Baines Johnson shows how Texas liberalism gradually developed in the 1930s and survived strong challenges in the 1940s. Texas liberalism sometimes coexisted with and even strengthened traditional sources of power rooted in large landowners and oil companies. At other times these forces clashed, even within the same person. Johnson was from the Hill Country west of Austin and San Antonio. Though his father served in the state House of Representatives and his grandfather was nominated for that body by the Populist Party, his family remained of modest economic standing. The relentlessly ambitious young Johnson—LBJ, as he was known—after a brief stint as a schoolteacher in Cotulla, became the administrative assistant for Congressman Richard M. Kleberg of the King Ranch in 1931. That post gave him an excellent position to watch President Franklin Roosevelt rapidly expand the federal role in economic life—regulation of banks, hiring the unemployed to build parks and infrastructure, establishment of old-age pensions and unemployment insurance, and the protection of labor rights, collectively known as the New Deal. Johnson became the Texas director of one such program, the National Youth Administration (NYA), which aimed to provide fun, work, and education for people between sixteen and twenty-five. In 1937, he won election to the U.S. House of Representatives as a staunch supporter of the New Deal.

Johnson was shrewd to ally himself with the politics and policies of the Roosevelt administration. Roosevelt's coalition depended on organized labor and included Black voters (in northern and western states, where they could exercise their

THE GOOD WAR   259

constitutional right to vote). Although southern Democrats generally scorned both of those groups, Roosevelt swept the vote in Texas by prodigious margins in 1932 (88 percent) and 1936 (87 percent). His commitment to ending the misery of the Depression, together with most of his liberal policies, clearly had overwhelming support. Programs like the NYA and labor protections made Democratic power brokers like Kleberg nervous that they would foster labor insurgencies and pushes for racial equality. Indeed, under Johnson's leadership 40 percent of NYA participants were Black, though segregated, as in the rest of the South, from their white and Hispanic counterparts. For Johnson and other ardent Texas New Dealers, racial discrimination was to be neither attacked nor celebrated, but rather avoided as a subject as much as possible. Kleberg and other leaders of the Democratic establishment supported the New Deal for the time being, joining most other southern Democrats in insisting on the exemption of agricultural and domestic workers (heavily Black and Hispanic) from minimum wage and labor protections as a condition for their support. Jim Crow lived on as a silent part of the New Deal order.

The money offered by jobs from programs like the NYA was not nearly enough to end the Depression. That came only with the wartime economic boom. But it gave people hope and kept millions from falling into abject poverty. Indeed, by the 1940s, millions of Texans came to believe that New Deal programs had not only maintained life, but improved it. Murals painted on post office walls depicting local history, new parks like Big Bend or Palo Duro Canyon, roads, and public spaces like San Antonio's River Walk were some examples. Electrification brought more fundamental changes to large portions of the state. The federal government built or subsidized thousands of hydroelectric dams in these decades, in Texas most notably on the lower Colorado River. This infrastructure dramatically expanded access to electricity and lowered its price. The creation of the Rural Electrification Administration (REA) in 1935 allowed farmers and small towns to pool their resources and form cooperatives eligible for federal loans to build electrical generating facilities and transmission lines in areas too sparsely populated for private power companies to make a profit doing so. LBJ's home territory of the Hill Country was perhaps the most transformed. In 1930, only 2 percent of Hill Country homes were electrified; in 1960, only 2 percent were not.

It is difficult for those of us who live with modern infrastructure to appreciate the dramatic changes brought by electricity, and the almost religious loyalty that it earned for leaders like Roosevelt and Johnson who made it possible. Without electricity, water was drawn from wells in buckets by hand and carried back to the house, many times each day. A writer visiting the Hill Country from the East Coast was struck by how stoop-shouldered local women were, even in their twenties. "My back got bent from hauling the water," one told him, "and it got bent when I was still young." Without electricity, it was difficult to keep food from spoiling, so fruits and vegetables had to be canned immediately after picking—weeks on end of labor over a hot stove in a Texas summer spent cooking the fruit, boiling the cans to sterilize them, emptying the ash tray, and constantly hauling and cutting wood to keep the fires going. The childhood family fights that Lyndon Johnson remembered were over who would haul the water and wood.

Electrification meant residents could read under light bulbs rather than flickering candles and smoking lanterns, store food in refrigerators, pump their water to taps rather than make endless trips back and forth to wells, and clean their clothes in electric machines rather than by hand. Although men built the power infrastructure and served on the co-op boards, women experienced the greatest transformation in their working lives. Before electricity, through the 1920s, all rural housewives cleaned their households' clothes by boiling them in a tub over an open fire or wood stove, pressing the dirt out of them by kneeling over washboards and kneading them with lye soap that burned the skin, rinsing them with well water or in a stream, and ironing them (a job that occupied a day or more each week) with heavy flatirons that had to be constantly reheated on a wood stove. After electrification, most put clothes in the washing machine, hung them to dry, and plugged in an electric iron. The Feds had saved women hours of grueling work every day. Women and their families could listen to the radio and go to town to see movies, entertainment and socializing that had been taken for granted by city people for a generation. No wonder rural households boasted framed pictures of Roosevelt—in my great-grandparents' house, hung on the wall next to an image of Jesus.

Electricity was new to such families, but co-ops were an old and familiar institution. Their importance to Populist politics and policies suggests the connections between New Deal liberalism and the agrarian political traditions of Texas, though New Dealers like Johnson were less interested in maintaining family farms and other independent businesses than they were in ensuring that salaries and wages were high enough to deliver a comfortable standard of living. The growing concern about the New Deal from more conservative Democrats also looked a lot like the politics of the 1890s. Leaders like John Nance Garner, an attorney from Uvalde who was Roosevelt's vice president in his first two terms, did not want a Texas where growing labor unions and higher taxes would crimp what they thought of as a fair and profit-generating private sector. They were also very concerned about the possibility that African

262   THE GOOD WAR

Americans and Mexican Americans would use the expanded power of the federal government to strike at the segregation codes of Jim Crow.

The conservative disenchantment with the New Deal and its Texas supporters rose in the 1940s with the replacement of Garner as vice president with the much more radical Iowa farm advocate Henry Wallace and the mobilization of hundreds of thousands of Hispanic and Black men as soldiers in a war against enemies that touted their belief in their own racial supremacy. "Loyalists," as Democrats who stuck with the Roosevelt administration called themselves, contended with more conservative Democrats for control of the state party and electoral offices. Neither side dominated the other. Wilbert Lee "Pappy" O'Daniel, a radio marketer and flour-milling sales manager who first won election as governor in 1938 on a platform of the Ten Commandments and old-age pensions, backed by his "Hillbilly Band" called the Light Crust Doughboys, became a central figure for the conservatives. "Pappy" appointed foes of the New Deal to important offices and railed against "labor leader racketeers." He narrowly defeated LBJ in a race for an open U.S. Senate seat in 1941 after the vote count for small counties controlled by his allies trickled in suspiciously late. The following year, he retained the seat after defeating another former governor, James Allred, who allied himself ardently with Roosevelt, but only by a narrow margin in a runoff election. In 1944, conservatives attempted to unseat Johnson and two other staunch New Deal congressmen. They also refused to support Roosevelt's bid for reelection, advocating a platform that called for the "restoration of the supremacy of the white race, which has been destroyed by the Communist-controlled New Deal." Their hope to return Texas to full control by a Democratic Party unwavering in opposition to civil rights, organized labor, and ambitious federal programs fell

THE GOOD WAR   263

far short. Support for a wartime president and the policies that
had alleviated the misery of the Depression remained strong.
Johnson and his compatriots held on to their seats, and Roosevelt won the state in his fourth run for the presidency with an
overwhelming 72 percent of the vote. "Gentlemen, the yokels
discovered they can outvote us," said one of the conservative
leaders to his friends.

Yet wartime changes had not destroyed the considerable
power over state institutions and the electorate held by conservative Democrats. In 1941, regents of the University of Texas
appointed by O'Daniel became irate that economists on the
faculty offered testimony in support of New Deal laws guaranteeing the right to form unions. They pressed the university
president, Homer Rainey, to fire them and to exert control
over the content of courses that touched on ongoing political
disputes. Rainey refused, but a year later, when four UT economists spoke in defense of minimum wage laws at hearings
in Dallas concerning strikes at war production plants, the regents dismissed them. Next they suppressed the teaching of
a novel critical of capitalism and attempted to fire the English
professor who had assigned it. Rainey furiously denounced
the regents to the faculty. The regents promptly fired Rainey.
The campus exploded in outrage. Students went on strike, and
8,000 of them marched in a mock funeral procession carrying
a coffin with a banner that read "academic freedom" from
campus to the capitol and the governor's mansion. The governor responded to the protests by appointing new regents and
offering jobs to the dismissed economists, but he refused to
bring Rainey back. Conservative critics of the university al-
leged that it harbored Communists, was "a nest of homosexuals," and had plans to admit Black students. It took more than
a decade for the University of Texas to regain credibility in
national academic circles and the ability to hire top-ranked

faculty. Rainey took his fight to the electorate. He ran for governor in 1946, promising to extend New Deal social programs and pay for them with taxes on key industries like oil and gas. Rainey made it to the Democratic Party runoff but was badly beaten by a candidate acceptable to conservative leaders. The struggles between liberals and conservatives had outlived the war, and neither had an overwhelming advantage.

The fate of Felix Longoria's body, four years after the end of the war that took his life, became another struggle for power among Texans. Longoria's parents and widow Beatrice assumed that they could hold a ceremony at the only funeral parlor in Felix's hometown of Three Rivers. But the nervous funeral director balked, worrying that "the whites would not like it." A stunned Beatrice turned for help to Hector P. García, a medical doctor in nearby Corpus Christi who had organized other Mexican American veterans into a group called "G.I. Forum" to combat discrimination. García called the director, pressing him to relent, but was told that "Latin people get drunk and lay around all of the time . . . we have not let them use it and we don't intend to start now."

The refusal was a routine humiliation of Jim Crow, of a piece with the dilapidated bathrooms, rancid water fountains, side windows, and back doors that were all too familiar to generations of Black and Mexican customers. But the changes brought by military service and wartime economic mobilization created new openings for the Longorias and García to fight back. The hundreds of thousands of Mexican Americans and African Americans who had answered the call to join a war they were told was for democracy no longer tolerated such insults. Increasingly, they felt that the federal government, with its reach now extended into providing electricity and

THE GOOD WAR   265

employing millions directly and indirectly on military bases and through military contracts, might be a weapon they could use to force Texas authorities to treat them as full-fledged citizens. Even before the United States entered the war, Black labor leaders who saw employment soaring in the defense sector made plans for a march on Washington to press for the hiring of Black workers at the same wage rates as their white counterparts. Roosevelt issued an executive order banning discrimination by federal contractors and creating a commission to investigate them. The march was cancelled in exchange for this measure, and the victory had its effect: membership in the National Association for the Advancement of Colored People grew nearly ten times over the course of the war, with Texas moving into second place in the nation in NAACP membership. Black soldiers served in segregated units, unlike Mexican Americans like Longoria who fought alongside their white neighbors. In 1948, President Harry Truman desegregated the military, eliciting howls of outrage from Jim Crow Democrats. Soon, in the dozens of military bases in Texas, Black soldiers lived and socialized with other servicemen, punching holes in the fabric of Jim Crow.

García also knew that wartime diplomatic changes had strengthened the hand he could play. A shared revulsion against fascism brought the Mexican and U.S. governments much closer together in the 1930s. Mexico declared war on Japan and Germany six months after Pearl Harbor when German submarines sank two Mexican oil tankers. Although a Mexican air squadron fought alongside American forces in the Philippines, the country's main contribution to the war was economic. Mexican copper, mercury, lead, and other resources fed manufacturing north of the border. When millions of American men began leaving farms, factories, and shops for the military, in 1942, the two countries signed the Bracero Agreement, allowing Mexican workers to come north for limited times under labor contracts that guaranteed a minimum wage, decent conditions, and freedom from discrimination. Texas farm associations opposed these protections, and the Mexican government struck back the next year by excluding Texas from the program "because of the number of cases of extreme, intolerable racial discrimination." Federal officials had reason to see the mistreatment of Mexican and Mexican American people as a matter of international relations and wartime urgency. Texas governor Coke Stevenson responded to federal pressure by establishing the Good Neighbor Commission, charged with investigating housing and health conditions for migrant workers as well as educational opportunity for and discrimination against all those of Mexican descent in the state. Mexico lifted the exclusion of Texas from the Bracero Program in 1947, and the commission continued its work. Although it had no formal power to change laws or working conditions, it was able to amplify the voices of those complaining about school segregation, working conditions, and discrimination.

The extent to which the war had changed Texas became apparent when Hector P. García and Beatrice Longoria called for an emergency meeting in Corpus Christi in January 1949 to settle the burial of Longoria. Hundreds of people poured into the "Mexican" elementary school from the fields, packing sheds, docks, shops, and the military base. The Good Neighbor Commission's leadership and Mexican diplomats expressed support for the effort to give Felix's body a dignified burial. A telegram from newly elected Senator Lyndon Johnson brought the crowd to its feet. "I deeply regret to learn that the prejudice of some individuals extends even beyond this life," it began. Johnson offered to expedite burial at Arlington National Cemetery in Washington, D.C., for "this Texas hero." The next month, the humble private from a small Texas town was laid

THE GOOD WAR 267

to rest in the company of his family, Senator Johnson, congressmen, State Department officials, and diplomats from Mexico and other Latin American countries.

Johnson may have needed Beatrice Longoria as much as she needed him. His election the previous fall came only after a ballot box from Jim Wells County came in late with a margin of 200 to 2 for Johnson over his conservative opponent in the Democratic primary, enough to put him over the top by eighty-seven votes out of nearly a million. The names from Box 13 were listed alphabetically, written by the same hand. Having once been cheated out of a Senate victory before, Johnson refused to be out-cheated this time. "Landslide Lyndon," as he was soon known, went to great lengths to reassure his more conservative financial supporters that his intervention in the Longoria case did not mean he was willing to see segregation dismantled. Johnson's dependence on one of the oldest and most corrupt political machines in the state showed how much he still relied on the old, crooked sources of power. But his willingness to intervene in such a high-profile civil rights case was not only a sign of how much the war had changed Texas, but a hint of how much more change would come in the following decades.

21

A Giant Reputation

Maybe the outsized reputation of Texas made it inevitable that the assassination of President John F. Kennedy would be blamed on the whole state. "We shot the President," my distraught grandmother told my fourteen-year-old father when he awoke from surgery in a hospital room in Midland in November 1963. Earlier that afternoon, a gunman had fired into the convertible auto carrying the president, his wife Jackie, and Texas governor John Connally through downtown Dallas. Bullets tore through Kennedy's neck and head, and into Connally's back. The motorcade rushed to Parkland Hospital, where Kennedy was pronounced dead, and then to Love Field, where a stony-faced Lyndon Johnson was sworn in as president on a plane that soon took the slain leader's body back to Washington, D.C.

Midland was more than three hundred miles from Dallas and my grandmother hardly wished Kennedy ill, yet her use of the word "we" reflected the immediate and lasting collective guilt placed on all of Texas. Two days later, the Dallas Cowboys played the Cleveland Browns in Cleveland, Ohio. Hotel employees refused to carry players' bags and Cleveland fans screamed "Dallas go home!" when the Cowboys took the field. The Browns' owner ordered the in-stadium announcer not to utter the city's name. Forty years later, when I lived in Dallas, visitors to the university where I worked would occasionally comment that it gave them chills to visit the same city where John F. Kennedy was assassinated. "I'll always think of November 22, 1963, when I come here," one professional colleague told me. The murder still tarnishes the reputation of Texas today.

It is curious to blame an entire state for a crime that one person committed in one of its cities. Five years after President Kennedy's assassination, a gunman shot his brother, Senator Robert F. Kennedy, in Los Angeles, California. Los Angeles happens to be the hometown of the visiting colleague so haunted by Kennedy's assassination, but I doubt that visitors tell her they have visions of Robert Kennedy bleeding to death in a hotel corridor whenever they land in her city. Nobody blamed California for this murder. The collective guilt put upon Texas reflected the huge reputation it had achieved in American culture by the 1960s. Big, brash, rowdy, maybe less civilized than other Americans, but also more honest and authentic: Texans embraced the stories told about their state and repeated them over and over again. So in a sense they also helped lay the groundwork for the collective guilt put upon Texas for the Kennedy assassination.

Texans' obsession with their own history became more systematic and institutionalized in the 1930s. By the 1950s, its outsized history and identity became a subject of interest in the country at large. The state's distinctiveness seemed to speak to a country that had not only survived the crises of the Depression and World War II, but emerged from these trials as the most powerful country in the world, with an economic, military, political, and cultural might rivaled only by the Soviet Union. Edna Ferber, one of the country's leading novelists, captured the drama of modern Texas history in her novel *Giant* in 1952. Her visit to the King Ranch several years earlier left her impressed (if not always positively) with the swagger of ranchers and oilmen. The novel is centered on the marriage between Virginia-born Leslie Lynton and Texas rancher Jordan Benedict, whose vast estate evokes the King Ranch. Leslie's struggles to understand the brash ways of her husband and his family stand in for the East Coast establishment's reckoning with the coming of age of the modern West as a center of power and wealth. Jordan's rivalry with Jett Rink, a poor ranch hand in love with Leslie who becomes fabulously rich after striking oil, captures the tensions between old ranching money and the coarse new oil-rich. The main characters are all white, even as depictions of the exploitation of the Benedict ranch's Mexican workforce and Rink's profane racism reflected the author's hope that her novel could help the country move toward greater equality.

The novel sold well, but it was Hollywood that brought its stories and characters to millions. The director George Stevens cast leading actors Rock Hudson as Jordan, Elizabeth Taylor as Leslie, and James Dean as Jett. He insisted on filming in and around the West Texas town of Marfa, where James Dean spent hours observing the speech and roping techniques of local cowboys. The film version of *Giant* was released in 1956 and gained enraptured audiences in the United States and abroad, along with nine Academy Award nominations. Stevens softened the novel's critiques of Texas without eliminating them. Late in the film, Benedict gets into a fistfight with a restaurant owner when his Mexican American daughter-in-law and grandchild are denied service. The film's end, a family scene of the aged patriarch Benedict looking on his multiracial grandchildren, suggests the possibility that Texas had a tolerant, humane future— a more subtle and quiet achievement than the brash history of ranching and oil, but a triumph nonetheless.

Ferber's novel and Stevens's film cemented the wildcat oilman and modern rancher as icons of Texas, themes that later dramas such as the television soap opera *Dallas* in the 1980s would extend. They joined older symbols that had endured. The 1960 movie *The Alamo,* directed by the legendary actor John Wayne (who also played Davy Crockett), reintroduced the central players of the Texas Revolution to national audiences. Like Ferber and Stevens, Wayne meant for his story of Texas to speak to the modern United States. "I'd read up on the history of our country and I'd become fascinated with the story of the Alamo," he said. "To me it represented the fight for freedom. Not just in America, but in all countries." In Wayne's film, the Mexican army the Texas rebels confronted looked less like the ill-clad and ill-equipped conscript force of 1836, and more like the robotic soldiers of a modern totalitarian state such as the Soviet Union. "*The Alamo* became a talisman of our defiance," remembers one journalist of his teenage years. "If John Wayne died to keep us from becoming Mexicans, who could doubt it was better to be dead than Red?" Here the Texas past showed the way to a future of resoluteness and courage in a worldwide confrontation.

Both films were wildly popular in Texas, despite the fury of some Texas writers at the depiction of open racism in *Giant.* "Texans delight in looking in the mirror, regardless of whether they are pleased with what they see there," observed the journalist John Bainbridge. In 1961 Bainbridge wrote the book *The Super-Americans,* which although much less well known today is the only work to rival *Giant* and Wayne's *Alamo* in cementing the enormous reputation of Texas in the postwar world. Bainbridge realized that rich Texans were compelling not because they were so different from their counterparts elsewhere, but because they took the American traits of materialism and self-confidence to extremes.

The Super-Americans replayed some of the greatest hits of the Texas mythos. Bainbridge found his subjects down to earth to the point of being crude, a theme in the state's reputation predating the 1936 Centennial and cattle kingdom and going back to Sam Houston's Indian beads and Davy Crockett's coonskin hats. He poked gentle fun at the underdeveloped nature of the state's universities, its allegedly crude cuisine (cooks there "are barely able to conceal their homicidal tendencies"), the maniacal insistence on bigness (houses, ranches, cars, the UT marching band's drum "Big Bertha"), murder rates and the ease of buying guns, and hostility to the federal government and liberalism. He also took his readers into art museums, corporate boardrooms, country clubs, and clothing stores in Dallas, Houston, Midland, and Fort Worth. In these places, Bainbridge's rich Texas subjects emerged not as throwbacks to the rough-and-tumble frontier, but as wealthy trendsetters in the boom times of the postwar United States.

High oil prices and sustained population growth (almost 25 percent over the course of the 1950s) made for flush times for the wealthiest Texans. They flaunted their riches in ways that would have given pause to their frontier predecessors, and even to some Rockefeller and other Yankee capitalists of the late 1800s. "When the temperature drops below ninety," said the manager of a suburban Dallas lunch spot, "out comes the minks. You've never seen so much mink under one roof." Bainbridge added the Dallas-based department store Neiman Marcus to outfits including the King Ranch and Texaco oil company among the state's legendary institutions. "The Alamo excepted," he wrote, "Neiman-Marcus has for years been the most celebrated institution in Texas."

People in this class showed off not just their clothing, but their private airplanes, their ranches, their shopping excursions to Paris (France, not Texas), and their home décor and landscaping. The Fort Worth oil magnate Ted Weiner bought a cemetery outside Kyoto, Japan, and had several dozen of its ancient headstones dug up and shipped back to Texas to adorn his garden. That was an extravagance, but it also reflected a new cosmopolitanism in Texas high culture, a wider interest and greater refinement than before. By the time Kennedy's assassination made Dallas infamous, frequent customers of Neiman Marcus included not just Texans like Weiner, but residents of all fifty states, England, France, Italy, and thirty-six other countries. (At one point during the filming of *Giant,* the cast was flown from Marfa to Dallas for a private shopping visit to the store.) Weiner's art collection featured sculptures by European luminaries including Picasso and Degas, but also home-grown talents such as Charles Umlauf and Charles T. Williams. His support for local operas and museums alongside national arts organizations was typical of the oil rich for boosting Texas while also appreciating and supporting a wider world of high culture. The rich men of Texas might be more profane and dress more casually than their counterparts in Massachusetts or France, but philanthropy and high style (the women's, at least) marked many wealthy Texans as fundamentally similar to John F. Kennedy and his elegant wife Jackie.

The Texas elite of this time was also a more open society in certain ways than it had been before. To be sure, the state's wealthy and socially influential remained an all-white caste, but one that had room for Jewish members such as Weiner and Stanley Marcus. This welcome certainly extended to members of the traditional New England Brahmin class, including the Connecticut senator and investment banker Prescott Bush, whose son George moved to Midland in 1948 after graduating from Yale College as part of the Ivy Leaguer or "Yalie" migration to West Texas. And despite the swaggering reputation of Texas men, many in these circles supported women's rights and were quite tolerant of divorce, which was regarded "like daybreak, as an everyday fact of life."

Rich Texans were different from their counterparts elsewhere, but no more so than their business and marriage partners in California or New England. In the end, Bainbridge found that they did not so much stand out from other Americans as point to a common future for the entire country, for better or for worse. "In the same way that America stands as the frontier of Europe," Bainbridge wrote at the book's end, "so Texas stands in the collective American imagination as the frontier of America—the land of the second chance, the last outpost of individuality, the stage upon which the American drama, in all its wild extremes, is being performed with eloquence and panache."

The Texas of *Giant* and *The Super-Americans* had its flaws, above all racism and violence. But in these books it nonetheless came across as a charming, fascinating, possibly even hopeful place. The Kennedy assassination and the multi-sourced rage and hatred that came to be directed at Lyndon Johnson during his presidency led people across the United States, and indeed the world, to see the same Texas characteristics in a very different light.

"Wanted for treason" screamed the headline on a flyer that littered Dallas in the days before Kennedy's visit. The sheet listed

A GIANT REPUTATION

a set of wild accusations against Kennedy—that he was soft on Communists at home and abroad, had turned over control of the United States to "the communist controlled United Nations," supported riots, appointed "Anti-Christians" to high offices, and hid a previous marriage (spelled "marraige") and divorce. An ad in the *Dallas Morning News* the day of his visit to the city hurled similar accusations under the title "Welcome Mr. Kennedy to Dallas." The president handed the paper to Jackie and said, "we're headed into nut country today." A few hours later he was dying in her arms.

These were the kind of details about Dallas that Americans and observers all over the world seized on after the assassination. Maybe some explanation for the shocking murder that seemed to mark the end of an era could be found in the anger of the right-wing circles in the city where he was slain. "A city of hate, the only city in which the President could have been shot," was how Dallas was later described by Judge Sarah Hughes, who administered the oath of office to Johnson on Air Force One.

It was true enough that the right-wing circles responsible for the flyer and ad were increasingly large, influential, and angry. Three years earlier, just before the presidential election of 1960 that pitted a Kennedy-Johnson ticket against Richard Nixon and Henry Cabot Lodge, women activists in Dallas surrounded Johnson and his wife, snatching the gloves from Lady Bird Johnson's hand and screaming and spitting at the couple as the television cameras rolled. Just a few weeks before Kennedy's assassination, his U.N. ambassador, Democratic Party luminary Adlai Stevenson, was heckled by a similarly well-dressed and heavily female Dallas mob. A woman married to an insurance executive hit him on the head with a placard, and the crowd began to rock his car until his driver made a quick escape. Stevenson, shaken up, urged the cancellation of his boss's upcoming trip, fearing greater violence would be directed against Kennedy.

The mob did not speak for all Texans. The Kennedy-Johnson ticket carried Texas in 1960, by a margin so narrow that it is possible Johnson's calm nerves and resoluteness in the face of the heckling pushed them over the top. Much to the irritation of the people who accosted Stevenson and Johnson in Dallas, outright liberals could contend for statewide power. "Smilin'" Ralph Yarborough, an attorney with a long set of victories against major oil companies, was serving the first of three terms as one of the U.S. senators from Texas (and was riding in the next car in the motorcade) when Kennedy was shot. Yarborough was an outspoken environmentalist and supported civil rights more than any other senator from a southern state. In short, Texas was not so different from of the rest of the country in its politics. Large and adoring crowds greeted President and Mrs. Kennedy in San Antonio, Houston, Fort Worth, and even Dallas, where three years earlier Kennedy had lost overwhelmingly. Moreover, there was no evidence that the open contempt for Kennedy had anything to do with the assassination. To the extent that the assassin, Lee Harvey Oswald, had a coherent political stance, it was more left than right. He spoke highly of the Soviet Union and Cuba and had visited both; Oswald had also shot at a retired army general much beloved by the Texas right, also in Dallas, just seven months before he succeeded in killing the president.

Nonetheless, the worldwide publicity surrounding the assassination brought the Texas right into public view. Newspaper readers and television watchers all over the world learned a lot about angry Texas conservatives. They heard about Bruce Alger, who won a breakthrough congressional election as a Republican in Dallas in 1954, and when in office condemned civil rights proposals and cast the sole vote against federal funding of lunches for impoverished schoolchildren. Carrying a sign that read "LBJ sold out to Yankee Socialists," he egged on the crowd that accosted Johnson and his wife. ("We lost Texas because of that asshole Congressman in Dallas," Richard Nixon reportedly said.) Alger and similar politicians were supported by W. A. Criswell, the pastor of the city's First Baptist Church. Like Frank Norris in Fort Worth a generation before, Criswell blended popular Protestantism (under his leadership, the church became the largest Southern Baptist congregation in the world) and firebrand politics, drawing attention for his condemnation of civil rights (based on the "spurious doctrine" of the "universal fatherhood of God and the brotherhood of man"). His comments before the presidential election of 1960, darkly warning that Kennedy's Catholicism threatened American democracy because he would follow the instructions of the Pope rather than the electorate, came into renewed prominence.

The traditionally Democratic political establishment of Dallas came in for heightened scrutiny as well. Observers noted that the previous mayor, the police chief, and the head of the homicide division charged with investigating the shocking murder by Oswald three days after Kennedy's death had all been in the Ku Klux Klan in their youth. In a clear sign that Dallas voters wanted to distance themselves from extremists, Earle Cabell, the mayor at the time of the assassination and a much more moderate pro-business southern Democrat, defeated Alger in the next year's congressional election. But the city could not shake its reputation as a toxic combination of wealth, intrigue, and hate. "Dallas is a woman who will walk on you when you're down," sang the Panhandle group the Flatlanders in 1976.

The press focused on prominent male leaders such as

Criswell, Alger, and one of their leading financial backers, the oilman H. L. Hunt. Hunt, a member of Criswell's congregation, made his fortune in the East Texas oil fields, where he had bought out Daddy Joiner's lease in 1930. By the 1950s, Hunt was one of the wealthiest men in the country. He built a mansion in Dallas on White Rock Lake modeled, with typical modesty, after George Washington's plantation home, that I used to run by when I lived there. Hunt was a key funder of the Wisconsin senator Joseph McCarthy's erratic and destructive anti-Communist witch hunt in the 1950s. Angered by Kennedy's bid for the presidency, Hunt paid for the printing of hundreds of thousands of flyers with Criswell's warnings about the dangers of electing a Catholic president. He was so closely identified with anti-Kennedy circles that, just hours after the assassination, agents from the Federal Bureau of Investigation warned him that they considered him a target for revenge killing.

The press coverage of people like Alger, Hunt, and Criswell was unfair when it implied that all Texans shared their extreme views. It was accurate enough, however, in portraying the right-wing political movement as increasingly powerful. Fueled by vast amounts of oil money and tapping the energies and large congregations of ministers such as Criswell, this coalition hoped to reverse New Deal economic regulations, especially protections for forming unions, minimum wage measures, and restrictions on banks and monopolies; to prevent federal support for civil rights; and to get the United States to assert its power on the world stage on its own rather than under the framework of multinational organizations such as the United Nations. The high-profile influence and swagger of these male figures sometimes hid the extent to which this right-wing movement relied on an active cohort of women grassroots leaders. The swelling ranks of Republican Women's

A GIANT REPUTATION 279

Clubs were one reflection of this leadership. So were organizations like Minute Women USA, formed in 1949 to combat what its leaders saw as Communist subversion, particularly in the form of university and school curricula on civil rights and international affairs. The Houston chapter, one of the largest, took over the city's school board for a time and fired and drove out several principals and teachers for supporting racial integration. One chapter even had a men's auxiliary. Minute Woman Ida Darden, a former opponent of women's suffrage, published *The Southern Conservative* out of Fort Worth for a decade, railing against the income tax and Edna Ferber's *Giant* as "Communist propaganda from cover to cover" for its depiction of children who repudiated their parents for becoming wealthy and dishonored them by marrying down. As one Neiman Marcus executive wrote in his best-selling book *Dallas Public and Private,* "compulsive right-wing women . . . have been, on the whole, more obviously numerous, more vocal, more absolute and sometimes more physical than men."

The day when conservatives such as Darden and Alger assumed dominance in the Republican Party and contended for statewide power in Texas had not yet come. But the depiction of them as a distinctively Texan mix of intrigue, rage against liberalism, and violence against their opponents became so entrenched that, ironically, it came to mark the reputation of one of their great enemies, Lyndon Johnson. After pushing through landmark civil rights measures and winning a landslide electoral victory in 1964, Johnson's presidency wrecked on the shoals of the Vietnam War. American involvement in Vietnam stretched back to the 1950s, when President Eisenhower supported France's efforts to retain control of its former colony. Kennedy stepped up U.S. support of the pro-American government of South Vietnam, which was locked in a struggle against Communist North Vietnam and a revolution inside its own borders, by sending more equipment and U.S. soldiers to train South Vietnamese forces. Johnson, in accordance with a bipartisan political establishment that believed the United States must support enemies of Communist regimes, deepened U.S. involvement by bombing the north and dispatching American soldiers and troops. By 1966, there were almost 400,000 U.S. soldiers fighting there, and a draft was in place to replenish their ranks. Every month hundreds died in a country that most Americans had not until then even heard of.

No factor was greater in heightening the country's social divisions than the Vietnam War, and no person was more associated with it than Lyndon Johnson. And Johnson was an easy stand-in for the state as a whole. "Everything about Lyndon—his size, his earthy way of speaking, his legendary gaucherie—was a caricature of Texas qualities . . . a sort of mythic Texas freak," remembered the Dallas-raised journalist Lawrence Wright. Given the gigantic reputation of Texas, Americans who thought U.S. involvement in the war was a mistake or even a crime were drawn to Johnson's Texas background to find an explanation. "Just about as important as any influence on Johnson's course in Vietnam," wrote a journalist in *Life* magazine in 1968, "is the battle of the Alamo fought 132 years ago just 60 miles from Johnson's birthplace." The novelist Norman Mailer similarly rooted his explanation for what he saw as a failed and pointlessly, shamefully bloody misadventure in the Texas past. His novel *Why Are We in Vietnam?* centered on a young Texan at a dinner party at his parents' mansion in Dallas, given in his honor the night before shipping out to Vietnam. Trying to understand why young American men were being sent to Vietnam, his thoughts keep going back to a hunting trip in Alaska that his father organized several years before. The recounting of his father's increasingly frantic efforts to kill a grizzly bear,

A GIANT REPUTATION 281

achieved only by the use of a helicopter, presents Texas culture as vulgar, materialistic, and gratuitously violent. "Texas" was the answer to the question posed in the novel's title.

Johnson seethed at being presented as a dumb hick from a backward and violent place. It played on his sense of inferiority in the shadow of the Kennedy glamour and mystique. He had good reason to be resentful about his portrayal: it was dubious at best to look at the Texas past to explain America's war in Vietnam. If Johnson had followed the wrong path, it was the same one that the entire American political establishment walked. Blaming Texas was easier than reckoning with the arrogance and disdain for life that came from Harvard, Yale, and the State Department. And precious few looked to the culture of the Lone Star State to explain why Johnson became an impassioned and effective advocate of civil rights, helping the movement remake American law and ensure actual equality. His grandfather had been a Populist when that movement practiced interracial politics, and his father was one of the few state representatives to stand with J. T. Canales in the confrontation with the Rangers in 1919. LBJ came from a long strain of racial egalitarianism. But the submerged histories of interracial solidarity were very, very far from what people thought of when they thought of Texas in the 1960s. Johnson also dug some of the ditch he was stuck in. "Hell, Vietnam is just like the Alamo," he told his National Security Council when he decided to increase the numbers of American soldiers. "Hell, it's just like if you were down at that gate and you were surrounded and you damn well needed somebody. Well, I'm going to go—and I thank the Lord that I've got men who want to go with me."

The first Texan president's time in office ended after the election of 1968, when mounting opposition to the war and his own despair over it led him to renounce a run for another term. The image of Texas by which he was judged lasted much longer, even as dramatic social changes were demonstrating how much more complicated the state was than the stereotypes cemented in the tumultuous 1960s.

Running for Freedom

22

Civil Rights

"My faith in the Constitution is whole, it is complete, it is total," intoned the speaker on prime-time evening television in early 1974 from her chair in a congressional committee room at the Capitol in Washington, D.C. "I am not going to sit here and be an idle spectator to the diminution, the subversion, the destruction of the Constitution," she continued in a resonant voice that fused precise, very formal enunciation of each syllable with traces of the twang of her Houston childhood. The speaker was Barbara Jordan, and the subject was whether President Richard Nixon should be impeached for covering up a break-in into the offices of the opposition political party.

Jordan's speech was widely credited with connecting the debate over Nixon's actions to the basic principles of democracy in the United States. The key role she played in the proceedings that drove a president from office for the first time in American history made her a household name across the country. When she won election to the Texas State Senate in 1966, Jordan became the first Black member of that body in eighty-three years, and when she was elected to represent her Houston district in 1972, one of the first two Black congressional representatives from the South since Reconstruction. The learned gravitas and careful yet passionate oratory she displayed in the Watergate hearings prompted speculation about future roles as a Supreme Court justice, cabinet member, or even vice president. Such possibilities were foreclosed when multiple sclerosis prompted her to leave electoral politics for an academic position at the University of Texas by the end of the decade.

The fact that a Black woman could win elections to such offices and gain the kind of prominence that Jordan did reflected the dramatic victories of the Civil Rights Movement both in Texas and across the United States. In some ways, the story of the Civil Rights Movement in Texas is one of thunder from distant battles that rolled across the state. As was the case with the decisive battles of the Civil War, the major conflicts that destroyed the Jim Crow system took place far to the east of Texas. Emboldened by the Supreme Court decision *Brown v. Board of Education,* in 1954, in which a unanimous court ruled that racial segregation in public schools violated the Fourteenth Amendment's promise of the equal protection of the law, Black southerners and their allies laid siege to the foundations of the social and political system of Jim Crow that had once seemed unshakable. A bus boycott in Montgomery, Alabama, in 1957 first brought Martin Luther King Jr. to prominence, and showed that ordinary southerners were willing to take great risks to regain the freedoms taken from their ancestors with the imposition of disfranchisement and systematic legal segregation in the wake of Populism's defeat at the end of the 1800s. Demonstrations for the end of segregation and dis-

CIVIL RIGHTS 285

franchisement and campaigns for voter registration in Alabama and Mississippi prompted mass jailings, open brutality against even child demonstrators, and the murders of civil rights workers by white authorities and vigilantes. But this terrible violence resulted in outrage that led Congress to pass the Civil Rights Act of 1964, which outlawed segregation in public accommodations such as restaurants, hotels, bus stations, and airports; and the Voting Rights Act of 1965, which ended wholesale disfranchisement by allowing the federal government to intervene to register voters and oversee election procedures in places with histories of voter suppression. President Johnson was instrumental in securing passage of both laws, most notably in an emotional appeal for the Voting Rights Act in which the white Texan uttered the civil rights slogan "We Shall Overcome" in front of Congress.

The laws and the movements behind them brought dramatic change to Texas, if unevenly and slowly. School systems began desegregation in the 1950s and 1960s, although when my father graduated from high school in Midland in 1968, his senior class was all white, and the school, which opened in 1961, was named Robert E. Lee and sang "Dixie" as its fight song. Many of the first Black students to attend previously all-white schools found their white teachers fair and nurturing. Annette Gordon-Reed, who grew up in Conroe in the early 1960s, wrote decades later that her first-grade teacher at Anderson Elementary "could not have handled my time in her care any better" and that the principal "and every teacher with whom I came into contact seemed committed to rising above the town's history to make things work." "I never experienced any different treatment from them," she wrote, "I felt nothing but their support." Texas universities admitted Black students before most southern schools. In 1950, trustees of Southern Methodist University authorized the admission of Black students to its seminary, regularizing a process that had begun a few years earlier when the seminary's dean invited students from all-Black schools to take classes, do coursework, and be assigned grades that would be forwarded to their official institutions. In 1954, the University of Texas at Austin admitted a small number of Black students in the wake of the *Brown* decision, although administrators worked behind the scenes to keep them out of positions as teaching assistants, band members, and football players. In 1962, SMU started admitting Black people as undergraduates; the same year, Rice University trustees began the legal process of amending the school's charter, which stipulated that the school was to educate only "the white inhabitants of the City of Houston, and State of Texas," to allow the university to admit all qualified applicants fairly and without regard to race.

Texas schools achieved some notoriety for their willingness to capitalize on Black athletic talent, again sooner than other southern institutions. In 1965, Beaumont's Jerry LeVias became the first Black athlete in the Southwest Conference to win an athletic scholarship when he joined SMU's squad, on his way to stardom in professional football with the Houston Oilers and the San Diego Chargers. A year later, the men's basketball team at Texas Western University—now the University of Texas at El Paso—fielded an all-Black starting lineup. In the national championship game, they defeated the perennial hoops powerhouse Kentucky, a program that was unwilling to recruit a single Black athlete.

Self-interest as much as high-minded principle motivated prominent universities such as SMU, Rice, and UT Austin to break from the vast majority of their counterparts across the South. The benefits of Black athleticism were readily apparent, as when in his freshman year LeVias led the SMU Mustangs to their first Cotton Bowl appearance in twenty years. Admitting

CIVIL RIGHTS 287

Black students, even if it was only a token number, allowed Rice to comply with increasingly strict federal anti-discrimination provisions, and therefore compete for federal contracts in the burgeoning defense and aerospace sectors. Rice could not have become a leading research university had it remained true to its original segregationist charter.

For the most part, the Texas business and political establishments embraced a similar preference for pragmatism over their previous virulent racism. Other former Confederate states pulled out all the stops to protect every single inch of Jim Crow's domain, a stance known as "massive resistance." The governor of Mississippi proclaimed "Segregation today, segregation tomorrow, segregation forever!" before armed federal marshals forced the admission of a single black student to the University of Mississippi. People in power refused to comply with the law. County officials in Virginia and Maryland, in unabashed displays of hatred, shut down entire public school systems rather than allow even small numbers of Black students to attend classes with white kids. Police in Alabama blasted peaceful demonstrators with fire hoses, turned dogs loose on demonstrating children, and charged and beat demonstrators with batons from horseback.

Most white Texas leaders saw this brutality, and the resulting television footage and newspaper articles that circulated worldwide, as a vindication of the judgment that they reached in the 1950s: it was better to bend in the wind of civil rights than to sacrifice harmony on the altar of massive resistance. Fort Worth, San Antonio, and El Paso began integrating city buses, swimming pools, railroad stations, and schools in the 1950s, well before the epic showdowns in the deep South. The distillation of the thinking behind this approach can be found in the remarkable film *Dallas at the Crossroads,* which was produced by the city's leaders in 1961 to pave the way for

288 CIVIL RIGHTS

the gradual integration of the city's public schools, beginning at the start of the 1961–62 school year with eighteen Black elementary school students enrolling at eight previously all-white schools. Narrated by the country's most revered television news celebrity, Walter Cronkite, the film portrayed a bustling city and a calm scene of a white suburban family with a grandfather puffing a pipe and playing with his granddaughter. "What we have created, we can also destroy," warned Cronkite. The images then changed abruptly to footage of a tornado in 1958 tearing apart downtown Dallas skyscrapers, armed soldiers surrounding the high school in Little Rock, Arkansas, and a mostly female white mob screaming at figures off camera. A procession of city leaders—a law school dean, a labor leader, elected officials, and the police chief—then spoke in somber tones of the dangers of violence and the importance of obeying the law. The film thus managed to pull off the trick of advocating for integration while showing only a fleeting glimpse of a single Black person. The end of strict Jim Crow in schooling was not so much a moral obligation as it was a matter of public safety.

Of course, there was strong opposition to civil rights measures. In 1951, on twelve separate occasions Black Dallasites moving into a previously all-white neighborhood in the city's south were welcomed with bombs. Five years later, Texas governor Allan Shivers dispatched Texas Rangers to ensure that three Black students, who were backed by a federal court order, did not enroll in Mansfield High School. Several Texas Rangers stood by while a mob kicked the students and threw gravel at them. "They were just 'salt of the earth' citizens," Ranger Jay Banks said later, "convinced that someone was trying to interfere with their way of life." Also under Shivers's watch, the state government attempted to ban the NAACP in 1956, setting

CIVIL RIGHTS   289

up legal and practical barriers that eroded some of the organization's local chapters. And white alumni sued Rice University over changing its charter to allow integration, delaying implementation of the amendment by several years. Aggrieved whites could show their opposition to integration in other ways as well: at SMU, white students made Jerry LeVias's life a "living hell" with social ostracism, slurs, and death threats. He wore the number 23, after the twenty-third psalm—"yea, though I walk through the valley of the shadow of death, I will fear no evil, for thou art with me"—to bolster his courage and help retain his self-control. In the end, the diffuse efforts to stop the implementation of basic legal equality failed: Dallas authorities convened an interracial grand jury to investigate the bombings and file charges against suspects; the would-be Mansfield students enrolled in Fort Worth's mostly white school district instead; NAACP chapters recovered; Rice won its court battle to change with the times; and LeVias played on.

The decisions of most white elites to avoid massive resistance meant that Texas saw fewer dramatic and newsworthy confrontations over civil rights than other southern states. That makes it easier to miss the long traditions of struggle against second-class treatment by both Hispanic and Black Texans. In the late 1940s and 1950s, the League of United Latin American Citizens (LULAC) and allied organizations filed fifteen desegregation lawsuits. Most notable was *Delgado v. Bastrop,* which resulted in a federal court striking down, in 1948, the exclusion of Mexican American children from predominantly white schools. Mexican American political rights were never as fully eliminated as was Black voting. Grassroots efforts to push for better school funding and for potential voters to pay their poll taxes resulted in increasing Hispanic success in electoral politics more than a decade before Barbara Jordan's breakthrough election. The San Antonio attorney and veteran Henry B. González won election to the San Antonio city council in 1953 and to the state senate in 1956 (where he was the first Mexican American member in more than a century). Two years later he won almost 20 percent of the vote in the Democratic gubernatorial primary. Three years after that, he made history as the first Mexican American elected to the U.S. Congress from Texas. Similar breakthroughs took place in local elections, as in Crystal City in 1963 when five Mexican American candidates swept the town's city council elections, lifted by support from an agricultural union and a long-standing voter registration drive. By the end of the 1960s, for the first time since the Populist movement seven decades earlier, white Texans did not have a monopoly on electoral politics.

Black Texans made their mark on the judicial side of civil rights generations before Barbara Jordan's ascent to national fame. Indeed, in some ways the road to *Brown* started in the Lone Star State, with three Supreme Court rulings from 1940 to 1950 paving the way. The strategy of the National Association for the Advancement of Colored People (NAACP) was to chip away at the legal basis of segregation by gradually leading courts to the idea that the Fourteenth Amendment's guarantee of "the equal protection of the laws" made segregated schooling and public accommodations unconstitutional. The horrific case of Bob White, a farmworker in Polk County, about eighty miles northeast of Houston, gave the organization an early opportunity. In 1937, White was seized with fifteen other Black men and identified by a white woman as the man who had sexually assaulted her, based on his voice alone. Texas Rangers removed him from the county jail every night for a week, chained him to a tree, and beat him until he confessed to the crime. After a Texas court found him guilty and sentenced him to death, the NAACP supported an appeal to the U.S. Supreme

CIVIL RIGHTS 291

Court. In 1940 the court ruled unanimously that White's confession was not admissible evidence because he had been denied the due process of law. The legal victory was a stepping-stone for civil rights. Yet it did Bob White no good. The following year the woman's husband, fearing he would be acquitted without the confession, shot him in open court in Conroe in front of the judge and dozens of other eyewitnesses, many of whom cheered the murderer and slapped him on the back. An all-white jury promptly found him not guilty of murder.

Forty miles away and six weeks after White's murder, the Houston dentist and NAACP member Lonnie Smith attempted to vote in the Democratic primary. Turned away because the Democratic Party, backed by the state government, prohibited Black people from voting in its elections, Smith filed suit. The NAACP won again, in *Smith v. Allwright,* issued in 1944, striking down the whites-only primary as a violation of the equal protection clause. Black voter registration tripled in a few years. In early 1946, Heman Sweatt, a sometime NAACP activist (and a patient of Lonnie Smith's dental practice), attempted to enroll in the University of Texas Law School. Although he met all criteria for admission, the state turned him down. NAACP attorneys again took the matter to the Supreme Court and again won a decision, in 1950, known as *Sweatt v. Painter.* A unanimous Supreme Court held that the state had to admit Sweatt and other qualified applicants for graduate and professional programs that did not have counterparts at all-Black schools, such as Prairie View A&M. Three Supreme Court civil rights victories coming from Texas in a decade, made possible by the nickels and dimes contributed to the NAACP by working-class Texans over a generation, set the stage for *Brown.*

Desegregation and a return to meaningful participation in electoral politics were welcome changes from exclusion and

292   CIVIL RIGHTS

disfranchisement. They also brought their own set of challenges to Black and Hispanic Texans. The two groups shared similar histories of exclusion from power and political rights, but that did not mean they cooperated or even respected one another. Before the NAACP's victories in court destroyed the legal basis for segregation, the easiest legal strategy for Mexican Americans was to claim they were white, and that therefore segregationist laws and policies did not apply to them. In the *Delgado* case, for example, LULAC attorneys argued that Mexicans should be allowed to attend white schools because they were in fact white people. In essence, they were not objecting to racial discrimination in principle, just to racial discrimination practiced against them. "Let the Negro fight his own battles," LULAC's national president said in 1957; "his problems are not mine. I don't want to ally with him." Some Mexican Americans actively supported anti-Black Jim Crow. One of the men arrested in Dallas for bombing Black families was named Pete García; and one LULAC leader, a Houston restaurateur named Felix Tijerina, refused to serve Black patrons at his restaurants (childhood favorites of mine) in the 1950s, even after other businesses began to do so.

On the other hand, many members of both groups felt a strong sense of solidarity with one another. Henry B. González condemned anti-Black racism throughout his career, and as a freshman state senator went to dramatic lengths to stop segregationist legislation, speaking for hours on end on the Senate floor in an effort to exhaust his opponents at a time when there were still no Black legislators in the body. One day soon, he predicted, "the strained interpretations of the law and even the Scriptures by the segregationists will sound as foolish and stupid as those same arguments used to support slavery 100 years ago." The state NAACP honored him with awards and

CIVIL RIGHTS 293

raised money for his campaigns. Barbara Jordan was a similarly fervent supporter of Mexican American interests in her career, playing an important role in Congress in ensuring that the provisions of the Civil Rights Act and the Voting Rights Act protected them as well.

By the 1970s, Jordan and González had become fixtures of the Democratic establishment, confidants of presidents and governors, comfortable in their congressional positions, secure in the knowledge that millions of Texans saw their lives as proof that society had become a much more equal and decent place. But they had Black and Hispanic detractors as well, especially in younger and more radical circles. Some young Mexican Americans began calling themselves "Chicanos," reclaiming a previously denigrating term for working class, uncultured people of Mexican descent. Chicano activists stressed their Indigenous rather than Spanish roots, saw the Vietnam War as a continuation of colonial violence, welcomed migration from Latin America, supported Black civil rights, and organized a separatist "Raza Unida" Party untainted by the Democrats' association with Jim Crow. In 1973, young activists staged a mock trial for González during his visit to a university and found him guilty "of being a traitor" to his own people by supporting the Democratic establishment and the war in Vietnam. This prompted the congressman to tell the "judge" that "I've had to fight chicken-shits worse than you" and "you're a dumb little shit." Jordan encountered similar rhetoric from Black radicals outraged by her support for the Vietnam War, some of whom called her "Aunt Jemima," after the stereotypical large southern Black woman.

These disputes between young militants and middle-aged politicians, like the tensions between some Black and Hispanic activists, were all signs that civil rights had transformed

Texas. It had not brought full equality. Black Texans in the twenty-first century, for example, remain more than twice as likely to be incarcerated. They have a median household income only 60 percent that of whites, and they live five years fewer, on average, than white Texans. But there are more Black officeholders in Texas than in any other state, nearly half of African American households are in the middle class (virtually the same proportion as white families), and Black professionals from all over the country move to the Lone Star State, especially the Houston and Dallas metropolitan regions. In 2022, the elementary school where Annette Gordon-Reed had become the first Black student six decades earlier, before going on to a professorship at Harvard and a Pulitzer Prize, was named in her honor. The Texas county that a generation earlier had tolerated the torture and murder of Bob White in open court, and the burning at the stake of another Black man on the courthouse lawn a generation before that, was a transformed place.

Barbara Jordan died at her Austin home in 1996, survived by her longtime romantic partner Nancy Earl, her mother, and two sisters. She was buried on Republic Hill near Stephen F. Austin's reinterred body at the Texas State Cemetery, becoming the first African American to be so honored. A life-sized bronze statue of her, seated in deep thought with glasses and a book in her lap, was placed in Austin's airport in 2002, in the terminal that bears her name. Her statue joined a bronze figure of a Texas Ranger rising twelve feet high on a granite pedestal in the main terminal of Love Field in Dallas, placed in 1963, as the state's most prominent airport art. The model for the anonymous Ranger was Ranger Sergeant Jay Banks. Banks had also achieved notoriety, in his case when a picture of him leaning back casually against a tree in front of Mansfield High School

CIVIL RIGHTS 295

in 1956 circulated across the world. Behind him, dangling from the school's main entrance, hung a dummy of an African American man from a noose. Between the two of them, the Austin and Dallas airport statues captured the dramatic changes brought by civil rights.

23

Luckenbach and Beyond

Hondo Crouch walked a very different path to fame than did Barbara Jordan. Born in the Hill Country town of Hondo and named John Russell by his parents, Crouch first achieved notoriety as an all-American swimmer for UT Austin. After his brief service during World War II, he moved back to the Hill Country and raised livestock that came to him from his wife Shatzi's wealthy stock-raising family. Crouch composed six hundred or so whimsical columns for the *Comfort News,* published in the old German town of Comfort, under the pen name "Peter Cedarstacker" starting in 1963. These pieces profiled local characters, offering humor and sometimes satire, and in the process earning him a reputation as a kind of bard of the Hill Country. Crouch leaned in to his persona as what one journalist called a "redneck Renaissance man," taking the name "Hondo," growing a chaotic beard, affecting a strong Texas accent, and always wearing a weathered cowboy hat, stained shirt, and loosely tied red bandana. In most of the country, people pretend to be more educated, worldly, and accomplished than they actually are. Crouch was a talented writer who had been recorded by the Smithsonian, an accomplished swimming coach, and an influential University of Texas athlete alumnus who raised considerable sums for his alma mater. He pretended to be a simple country boy.

His purchase of the town of Luckenbach in 1971 expanded Hondo's fame. Hondo himself told it as a simple story of seeing a newspaper ad that read "town for sale, pop. 3" while on a beer break traveling between his two ranches, and immediately deciding that running a general store, saloon, and dance hall was the perfect fit. His business partner, Guich Kook, remembered it as Shatzi's idea. By this account, the purchase of Luckenbach came from her hope that it would give her husband a satisfying occupation and a platform for his hayseed persona. Whatever the truth, it worked. Crouch and Kook made Luckenbach a brand as much as a town. Its logo was a Texas Lone Star set in an oval with the text "Luckenbach, Texas," and, inside the star, the inaccurate "est. 1849" (a date Kook said "we just made up"). Crouch presided over the store, made-up celebrations like "Luckenbach World Fair," and chili cook-offs as the town's "clown prince." The festivals, marketed by a professional public relations firm, attracted tens of thousands of visitors. The Texas musicians Willie Nelson, Jerry Jeff Walker (who succeeded in masking his New York roots by gluing a cowboy hat to his head and speaking with a Texas accent), and Waylon Jennings headlined early World Fairs, mingling the town's reputation with their own.

Hondo's premature death at age fifty-nine, in 1976, only cemented his reputation. The next year, Waylon Jennings recorded "Luckenbach, Texas," an ode to the town that reinforced the national fame of both Jennings and Luckenbach.

"Maybe it's time we got back to the basics of love," crooned Jennings, lamenting the shallowness of conventional middle-class striving. This anthem to the simple life of Texas remains wildly popular two generations later. When I taught Texas history in Dallas, more than half of my students could recognize the song based on the opening chord alone, though none had even been born when it came out.

The contrast between the conventional urban world and the simple virtues of rural Texas made the song "Luckenbach" work. The irony was that the more most Texans' lives looked like everywhere else, the greater the appeal a Texan identity held. Luckenbach remained a real place, but it had also become an idea that could be invoked and sold by anybody who understood this paradox—Jennings's songwriters (from New York), Jerry Jeff Walker, native Texan Willie Nelson, the marketing companies that made the Luckenbach logo a mainstay of Texan bumper stickers. The more that Texans actually lived like the rest of the country—with suburban tract housing, offices and factories, the same products in the same stores, with people who had moved from the rest of the country and the world—the more many of them felt the need to distinguish themselves from this homogeneity. By the 1970s, you could hear this in people's voices. Linguists found that the classic Texan drawl, with a flattened vowel sound that makes "night" sound like "naht," was becoming more rather than less common, and distinctive expressions like "y'all" and "fixin' to" were growing in popularity. Texans were more likely to use these terms, and turn up their accents, when they visited barbecue restaurants and small towns. They were sincere about their Texanness, but like Hondo Crouch, they were also performing.

Dallas's reputation also grew over the decade. It was the Texas city at the other end of the spectrum from Luckenbach, a place of flashy materialism and swagger. Like Luckenbach, the Dallas Cowboys and their cheerleaders belonged not just to Texans, but to anybody who claimed them. And like Luckenbach, they were the products of careful marketing and a corporate approach to entertainment that was as much Madison Avenue as Texas.

Modern professional football is the child of Texans Lamar Hunt (one of the heirs of H. L. Hunt's enormous oil fortune) and Earnest "Tex" Schramm. In 1960, Hunt founded the American Football League (AFL) to compete for players and fans with the National Football League (NFL). The same year, Schramm was hired as general manager of the new NFL team, the Dallas Cowboys, by their owner Clint Murchison Jr., the heir to another Texas oil fortune. Six years later, Schramm and Hunt orchestrated a merger of the two leagues into an organization that kept the name NFL and picked its champion in a "Super Bowl" (Hunt's name) played between the champions of the old and newer leagues. Under Schramm's management, the Cowboys earned twenty straight winning seasons and two Super Bowl championships. Schramm, a former journalist and public relations director, recognized professional football's potential as mass televised entertainment. Basic aspects of the game were his creations, including instant replay and referees with microphones. Schramm ensured that the Cowboys were among the first teams to play games on Thanksgiving Day and Monday nights, earning them national media coverage as football eclipsed major league baseball as the nation's most popular sport.

In 1978, an NFL executive dubbed the Cowboys "America's team," a label that stuck. The loyal following for the Cowboys (and my hometown team of the Houston Oilers, who played in the Astrodome, the country's first indoor stadium) owed something to the Texan mania for football. Over the previous generation, better roads and then postwar prosperity allowed even small towns to field high school teams that traveled to compete with towns near and not so near. Millions who grew up playing, cheering, and partying under the Friday night lights became avid fans of professional and big-time collegiate football. Nowhere was the sport bigger than in Texas.

The Cowboys, more than any other professional sports franchise, used the tools of corporate America to build a money-making machine on this foundation. Most teams centered on the charisma and talents of a coach and key players. The Cowboys had their personalities, to be sure—Schramm himself, his longtime coach Tom Landry, and the star quarterback Roger Staubach chief among them. But they were successful because they operated like a soulless bureaucracy. Drawing from Murchison's deep pockets, Schramm hired a computer programmer to develop rigorous measurements of potential recruits, with data inputted by a scouting staff. Where other team owners constantly inserted their own judgments into recruitment and strategic decisions, Murchison followed the well-established corporate principle of a separation between ownership and management. He let Schramm run the team. Schramm in turn delegated coaching to Tom Landry, whom he hired away from the New York Giants. Landry was a high school star from Mission who played a few seasons in the NFL. His suits, ties, elegant fedora hat, and unemotional demeanor (one player famously called him "a plastic man . . . actually, no man at all") bore the marks of his business degree. Another sign of the Cowboys' bottom-line approach came in the form of player recruitment. They hired Black players, even publicly assertive ones with Ivy League degrees that gave other teams pause, and worked behind the scenes to make sure that they could buy homes where they wanted and play in front of integrated audiences. "The sports world is run by the win-loss column," Schramm matter-of-factly told a reporter asking him about his

Black players. And the team paid all of its players, even its biggest stars, less than almost all other teams. The Cowboys were the relentless, bare-knuckled, number-crunching love child of Texas brashness and Yankee capitalism.

One of the most notable innovations of the 1970s Cowboys was that the team's cheerleaders became as much of a draw as the players themselves. What were fans supposed to look at during the long breaks between plays? These fit women with big hair who strode out onto the field in 1972 wearing halter tops, white hot pants, and go-go boots answered that question. Exaggerated dance moves and enormous pom-poms made their motions visible to fans at the stadium as well as on television. Cheerleading, like football, was much older than the NFL, but the barely contained sexuality of the Cowboys Cheerleaders was new. "We're looking for an all-American, sexy girl," said the squad's first instructor, Texie Waterman, who had danced at New York clubs and on television in her younger years. Management brought the same bottom-line mentality to the cheerleaders as to the rest of the franchise. They were directed by Schramm's secretary, on top of the rest of her duties, and paid all of $15 per game. That's worth more like $70 in 2020s dollars, but since the team did not pay anything for the required daily practices or travel time, it was next to nothing. And it came with a huge set of restrictions on their private lives: no dating players, no smoking where they could be caught on camera, no gaining weight. Most Cowboys Cheerleaders of that era look back fondly on their time in the limelight, but with the knowledge that they gave the team much more than it gave them.

The cheerleaders' national fame built on and reinforced Dallas's reputation as a center of wealth and excess. The year 1978 saw the Big D invoked in film and on television. The film *Debbie Does Dallas* spoofed the Cowboys Cheerleaders squad and became one of the top-earning pornographic features. The CBS network began broadcasting the soap opera *Dallas,* which ran for thirteen years and was a worldwide hit. (Colleagues of mine who grew up in the Middle East and eastern Europe remember it as one of the few shows that ran on their countries' television networks.)

Dallas centered on the schemes and feuds of the Ewing family, a fictitious composite of Texan oil and ranching dynasties. A decade after the show's debut, Dallas entrepreneurs paid tribute to it by opening two bars, J.R.'s and Sue Ellen's, named after the show's leading couple. The first marketed itself mostly to gay men, the second to lesbians. The opening of these venues reflected not only the influence of the soap opera, but also the enormous social changes that had taken place in the daily lives of countless Texans. Beyond the images of a glitzy Dallas and a simple Luckenbach, Texans were at the forefront in changing public attitudes toward sexuality and gender roles.

The overt if managed sexuality of the Cowboys Cheerleaders reflected a fundamental change in American life: a more open recognition that human beings were sexual creatures. Marketing women with revealing clothing departed from earlier, more conservative social mores. Greater challenges came in the form of a push for legalized abortion and for gay rights. The two most consequential Supreme Court cases since *Brown v. Board of Education* were *Roe v. Wade* (1973), which created a partial right for pregnant women to abort their fetuses, and *Lawrence v. Texas* (2003), which struck down state bans on sex between consenting adults. Neither became part of the reputation and history of Texas in anything like the same way as the Cowboys football team and cheerleaders or Luckenbach. But when Americans fought over whether abortion or same-sex marriage should be legal—as they have for decades—they were unknowingly living in a world made by modern Texas, just as much as when they cursed the Cowboys or listened to Jerry Jeff Walker.

Henry McCluskey Jr. did not live long enough to see it, but the roads to both *Roe* and *Lawrence* ran through his simple law office in east Dallas. A Mason, Shriner, church-going Baptist, and graduate of Baylor's law school who lived with his parents, McCluskey made his living doing adoption paperwork and defending clients charged in criminal cases. As a gay man in an age when many saw homosexuality as a sin, he was willing to represent clients that other attorneys were not, including gay people who got in trouble with the police.

And gay people, especially men, got in trouble with the police a lot. It was not illegal to be gay—not exactly. But it pretty much was if you did anything about your feelings. Article 524 of the Texas Criminal Code, updated in 1943, made it a crime to have "carnal copulation . . . in the opening of the body, except sexual parts, with another human being" and also applied to "whoever shall use his mouth on the sexual parts of another human being for the purpose of having carnal copulation." In theory this made anyone who engaged in anal or oral sex, even if they were a man and a woman married to each other and doing so in their own home, a criminal. In practice, however, this law was only ever enforced against partners of the same sex, mostly men. It allowed police to raid the bars with predominantly gay clientele that had started to become more visible in some Texas cities, especially Dallas's Oak Lawn neighborhood and Houston's Montrose district. As in other states, in Texas urban police departments had "vice squads" that enforced these laws by spying on gay citizens and arresting them when they broke the law. On this basis, 451 people were arrested in Dallas alone between 1963 and 1969. A bar or restaurant frequented by a predominantly gay clientele could effectively be closed by repeated police raids and arrests.

In 1969, after the Dallas vice squad arrested Alvin Buchanan and charged him with having sex with another man, he hired McCluskey to represent him. They lost the first trial and a state judge sentenced Buchanan to five years in prison. McCluskey appealed the conviction to a federal court, arguing that the enforcement of the law meant that homosexuals were not "treated as their heterosexual equals." The attorney recruited a heterosexual married couple and another gay man to join the lawsuit. None of these three had been convicted of violating the statute. But representing them allowed McCluskey to argue that they lived in fear of being arrested for private sexual behavior, and thus that the law was a violation of their privacy, a right that the Supreme Court had recognized in the previous decade when it struck down bans on birth control by married couples. McCluskey wanted not only to free his client, but to have the law struck down as unconstitutional. His appeal named the Dallas chief of police, two vice squad officers, and the Dallas district attorney (who was in charge of enforcing the law), a man named Henry Wade.

A few months after Buchanan's first trial, a woman named Norma McCorvey came to McCluskey's office. Pregnant and fearing she was unable to support a child, McCorvey had been referred to McCluskey by her doctor because the attorney had arranged many adoptions. But McCluskey, understanding how rapidly the law and society were changing, suggested that McCorvey might have a legal case. He passed her along to an old friend from law school, who then brought in the attorney Sarah Weddington. Weddington had grown up in Abilene and graduated from the University of Texas Law School. She wanted to find a way to get the courts to strike down the Texas laws that banned abortion. Weddington had had an abortion while a law student (in Mexico, where it was more easily available), and she also resented the discrimination she had faced in the job market (despite her obvious brilliance and strong performance in law school, most law firms refused to hire her simply because she was a woman). Weddington believed strongly that the state's anti-abortion laws were unjust and an encroachment on women's freedom. She filed a suit, naming Henry Wade as the defendant, and using the name "Jane Roe" to protect McCorvey's privacy.

The lawsuits came through McCluskey's office at a time when gay people and women were pushing to open greater opportunities for themselves in public life. Despite better protections for women's property rights (relative to other states) passed down from Spanish law, married women in Texas could not enter into a contract, write checks, or file lawsuits without their husbands' permission. This left them with only the same rights as "infants, idiots, and felons," in the words of the pioneering female attorney who persuaded the legislature to change this in 1967. Five years later, as the courts contended with the *Roe* and *Buchanan* lawsuits, Representative Francis "Sissy" Farenthold—the only woman in the Texas House— succeeded in passing an equal rights amendment to the state constitution that read: "Equality under the law shall not be denied or abridged because of sex, race, color, creed, or national origin." Texas joined a handful of states with such provisions, more than two decades before famously liberal California succeeded in passing equal rights legislation. In 1972, Farenthold also ran for governor, forcing a runoff election for the Democratic nomination.

Similar changes with respect to sexuality were also afoot. People who found themselves attracted to members of the same sex used to hide it, or even seek medical help for what was still considered by psychologists to be a mental disorder.

But by the time McCluskey filed his suit for Buchanan, they could meet potential partners in gay bars. They could also join organizations like Dallas's Circle of Friends that fought discrimination. Three hundred people marched in Dallas's first gay pride parade in 1972, with Houston following suit with a similar event in 1976. Increasing numbers of heterosexuals began supporting them. If many gay people still faced ostracism from their own families, others saw their parents and siblings welcome their dates and partners. A state bar committee charged with overhauling criminal law received numerous recommendations for eliminating laws punishing same-sex conduct. One judge advocated removing all laws regulating sex between consenting adults, and most committee members found the rationale for such laws unconvincing.

Sarah Weddington scored a stunning victory in 1973, when the U.S. Supreme Court ruled in *Roe v. Wade* in favor of Norma McCorvey's lawsuit and forbade states from banning abortion in the first three months of pregnancy. It came far too late to help McCorvey, who had given birth to her third daughter, whom she gave up for adoption. *Roe* was a legal earthquake, creating access to legal abortion in the forty-six states with abortion bans. Soon it was a political earthquake as well, bringing evangelical congregations and Catholic voters, once reliably Democratic, into the Republican column. McCluskey faced stronger headwinds. His appeal to a federal court resulted in the court striking down Article 524 as an unconstitutional infringement on the right to privacy, as he hoped it would. It was the first such decision in U.S. history. But Buchanan remained imprisoned pending appeal. District Attorney Henry Wade, privately supportive of abortion rights but adamantly opposed to homosexuality, appealed the decision to the Supreme Court, which eventually threw out the federal ruling and upheld the law banning non-vaginal sex.

Lawyers fought over the legality of bans on same-sex intimacy for decades. Wade was again named the defendant in a lawsuit filed in 1979 by the Dallas schoolteacher Don Baker, who was fired after he acknowledged his sexuality in a television interview. When a federal judge sided with Baker and struck down the updated state law, gay rights activists celebrated the decision date of August 17, 1982, as "Gayteenth," invoking the emancipation from slavery as a model for their own victory. That decision was reversed by an appeals court three years later, and in 1986 a Supreme Court ruling that a similar law in Georgia was constitutional was another setback for Baker and his allies. But many jurisdictions stopped enforcing the law, as gays and lesbians in Texas and elsewhere found greater social acceptance. Gay rights organizations came to the defense of two men arrested in Houston in 1998 for violating the statute, and supported legal challenges that again went to the Supreme Court. In 2003, the high court reversed itself and struck down bans on same-sex intimacy as violations of the right to privacy and to the equal protection of the laws. Henry McCluskey, murdered in 1975, did not live to see the decision, but its rationale was the very same one that he had argued for thirty years before. In 2013, the Supreme Court mandated that marriage be open to same-sex couples in *Obergefell v. Hodges,* on the same basis. Unlike football or country music, gay rights has never been associated with Texas, but it should be.

As of this writing, the gay rights decisions that McCluskey helped to put in motion remain the law of the land. *Roe v. Wade,* on the other hand, does not. When the Supreme Court overturned it in 2022, state laws that banned most (and sometimes all) abortions went into effect in fourteen states. Texas was one of them. Over the decades, protesters who believed that abortion was murder moved from picketing clinics where the procedure was performed to electing politicians who vowed to outlaw the practice. The abortion fault line ran straight through Norma McCorvey herself. Although her diary for 1973 failed to even note *Roe v. Wade,* eventually her role in the case came to dominate her life. She worked as an aide at a North Dallas abortion clinic for years and went on the national speaking circuit to advocate for legalized abortion. In the 1990s, she converted to evangelical Christianity (and then to Catholicism) and started earning money as an anti-abortion speaker and activist. She never fit well in either camp. McCorvey was looked down on by educated activists like her former attorney Sarah Weddington as vulgar and uneducated. At the same time, her heavy drinking and thirty-year romantic partnership with the woman she lived with in North Dallas rankled the anti-abortion activists who found her conversion so energizing for their cause.

The Texas of Norma McCorvey's life was many things—Luckenbach and Dallas; simple and corporate; wholesome and sexy; feminist, gay, and conservative—all at the same time and sometimes even in the same person.

BARTON SPRINGS

24

Urban Cowboys

People spilled out into the Austin street in June of 1990. Some stood patiently in a long line, and others milled about talking excitedly almost until dawn. Most were casually dressed for the muggy night, while others came in suits and ties; denim and cowboy hats could be seen alongside bell bottom jeans and tie-dye t-shirts.

The sight was a familiar one for a city that was beginning to be called "the live music capital of the nation," where honky-tonks such as the Broken Spoke and a stretch of clubs and bars on Sixth Street regularly drew such gatherings. But this was a city council meeting, and people were waiting for their allotted three-minute slot to speak about a proposed real estate development.

It was the fate of a body of water, called Barton Springs, that had the crowds worried enough to keep them there all night. The spring's name dates back to the 1830s, when settler Billy Barton began charging Austinites for the privilege of swimming there, although the proliferation of Indian trails along the creek and Spanish documents from the 1700s suggest that the clear and cool (a constant 68 degrees) spring waters had drawn people long before that. Icemaker A. J. Zilker gave the spring and surrounding land to the city in 1918. A small dam built in the 1920s expanded the swimming hole into a long swimming pool, with the clear water and limestone floor remaining. There is no place more loved in Austin and maybe in the whole state. "You don't cut up the Mona Lisa to make a buck," one speaker said that night in defense of the springs, "and you don't chip away at David for a few tax dollars."

The water in Barton Springs comes from an enormous aquifer, which is fed by rain that falls on the hill country to the north and west, and then seeps through the limestone. Buildings, parking lots, lawns, and golf courses constructed on the aquifer's recharge zone can pollute that water with sediment, chemicals, and fertilizers. By the late 1970s, after upstream development, heavy rains would turn the pool's water cloudy and silty a few days later. By the 1990s, swimmers encountered huge algae blooms fed by lawn and golf course fertilizers. The algae clogged their eyes, stuck in their hair, and pulled out enough oxygen from the water to kill plants, fish, and salamanders. "The Estates at Barton Creek," a huge development that proposed to integrate several thousand homes and apartments with a large mall, office space, and four golf courses, meant more changes to the watershed. It required the approval of Austin's city council.

The developers, led by a former UT football tackle turned corporate executive, lost. They came into the meeting confident of victory; the path to approval for their plan was well oiled by personal connections, campaign donations to the mayor and most of the city council, and the widespread assumption that real estate development was a good thing. A little after five in the morning, when the mayor gaveled the discussion closed, every single member of the city council voted against the proposal. The hundreds of speakers who voiced their opposition and hundreds more who had gathered to cheer them on and stayed through the night had won. They went on to play offense, founding the organization Save Our Springs, which successfully pushed for a city ordinance that preserved open space and limited runoff in the Barton Creek watershed. Save Our Springs later secured land for city and suburban parks and greenbelts. In the next generation, Austinites made the city a leader in park space and urban trails, solar power, and incentives for water recycling, insulation, and other environmental measures. The city council meeting in 1990 was a turning point for Austin's development.

On one level, there was nothing new for Texans about living in cities in the 1980s and 1990s. Texans had been mostly urban for a generation. Houston broke into the ranks of the ten largest metropolitan areas in the country in 1980, at number ten, still smaller than not only New York, Chicago, Los Angeles, and Philadelphia but also Miami and Detroit. Dallas was right behind at number eleven. Despite a slump in the mid-1980s driven by low oil prices and resulting bank failures, Texas cities continued their dramatic growth. Houston, Dallas, San Antonio, Austin, El Paso, and a host of smaller urban areas attracted people not only from across the United States and from Mexico, but increasingly from farther-away places like India, China, Nigeria, Vietnam, and Saudi Arabia—few of which had ever seen people move to Texas in significant numbers before. As of the early 2020s, Texas is the only state with two metropolitan areas in the top ten: Dallas–Fort Worth in the fourth position, followed closely by Houston in the fifth. If you cut out the suburbs and look only at populations within city limits, San Antonio and Austin join the Big D and Houston to make Texas account for four of the nation's ten most populous municipalities.

The Austin protests suggested that Texans were beginning to catch up with this urban reality, to understand that the cities and suburbs in which they lived were important enough to fight over, in the same way that earlier generations debated cotton prices, prohibition, oil monopolies, and civil rights. It was a sign that Texas, heir to a powerful historical mythology that was all about the countryside and open spaces, was coming into its own as an urban civilization.

Cities grow because people can do things there that they cannot do in the countryside, at least not as easily and cheaply. Shipping and military bases drove the growth of Galveston and San Antonio in the nineteenth century, cotton and cattle gave life to Fort Worth and Dallas, and oil propelled Houston into a sprawling metropolis by the late twentieth century. When protesters blocked the Barton Creek development to save the springs, Austin was a city made by state government and the flagship university, expanded by a vibrant arts and music scene, and entering a period of meteoric growth fueled above all by the computing industry. By 1990, Michael Dell's business had moved into sixth place in the country for sales of personal computers. Dell, who grew up in Houston, started the company from his UT Austin dorm room, where he sold upgrade kits for personal computers. Believing in the quality of his computers and the business plan of selling directly to consumers (first by telephone, later by orders over the internet), Dell dropped out of college at the end of his first year. He rented a small office in North Austin where "three guys with screwdrivers sitting at six-foot tables" assembled his products. Within a year his company brought in $6 million in annual revenue. By 1992, Dell, all of twenty-seven years old, was the youngest chief executive officer of a Fortune 500 company. In 2001 his company passed another Texas firm, Compaq, to become the largest manufacturer of personal computers on the planet. By that point, though still based in Austin and employing thousands there, it had offices in the British Isles, mainland Europe, Mexico, India, and elsewhere. Dell servers helped run the internet, and the company's reliance on just-in-time inventory, direct sales, and effective information management served as models for the larger business world in much the same way that the Dallas Cowboys showed the sporting world what a successful corporate team looked like in the 1970s.

Dell's ascent ensured that Austin would be the Texas place most marked by the computing industry and most associated with it. By 2010, about 15 percent of the city's employment and almost 30 percent of its payroll came from the high-tech sector. People moved to Austin from all over the world, this time drawn not by cheap land that could grow cotton or rising oil prices, but instead by the chance to work for or do business with Dell and other tech companies. Houston, where Compaq is based, and Dallas, home of the older but still important companies Electronic Data Systems (EDS) and Texas Instruments (TI), also hosted significant high-tech businesses, though in cities that were much bigger and more economically diversified. *Doom*, the online video game that sucked up far too much of my time as a young adult in the 1990s, came out of a North Dallas cyberstudio. By the mid-1990s, Texas had become the leading source of semiconductors in the country, soon accounting for a quarter of American production. And all of the people who moved to Texas to work in the tech sectors needed houses and apartments, places to shop, golf courses, swimming pools, lawns . . . in other words, the real estate developments of the sort that threatened to foul Barton Springs.

Cheap land and plentiful oil were the key factors in the early waves of Texas urbanization. Dell and Compaq owed some of their success and location to this previous development. The building block of the modern computing era, the integrated circuit, came out of a Texas Instruments lab in Dallas in June 1958, when newly hired engineer Jack Kilby was left to his own devices while most of his co-workers were on vacation. Kilby's invention, for which he was later awarded the Nobel Prize, revolutionized computing by shrinking bulky capacitors, resistors, and transistors into small chips. A decade later, TI marketed the first handheld calculator. Over the years Kilby's invention became the wellspring for modern tech, allowing for the creation of personal computers, smartphones, and microcomputers in cars and appliances like washing machines and thermostats. Texas Instruments started in 1930 as Geophysical Service Incorporated, a company that made equipment for oil exploration and later electronics for the military during the Second World War. The oil tycoon and the tech bro may be very different types, but in Texas a direct line runs between them.

Cultural capital and universities, rather than natural resources and manual labor, were the seedbeds of the tech industry and other dynamic aspects of late twentieth-century Texas. Dell Computers is located in Austin because the University of Texas is based there. UT drew the Houston teenager Michael Dell to Austin, and its graduates and cultural amenities made it a suitable platform for a tech company with a world reach. Austin nurtured and kept cultural entrepreneurs as well. It emerged as a funkier (and initially cheaper) twin to Nashville, Tennessee, as a hearth of country and western music in the 1970s. *Austin City Limits,* a television show featuring live music performances, debuted in 1974 with a pilot episode featuring Wille Nelson. Its rise to national circulation helped to cement Austin's reputation as a center for live music.

In the same years, a twenty-something named John Mackey figured out how to fuse the eating habits of the 1960s counterculture with corporate branding. Mackey and his then girlfriend Renee Lawson opened a natural grocery store in Central Austin. The natural foods movement emerged in the early 1970s as part of the countercultural rebellion against mainstream, generic middle-class culture. It valued foods that could be grown without harming the environment and sold to the benefit of employees and customers rather than owners. Mackey lived as a member of one of Austin's vegetarian communes, an experience that transformed the way he ate.

The business at first looked a lot like a commune. The couple's store was small, the size of a living room, as my parents remember from their visits. Mackey and Lawson stored bags of rice, flour, and other bulk goods in their own apartment, and just moved into the store when their landlord evicted them. When a flood ruined most of their inventory, friends and neighbors pitched in to clean and rebuild. When they did not have time to get to Barton Springs, the couple used a hose attached to the industrial dishwasher to shower. A few years later, the company, now named "Whole Foods" and boasting locations in Houston, Dallas, New Orleans, and Palo Alto, made a modest contribution to Save Our Springs. But Whole Foods did not make much money until Mackey started stocking meat, alcohol, and sugar. They refused to sell preservatives or products artificially colored or flavored, but this was enough of a break with countercultural orthodoxy that they were seen as capitalist sellouts by much of their former hippie crowd in Austin. Mackey, who continued running the company after he and Lawson split, was unrepentant, maintaining that "if your business motives are so pure that you can't create a business around them, you'll never accomplish your mission." As the store went national and began shaping grocery retailing in the same way that Compaq shaped the PC market, he accepted only a nominal $1 salary. Human and environmental health, he insisted, remained his priority. "We're not like every other corporation. Whole Foods Market doesn't primarily care about money," he said. "It primarily cares about fulfilling its purpose."

Mackey used the national platform that the success of Whole Foods had given him to argue for "conscious capitalism" (a phrase that he coined), the belief that entrepreneurs "solve problems by creatively envisioning different ways the world could and should be." The government provision of health insurance, a goal of leftists for a century, he argued, was unnecessary if people would eat the kind of diet made possible by Whole Foods. This sense of mission and his casual dress and demeanor were the signs of the maturation of Austin's countercultural scene into middle age. They certainly made for a different vibe than Tom Landry's Cowboys or the oil tycoons of the 1930s. But in other ways, Whole Foods looked like any other corporation. Mackey was worth $100 million, a small fraction of Michael Dell but still far more money than most of us will ever see in a lifetime. Its products were for sale to those who could afford them, and they were not cheap. When declining revenue in established stores scuttled plans for more expansion and sent stock prices tumbling, investors forced Mackey to sell the company in 2017. The online retail giant Amazon, whose leader was the world's richest man and who certainly did not argue for conscious capitalism, bought it, for almost $14 billion. The Austin co-op scene had left its mark on the ways Americans buy and eat food, but was ultimately swallowed by mainstream capitalism.

In the same year that Whole Foods took off, Texas returned to the television screen, if in very different ways than with *Dallas.* Mike Judge, a young engineer repulsed by the corporate culture of California's Silicon Valley, the heart of the American computing industry, moved to North Texas in the late 1980s and started taking math classes at UT Dallas (itself established with the support of Texas Instruments executives). He turned to animation and comedy, first in *Beavis and Butt-Head,* a show about two clueless and obnoxious teenagers in the fictional town of Highland, Texas, that should not be funny but somehow is. Texans who broke through in television and film in earlier generations generally moved to Hollywood or New York, but Judge settled in Austin. There he made *King of the Hill,* a less offensive and much funnier show profiling the middle-class Hill family. The show pokes gentle if loving fun at its characters for their Texanness. Hank Hill, the father in the family, opines at great length on the best barbecuing technique, and one of his friends constantly mouths satires of right-wing conspiracy theories about black helicopters, while another speaks in a nearly incomprehensible Texas dialect. The action is set in a conventional suburb, which despite the alleys and fences that look a lot like Garland, could be most anywhere in the United States. Mike Judge's Texas looks above all suburban.

In 1986, a few Austin journalists and music promoters decided that it would be good if Austin's music scene drew more visitors from around the country. The inaugural run of what they called "South by Southwest" was a modest success that managed to draw a crowd of seven hundred. Twenty years later, the annual gathering hosted thousands of performers, brought Austin's already bad traffic to a standstill, sent lodging prices out of sight, and strained cell service. It is now an international venue for major deals in music, movie production, and tech, drawing leading artists and producers, politicians, business leaders, and several hundred thousand spectators every year.

As a result of these high-profile events and businesses, by the 1990s the cultural and intellectual assets and institutions of Texas drew people from across the globe, in ways that they never had before. Growing engineering companies, a medical center that was beginning to earn a strong reputation, and tech-oriented graduate programs at Rice and the University of Houston made the Bayou City, once just an oil and petrochemical town, an attractive destination for professionals from across the United States and abroad. Early connections between Houston's universities and India and Pakistan were made in the 1960s and 1970s, expedited by federal programs designed to cement economic and cultural ties with newly independent countries. Many South Asian students who came to study at Rice, the University of Houston, and Texas Southern University (established to educate Black Texans) found Texas a congenial place to live. The family unification provisions of immigration law made it easy to get visas for parents and siblings, and the educational opportunities continued to be appealing, so South Asians continued to migrate to Houston. By 2010, more than 135,000 South Asian immigrants lived in Houston, making it the second-largest Asian American metropolis in the South, following Washington, D.C.

The educational level of the most recent South Asian–American community has drawn closer to the overall American pattern, but for a long time Texans from South Asia were about the most educated demographic in the country. In the mid-1980s, more than a third held Ph.D.s (fifteen times the rate of the general population) and 80 percent were college graduates (five times the rate of the general population). If they had a rival in terms of educational achievement, it was the Nigerian immigrant population, which had formed significant communities in Houston, Dallas, and Austin by 2000. More Nigerian immigrants live in the Lone Star State than in any other.

Not since defeated German revolutionaries flocked to the state in the mid-nineteenth century had Texas seen such an influx of highly educated immigrants. Like their German predecessors and countless other immigrant groups in American history, South Asian arrivals to Texas created their own distinctive landscapes. Houston and its suburbs were too populous and complicated to be dominated by any one group's culture in the same way that swaths of the nineteenth-century Hill Country were marked by distinctively German fencing and homes. But by the 2010s, the suburbs of Sugarland and Alief were dotted with Muslim mosques and Hindu temples, Indo-Pak grocery stores, and South Asian dance schools. Streets were named after Mahatma Gandhi and other Indian historical figures and store marquees bore the names of states in Pakistan and India. Asian Americans made up a third of Sugarland's population, and Houston's Nigerian community was the second largest after New York City's.

These migrants were lucky to arrive after the victories of Black and Hispanic civil rights movements. But they did not always have it easy, as families who fled South Vietnam in the late 1970s after its loss in the war that destroyed Lyndon Johnson's presidency found out. Most of these transplants were conservative Catholics whose men had fought against a Communist regime, but they were still marked as Asian outsiders in their new home. Those who settled around Galveston Bay and took up shrimping and crabbing saw their boats firebombed by white neighbors egged on by the Ku Klux Klan. They stood

320 URBAN COWBOYS

their ground and enlisted civil rights organizations in suing and securing police protection. Their victories in court crippled the Klan, and they refused to leave their new home. The Vietnamese American community on the Gulf Coast of Texas numbered close to 300,000 by 2020, making it second in size only to California's.

South Asians and Vietnamese were greatly outnumbered by migrants from Mexico and the rest of Latin America. Some of these were also educated professionals seeking better opportunities in the United States. Many more were blue-collar workers who found employment in construction, agriculture, manufacturing, and the service economy. U.S. government policies, especially support for modernizing farming and better integrating the U.S. and Mexican economies, encouraged this migration, if not always intentionally. The implementation of the North American Free Trade Agreement (NAFTA) in 1994 tore down barriers to conducting business across the United States, Canada, and Mexico. It had a bigger impact on Texas than any other state because of its booming economy and long border with Mexico. By 2020, Mexico accounted for more than a third of Texas imports and exports, far more than Canada, China, or any other country. The popular image of Texas encourages us to think of it as parochial and inward focused, but with exports and imports adding up to more than a quarter of economic activity, the Lone Star State was one of the country's most globalized economies.

Mexican border towns became key sites for the manufacturing of consumer electronics powered by semiconductors and software designed in Texas. Laredo became the nation's largest inland port. And where goods and services flowed, people followed, with or without authorization. In the early 2000s Texas became "majority-minority" for the first time since Stephen F. Austin's colonists moved there in the 1820s—in other words, no one demographic group formed a majority. Decades of sustained economic growth and globalization made scenes like Sugarland's Indo-Pak districts, North Austin's Nigerian churches, and Houston's Little Saigon normal parts of the landscape, signs of a cosmopolitan society.

The crowd outside Austin City Hall that night in June 1990 was a sign of the Austin of the future—a city that blended growth with culture, the outdoors with high-tech, environmentalism with business. A more routine sight in the decades to come was men and women (but mostly men) standing in Home Depot parking lots and at major intersections, waiting to be picked up for a few hours or maybe even a day of work. These gatherings were another sign of Austin's growth, if a less heartening one. Office parks, shopping malls, houses, and restaurants could not be built without roofers and drywallers, or run without waitresses and janitors. The gushing profiles of booming Austin that became commonplace in the national press rarely mentioned the ordinary and very physical labor that lies behind smartphones, solar panels, and organic produce retailing. To do these jobs was not necessarily to share in the wealth that they produced. After decades of meteoric economic growth, in the 2010s, 23 percent of Austin residents lived below the poverty line, substantially more than the 16 percent of people who did across Texas and the country as a whole. By driving up housing costs, Austin's sustained growth—and limits on housing construction, a consequence of the measures that Save Our Springs advocated—might have effectively impoverished more people than it enriched. This paradox has not become a central focus of politics in the twenty-first century in the way that it did in the heyday of Populism more than a century before. But it is a reminder that solar panels, smartphones, and new skylines did not mean that the old questions of economic inequality, security, and dignity in Texas society had been answered.

WACO BURNING

25

An Age of Disquiet

A huge pillar of smoke rose east of Waco in April of 1993. The source of the billowing dark clouds was not a runaway grass fire or a factory blaze. For fifty-one days, agents from the Federal Bureau of Investigation (FBI), the Bureau of Alcohol, Tobacco, and Firearms (ATF), and a host of state agencies had surrounded the home of a religious group known as the Branch Davidians. In late February, around eighty ATF agents raided the settlement in an effort to arrest its leader, David Koresh, on suspicion of possessing banned firearms. The conversion of semi-automatic weapons into automatic weapons and their subsequent sale had attracted the notice of the ATF. Moreover, the group was increasingly notorious for Koresh's sexual abuse of teenage girls, to whom he claimed a divine right to marry. By coercing girls and convincing their parents that being his bride was a gift from God, Koresh had gained as many as twenty wives, some as young as twelve years of age.

The raid, dubbed "Operation Showtime" by ATF commanders, was a disaster. The Davidians knew that they were being spied on, and were tipped off by Koresh's brother-in-law, who learned about it from a television reporter invited by the ATF to watch the raid who got lost and asked him for directions. When the ATF arrived, gunfire broke out. The agents said it first came from the Davidians; the Davidians said it was the other way around. Six residents and four agents were killed. Law enforcement surrounded Mount Carmel, as the Davidians called their settlement. Almost two months later, on April 19, tired of waiting them out, government forces drove armored vehicles to the buildings, punched holes in them, and pumped in tear gas. The gas proved to be flammable, and fires, with origins that remain disputed, broke out. Koresh and seventy-five of his followers, a third of them children, were killed, either shot or burned in the ensuing inferno.

Looked at one way, the destruction of Mount Carmel was a one-off, a bizarre and horrific story of a collision between an apocalyptic religious cult and the government. The Branch Davidians were a tiny and isolated movement with no real following in society as a whole. They are still badly misunderstood. Had the ATF arrested Koresh on one of his regular errands into town instead of staging a dramatic paramilitary raid, or waited out the siege instead of acting in ways that seemed to confirm the Davidians' apocalyptic fantasies, this conflict would remain a little-known curiosity of the past. Instead, the siege became a symbol to an increasingly violent right-wing movement that emerged in tandem with the rise to dominance of more mainstream conservatives. The numbingly frequent mass shootings by highly armed civilians and increasingly violent policing over the following decades also made the siege look more like a prophecy of things to come than the relic of an irrational past. Texas continued its astounding growth into the 2020s, becoming steadily wealthier and attracting people from across the country and the globe. It had never been so diverse, so rich, or so influential on the country as a whole. Yet a cloud of violence, division, anger, and disillusionment hung over it.

The dramatic siege and mass death galvanized right-wing militia movements in Texas and beyond. These organizations, like the long-established Ku Klux Klan chapters that tried to bomb out Vietnamese settlers on the Gulf Coast, met in secret, stockpiling military weapons and sometimes drilling with them, in preparation for the collapse or overthrow of the U.S. government. The destruction of Mount Carmel was a signal event for them, a shorthand for the violent suppression of their rights, especially to own and bear weapons. Since 1993, being "Waco'd" meant in these circles to be surrounded and murdered by your own government. On the second anniversary of the siege's tragic end, Timothy McVeigh, a former soldier who had come to Waco during the siege and wept when Mount Carmel erupted in flames, parked a moving truck packed with fertilizers beneath Oklahoma City's federal building and lit a fuse. One hundred and sixty-eight people, including nineteen children in the second-floor daycare, lost their lives in the resulting explosion. The Federal Bureau of Investigation considered it the worst act of domestic terrorism in the country's history.

The Texas militia organizations for whom Waco was so important argued for a restoration of the Republic of Texas as an independent country. Or at least they assumed that that is what would happen if the U.S. government collapsed or was overthrown. Richard McLaren, a property owner in the Davis Mountains, achieved brief notoriety in the years after the siege by establishing an embassy for the "Republic of Texas," proclaiming federal taxes illegal because Texas had not legally joined the union, and filing liens against neighbors that made it difficult for them to sell their property. He was convicted of kidnapping and wire fraud in 1997 and sentenced to prison for decades. Others took up his calls for a return to Texas independence, forming small organizations and hosting rallies for secession. And his hostility to the federal government, vigorous defense of the right to own and bear military weapons, and general celebration of Texas resonated with growing numbers of conservative officeholders and voters. In 2009, Republican governor Rick Perry made a wisecrack about Texas having to secede if the country continued to be governed by Democrats. Perry was quick to clarify that he was only joking, but talk of leaving the United States became more and more common among leaders of the party over the next decade.

The Branch Davidians obsessed McVeigh and McLaren because the fiery destruction of Mount Carmel fulfilled their apocalyptic fears of a federal government willing to slaughter its own citizens. But the Davidians' full history was not a good fit with the violent white supremacy that animated the Oklahoma City bomber. For sixty years before the siege brought them international renown, Davidians had lived in rural Texas by a social code that was radically at odds with mainstream society. Victor Houteff, a Bulgarian immigrant and convert to Seventh-day Adventism, led a splinter group of a Los Angeles congregation to a farm outside Waco in 1935. There the Davidians, as they called themselves, lived a purified existence in conformity with what they saw as the true teachings of Jesus, whose return to this world they expected to happen soon. For Houteff's followers, this meant vegetarianism, pacifism, and a love for all people regardless of race. Power struggles and theological struggles after his death led to the formation of the

Branch Davidians, so named not only because they were an offshoot, but because the name evoked the return of Christ and the end of human time. Black members and converts, by way of the original Los Angeles congregation and from the Caribbean and British Isles, were a consistent presence. A third of those who perished on April 19, 1993, were Black. This is a fact rarely noted in press accounts at the time or in the coverage of anniversaries of the slaughter. It hardly exonerates Koresh's tyrannical rule and serial rape of children, but does suggest that the reality of Texas continued to be more complicated, curious, and unpredictable than the wider world's ability to understand it.

People like Richard McLaren drew television and newspaper reporters to them like fire ants to watermelon. Their talk of secession and violence fits into an easy story about Texas as its own place, a little crazy and definitely different from the rest of the country. Yet McLaren and his ilk remained curiosities, with no real power and not enough of a popular following to be elected to any office. Republicans, on the other hand, rose to statewide dominance in the decades after the catastrophe in Waco. Ann Richards, the feisty liberal Democrat who was governor during the siege, was defeated the following year by the Republican George W. Bush. As of this book's publication, no Democrat has occupied the governor's mansion since then, and no Democrat has won a statewide election since 1994.

Republicans chiseled away at the Democratic fortress for decades before they were in a position to become the state's dominant party. John Tower's victory in a special election for the U.S. Senate in 1961 marked the first time since Reconstruction that a Republican had held that office. A handful of Republicans, including George Herbert Walker Bush in Houston in 1966, won congressional seats. Oilman William Clements, striking a pragmatic pro-business note and invoking his service to two Republican presidents, won the governorship in 1978. But Tower, Bush, and Clements still swam in a Democratic ocean, with that party continuing to hold both houses of the state legislature, almost all statewide offices, and most congressional seats. Republicans won presidential elections statewide, but as elsewhere in the South, they had difficulty translating the popularity of Republican presidents into down-ballot victories. George H. W. Bush, after serving as Ronald Reagan's vice president, became the second Texan president with his election victory in 1988, without ever holding statewide office back home.

Twelve years later, in 2000, his son George W. Bush narrowly lost the national popular vote but then became president after the Supreme Court determined that he had won Florida's disputed electoral college votes. This time, with a Texan in the White House, Republicans won control of both houses of the Texas legislature and, after a controversial redistricting spearheaded by Bush's chief political strategist, a majority of the state's congressional seats. The redrawing of electoral districts by Texas Republicans became a model of what is known as "gerrymandering," slicing up the electorate in ways to deliver outsized victories based on a slender majority or even a minority of the overall vote. Republican strategists adopted the technique elsewhere, especially in North Carolina, Ohio, and Wisconsin. Texas itself looked from one vantage point like a one-party state, which it had been except during Reconstruction since joining the United States in 1845. The only difference was that it had switched from Democrat to Republican. But Republicans have never exercised the dominance that Democrats did for nearly a century. In the 2020s, a third of Texas congressional representatives remain Democratic. Democrats routinely win races for mayor and county judge in the cities. Openly gay candidates including Annise Parker (Houston's mayor from 2010 to 2016) and Lupe Valdez (Dallas County Sheriff from 2005 to 2017) win heavy majorities in these jurisdictions. Republican Donald Trump won the state in 2020, but by a margin of less than 6 percent. Texas politics tilt conservative but are fundamentally not so different from those of the rest of the country.

As with Lyndon Johnson's time in office, the two Bush presidencies ushered Texans to the height of national power. George W. Bush's two terms in office (2001–9) brought Texas funders, strategists, and officeholders such prominence that journalists began to refer to the "Texanization" of national politics. Bush invoked his Texanness as part of appealing to voters nationally, more than his Connecticut-born and -reared father did or could. He spoke of Texas as a model of freedom and opportunity for the rest of the country. Bush had himself photographed using a chainsaw on his ranch outside Crawford (twenty miles west of Waco) and read Travis's "Victory or Death" letter from the Alamo to American golfers in the midst of his presidential campaign. So perhaps it was inevitable that when President Bush led the United States into a war with Iraq in 2002, invoking the supposed macho pathologies of Texas became one way of explaining why the country was mired in such a catastrophe. "Until America invaded Iraq," lamented San Antonio native and *New York Times* journalist Mimi Swartz, "it was possible to go through life for long periods without falling victim to the Texas stereotype . . . [but] now Texas bashing has returned as a global pastime." It was Lyndon Johnson and Vietnam all over again. As increasing numbers of Americans turned against a war that had not delivered freedom to

Iraq or stability to the Middle East despite the mounting death toll, the reputation of Texas became another casualty of the war. Bush was a "cowboy" who shot first and asked questions later. Never mind that he was a Yale graduate and son of a president, or that most of the national political establishment, including a majority of Democratic senators, had gone along with the war.

Republicans in Texas after Bush left to become president grew more conservative even as they grew more powerful. As governor, Bush advanced the conservative priorities of reducing property taxes, increasing punishments for crime, and more access to firearms. He also tried hard to increase funding for public education, refrained from presenting migration from Latin America as a problem or threat, and generally avoided social issues such as same-sex marriage and abortion. Bush won about 40 percent of the state's Hispanic vote in his presidential race, then a high-water mark for Republicans. Indeed, even after Bush's political career ended with his presidency in 2009, Texas Republicans successfully appealed to a significant proportion of the Hispanic population and ran successful Hispanic candidates such as Ted Cruz (elected to the U.S. Senate in 2010) and Monica de la Cruz (elected to Congress from South Texas in 2022). A heavy majority of Hispanic officeholders are Democrats, but Republicans avoided becoming an all-white party—necessary in a state that became majority-minority in the early 2000s.

A comparatively inclusive political coalition did not mean moderation in terms of policy. Pro-business officeholders who followed Bush's lead in avoiding social issues were replaced by candidates like Dan Patrick, who described Latin American immigration as an "invasion," passed measures that made it harder and harder for abortion clinics to remain open, and legalized the possession and open display of even military-grade firearms. Patrick's election as lieutenant governor in 2014 marked the dominance of very conservative Republicans in the party and thus the state as a whole. By the early 2020s, centrist Republicans had failed to organize themselves into an influential faction within the party in the way that Populist and liberal Democrats had in the decades in which Texas was a one-party Democratic bastion.

Politically engaged evangelical Christians played a critical role in making Republicans more powerful and more conservative. Substantial Middle Eastern and Asian American communities meant that twenty-first-century Texas was more religiously diverse than ever before, with Muslims, Hindus, and Buddhists joining Jews and less numerous adherents of Native American religions in practicing religions outside of the Christian tradition. But Texan life remained overwhelmingly Christian. Three-quarters of Texans believe that Jesus Christ was the son of God who sacrificed himself to redeem humanity. And most Texans are devout: 88 percent are "absolutely certain" or "fairly" certain of their belief in God, and almost 90 percent pray weekly or daily. In this regard, Texas continues to look very much like the rest of the South, and for all of the changes it has experienced, a time-traveling visitor from nineteenth-century Texas would find the passion of Christian belief to be quite familiar.

Not all Christians are conservative. But the branches of Christianity that grew the fastest (Southern Baptists and Pentecostals) were the most engaged with conservative politics, and those that lost the most congregants ("mainline" Protestant denominations such as Presbyterians and Methodists) tended to skew more liberal. The rise of fundamentalist ministers like Frank Norris propelled conservative Democrats in the 1920s and 1930s in their campaigns against alcohol and open sexuality. Predominantly white evangelical congregations played a similar role in Republican ascendance in the late twentieth and early twenty-first centuries. Robert Jeffress, for example, used his pulpit at First Baptist Wichita Falls, and later First Baptist Dallas, to encourage businesses to openly celebrate Christmas, endorse Republican candidates for state office, and warn of the dangers of Mormonism and Catholicism. He had grown up conservative, as a childhood member of the First Baptist Dallas congregation, but refrained from advocating for particular policies or candidates. That changed in the late 1990s when a distressed member of his Wichita Falls congregation brought him two children's books from the local public library that portrayed families with parents of the same sex. Believing homosexuality to be sinful, Jeffress fought to keep such books out of libraries.

Jeffress's open support for not only policies supported by Republicans, but specific candidates, earned him the support of president-elect Donald Trump in 2016, and a regular column for Fox News, the country's leading conservative television network. Jeffress preached at a private service for Trump the day before his inauguration in 2017. His leadership at First Baptist Dallas not only continued a seventy-year alliance between that large and wealthy congregation and conservative Texas Republicans, but expanded the congregation's numbers, reach, and facilities. The insistence on the separation of church and state by evangelical Christians that had marked Texas Baptist leaders in the nineteenth century had been entirely banished and replaced with a fusion of divine and earthly power.

Many advocates of this political Christianity believed in what scholars call the "prosperity gospel," or the belief that adherence to God's word brings wealth and other forms of worldly success. "If you will invest in winning the lost, God will give you the abundance you cannot contain," one San Antonio pastor explained. This is a much more optimistic view

AN AGE OF DISQUIET
333

of the world than the hardscrabble pioneer Christianity of the nineteenth century, which assumed that suffering hardship was a part of this world, to be left behind by the faithful only in the afterlife. Joel Osteen, the pastor of Houston's Lakewood Church, became the most prominent prosperity gospel proponent in the nation early in the twenty-first century. After succeeding his father as the pastor of Lakewood Church, he drew so many to its services that soon the church purchased the Compaq Arena, former home of the professional basketball team the Houston Rockets, to seat the tens of thousands who came every Sunday to worship. Osteen reached millions more through his books and television ministry. Suffering and sin, which traditional Christianity held were inescapable facts of life that required salvation by Jesus, were so de-emphasized in his preaching that his Baptist critics accused him of preaching "Christianity without a cross" and treating God like "a cosmic slot machine" that disgorged money if you played him right.

Osteen's success indicated that the prosperity gospel spoke to the experiences of Texans who lived wealthier lives than their parents and grandparents had. Like the Republican Party's success with Hispanics, the appeal of the prosperity gospel crossed racial lines. Pentecostalist congregations, where the prosperity gospel was particularly strong, attracted many more Hispanic than white congregants and ministers. Black Christians could find the prosperity gospel appealing, too. When T. D. Jakes, a charismatic and ambitious minister in West Virginia, looked to move his congregation to a place with a larger base of middle-class African Americans, he chose Dallas and founded the Potter's House in the southwestern corner of the city. Three of the top twenty-five cities for African Americans in the country, as measured by education level, median income, and employment rates, were suburbs of Dallas. It would have been hard to predict in the decades of Jim

Crow, to say nothing of slavery, but Texas had become a magnet for well-heeled Black people.

In August of 2017, Joel Osteen made national headlines. Hurricane Harvey smashed into the Gulf Coast, stalled out over Houston, and dropped an astounding sixty-one inches of rain in what meteorologists deemed "the single greatest rainfall event in North America in recorded history." More than thirty people were killed, 150,000 homes were damaged, and at least $125 billion in property damage was done. Some of the displaced made their way to Lakewood Church, where they were initially turned away. Osteen and his staff maintained that conditions were not safe, while critics pointed out that one of the country's largest and wealthiest churches, whose main facility was on high enough ground for the flooded out to walk there, should have been ready to follow the biblical commandment to give shelter.

Events like the flooding that sent so many Houstonians heading for higher ground in 2017 are often referred to as "acts of God," meaning that they are unpredictable one-offs. Meteorologists estimated that storms carrying that amount of rainwater took place only once every five hundred years. But Harvey was just one in a string of five 500-year floods in consecutive years. Scientists argued that the explanation was climate change—the increased retention of energy from the sun caused by all the carbon dioxide and other greenhouse gases emitted by burning fossil fuels like Texas oil for the two centuries or so since the Industrial Revolution. In that sense, Hurricane Harvey, or at least some of its impact, was an act of humans. And more such storms were in the offing. Since hurricanes gather their energy from warm ocean waters, and the gasoline burned in cars and methane vented in natural gas production warm those waters, an increased frequency and larger size of storms was one inadvertent legacy of Texas to the world. The same forces powering more and stronger storms were causing the oceans to rise dramatically, by two feet at Galveston by the 2020s, with between two and ten feet more predicted by 2100. Most models of future climates predicted dangerously warmer temperatures in much of the state for prolonged periods, a greater likelihood of long droughts (especially north of Dallas and around San Antonio), and an increased prevalence of mosquito-borne diseases such as the West Nile and Zika viruses.

Twenty-nine years after police, Texas Rangers, and federal agents drove helter-skelter to Mount Carmel, a similarly disastrous scramble of law enforcement personnel took place in Uvalde. In May of 2022, a young man crashed his car outside Robb Elementary, and a caller reported that he had entered the school and was shooting. Local police, state troopers, Texas Rangers, U.S. marshals, and federal immigration agents rushed to Robb, entered the building, and assembled outside the connected classrooms occupied by the shooter. They waited outside for an hour until finally some of the officers stormed the room and killed the shooter. By then, nineteen students and two teachers were dead. The death toll, the youth of the victims, and the inexplicable wait made the Uvalde massacre especially horrific. But it was a numbingly familiar horror: eight mass shootings (in which a lone gunman killed four or more people) took place in Texas between 2009 and Uvalde, in schools, churches, and offices.

Federal Bureau of Investigation data indicate that homicide rates in the Texas of the 2020s were a third of what they had been in the 1980s and 1990s, and just a small fraction of the rate of the nineteenth century. Despite the state's violent reputation, Texans killed one another less often than the national average. Yet these facts brought little consolation to the grieving families of the victims in Uvalde and other mass shootings. Like the rest of the country, Texans lived with a murder rate higher than any other wealthy nation. In the twenty-first century, lawmakers liberalized gun laws to the point of letting residents openly carry weapons without a license and allowed the sale of semi-automatic weapons such as the AR-15 used at Uvalde to anyone eighteen or over. The Texas government imprisoned more and more of its population—a third more than the United States as a whole did, six times that of the United Kingdom, more than any country on earth. Yet these measures had not delivered safety; by the 2020s, Texas children were more likely to die from a gunshot wound than any other cause, including automobile accidents.

For all the changes brought by modern life—organic produce from all over the world, tiny computers, space flight, automobiles, gigantic cities—the challenges faced by modern Texans in the twenty-first century were not so different from those of the generations that had come before. Inundated by floods, baked by droughts, and knowing that death could come for them and their children at any time, modern Texans lived in a world right out of the Bible that guided so many of them.

Epilogue

This book began with the digging up and reburial of Stephen F. Austin's body in 1910. Texans brought his decayed remains from the cemetery in Brazoria County to Austin, where they were buried in a place of honor in the state cemetery after much pomp and ceremony.

More than a century later, as I finish this book, Texans are just as invested in their own history as were their predecessors who reinterred Austin. Some of this commitment can be seen at the Alamo, the Spanish mission that became the site of the crushing defeat that preceded the improbable victory of Texan rebels against Mexico's tyrant. The state government has pledged more than $30 million, major business and philanthropic supporters are lined up for millions more, and architects and design firms have been contracted to envision a major overhaul of the Alamo's surroundings. The project will bring a dramatic change to the areas surrounding the church (often referred to as "The Alamo," though it was just one part of the mission complex). Storefronts located where the mission's west wall once stood used to house businesses like Ripley's Believe it Or Not!, a wax museum, and a movie theater. The trinkets and generic mass culture had been part of Alamo Plaza for decades—as a child, I'm pretty sure that I thought Ripley was an Alamo defender. Now they are gone, and soon visitors' attention will be drawn to depictions of the long-gone gatehouse and defensive works. The city street that funneled cars and buses right through the center of the plaza is now closed to traffic. A 24,000-square-foot building for displaying traveling exhibits has been constructed, tastefully located so as to not alter the view of the church from the plaza. Artifacts gathered over decades by Phil Collins, a British rock star who became enraptured by the Alamo story, have greatly augmented the collection held at the Alamo museum.

The new plans under way at the Alamo are much more inclusive of different kinds of Texans and different experiences than were the celebrations in 1910. White Texans were the only participants with any power in the reburial of Austin. In that event, they told a story of their triumph over Mexico and Mexicans. Indians and Black people were at best bit players in the stories they told. In the twenty-first century, Alamo docents are charged with telling the history of the mission long before Austin's colonists showed up in Texas, particularly the role of local Indigenous peoples in its construction and survival. They will mention not just the legendary battle, but also the practice of slaveholding so central to Anglo Texan society, and the worldwide fame of the Alamo in the twentieth century. Statues of Black participants in the Texas Revolution and Tejano defenders (including Juan Seguín, who fought for the Revolution only to be driven into exile by the republic that he helped to birth) have joined those of the classic Anglo heroes of the Alamo in the statue garden.

EPILOGUE   339

These changes in the way the story of the Alamo is officially presented do not mean that Texans agree about their history or how it should be told. Earlier versions of the Alamo redesign prompted enormous criticism. Some complained that they remained focused on the Anglo history of Texas, while others worried that telling centuries of the site's history disrespected the pivotal events of 1836 and the heroic sacrifices that brought independence to Texas. Unknown parties spray-painted graffiti linking the Alamo with "white supremacy" and "profits over people" on the cenotaph of Alamo defenders, a sixty-foot-high marble shaft placed in 1939. Outraged by the graffiti and the suggestion that the cenotaph would be moved from its location at the heart of the plaza, men armed with assault rifles stood guard. When excavations at the chapel uncovered human remains, both the Tāp Pīlam Coahuiltecan Nation and the Alamo Defenders Descendants Association sued for the right to participate in oversight of excavations and the treatment of any remains found. They lost in court, but subsequent negotiations resulted in the extension of Saturday visiting hours that will allow the Indigenous group to perform a religious ceremony at sunrise, and the state agreed to consult them on future cultural and historical programming at the Alamo. When it comes to the telling of Texas history in public, many more voices are at the table than a century ago.

The contention over the Alamo and how its history should be told was not the only high-profile fight over Texas history to take place in the 2020s. Angered by books and lectures that described the role of slavery in the Texas Revolution and the republic that it created, in 2021 conservative lawmakers passed laws tightly regulating what public school teachers could and could not say about the histories of the United States and Texas. Some of these legislators want similar measures in place at universities, and to be able to fire professors who break them.

Texas was only one of more than a dozen states that passed similar laws, but in the Lone Star State much of the debate centered around how the history of Texas is told. Lieutenant Governor Dan Patrick, who enthusiastically supported the legislation, prevented the authors of a book on slavery and the memory of the Texas Revolution from speaking at the state history museum. Patrick and his allies wanted Texas history to be told in much the same way that the people who reburied Austin in 1910 did—as the heroic story of the triumph of freedom-loving Anglos over others. If there were blemishes in the republic (and later, the state) that they created, like slavery, they were, as the law said, to be explained as "deviations from, betrayals of, or failures to live up to the authentic founding principles."

Others thought it was important to tell different accounts of Texas history. The state museum sponsored an exhibit about the violence perpetrated against Tejanos and Mexicans by the Texas Rangers and vigilantes in the 1910s. In the circles of professional historians in which I work, books about violence, slavery, and migration in Texas history got the most attention and garnered the most awards. Students and educators successfully convinced the state to create a class in Mexican American studies in 2018, and in later years pushed the Texas Board of Education to include more content about Asian American experiences. In 2023, the city of Waco put up a state historical marker commemorating the lynching in 1915 of Jesse Washington. Markers commemorating similar outrages went up in Anderson County and Presidio County, and were proposed in others. Researchers found what they think is a mass grave of the victims of Texas Ranger executions, including of fugitive slaves, under the parking lot of Seguin's Chamber of Commerce. Around the corner, a mural lovingly portrays the Rangers who were so important to the town's early history.

There is no sign in sight that these debates over Texas his-

EPILOGUE 341

tory and the different approaches to it will end. The Texas of the twenty-first century is a complicated society made up of many different kinds of people, and they have access to newspapers, museums, universities, and state agencies. They care about their past, enough to fight over it.

Telling stories about our past is one of the main ways we define who we are. My hope is that the stories in this book convince readers that Texas is interesting, important, sometimes inspiring and sometimes horrifying; that you can't understand its past or present without paying attention to all of the different kinds of people who have lived in the place; and that you have to know about the Texas past if you want to understand the United States as a whole. Of course, this book is just one history. There are other stories to be told about Texas, and other ways of telling the ones in these pages. As long as there is a Texas, there will be arguments about how we should remember its history.

Essay on Sources

As I hope I've shown in this book, Texas is an outsized place, identity, and idea, all at once, and has been since the nineteenth century. Little wonder, then, that it has inspired such an enthusiastic body of historical narratives, by amateurs and professionals alike: from dime novels about the lives of Davy Crockett and Sam Houston; to widely read histories by Walter Prescott Webb, T. R. Fehrenbach, James Michener, Randolph Campbell, James Haley, Stephen Harrigan, and Annette Gordon-Reed; and historical fiction in print and on screen, from Edna Ferber's and George Stevens's *Giant* and Larry McMurtry's *Lonesome Dove* to Philipp Meyer's *The Son*. As John Steinbeck once observed, "like most passionate nations, Texas has its own private history based on, but not limited by, the facts." This book necessarily relies on the large body of work about the Texas past written over the generations. More detailed information about specific quotes and citations can be found at a companion website, www.Texas AnAmericanHistory.com. Here I discuss some of the most important sources and resources that went into writing this book.

344   ESSAY ON SOURCES

Growing up in Texas and decades of reading about its past have gone into the sensibility that I bring to this book—a sometimes unsteady mix of fascination, admiration, and curiosity infused with occasional doses of horror and sorrow. John Graves's *Goodbye to a River* (1960) and Annette Gordon-Reed's *On Juneteenth* (2021) are very different books written generations apart. Both authors understand and accept that Texas shaped who they are, and both portray a land haunted by its history, from frontier violence between Anglos and Comanches to the cruelties of slavery and Jim Crow. They're honest about the brutal chapters of the past even as they see its achievements and claim its history as their own. I'm not the only reader they've moved and inspired.

This investment of Texans (and many non-Texans) in their distinctive past and culture has given rise to major historical resources. Three were indispensable to the writing of this book. The enormous Handbook of Texas online is a good starting point for most places and topics in Texas history, which makes the recent changes in the leadership of its sponsoring institution, the Texas State Historical Association, all the more disappointing. The Portal to Texas History, sponsored by the University of North Texas libraries, provides easy access to hundreds of thousands of documents, newspapers, and archives about Texas history. A search of the website of the magazine *Texas Monthly* never fails to yield valuable reporting and excellent writing about various figures and topics in Texas history.

I wrote *Texas: An American History* in part because of the shortcomings I see in many popular histories of the state. Countless authors achieve the difficult feat of patronizing Texas even as they glorify it. They take their subjects, by turn, both too seriously and not seriously enough: hagiography substitutes for analysis, triumphalism for sober reckoning, and celebration for more balanced judgment. Accessible and synthetic writing about Texas history focuses too heavily on white Texans and far too heavily on the nineteenth century, downplaying the fascinating Native histories and colonial encounters. It risks making a backwater and sideshow of a place that has been a powerful influence on the modern history of the United States. These shortcomings are particularly apparent in T. R. Fehrenbach's *Lone Star,* first published in 1968 and still to my knowledge the single best-selling volume on Texas history. Fehrenbach treated his Anglo heroes like El Cid or Sir Lancelot, as embodiments of timeless masculine virtues. Because he treated Texans as a hardy frontier people whose distinctive consciousness was forged in the hearth of conflict with Indians and Mexicans, the nineteenth century devoured his attention. Fehrenbach reached the twentieth century 632 pages into his book, and seemed to regret having to do so at all. The more Texas seemed a part of the modern world, the less it could speak of having a history at all: "when the office-working, car-driving Texan is completely indistinguishable from his Northern counterpart," he insisted, "the history of Texas, as Texas, will be done."

James Haley and Stephen Harrigan are two nonacademic authors of compelling treatments of Texas history that aim to replace Fehrenbach's unabashed Anglo triumphalism. Both Haley's *Passionate Nation* (2006) and Harrigan's *Big Wonderful Thing* (2019) are engaging and well-written accounts upon which I sometimes draw. I particularly admire Harrigan's wry sense of irony and appreciation of modern Texas; you can tell from his prose that he is a novelist and a journalist as well as a historian. At the same time, I think it's fair to say that both accounts are more focused on Anglo Texans than other groups, even when describing eras when Indigenous and Mexican people were the overwhelming majority. The explosion of historical scholarship on Texas since the publication of *Passionate*

346   ESSAY ON SOURCES

Nation, and the huge size (more than eight hundred pages!) and episodic nature of *Big Wonderful Thing* led me to think that there was a place for a shorter, even more inclusive Texas history.

Randolph Campbell's *Gone to Texas* (Oxford, 2003, with a more recent 2017 edition), the best-selling comprehensive Texas history outside of Fehrenbach, is the other major treatment of the sweep of Texas history. It is rigorous, deeply researched, and well written, and served as a helpful reference to me for major political and economic developments. The framework of migration suggested in his title allows for a somewhat broader treatment of Black and Mexican experiences than Fehrenbach and previous authors. Yet Campbell structures his narrative around elite political history, consistently minimizing conflict within Texas society, as in his dismissal of the enormous opposition to joining the Confederacy and downplaying of the radicalism of 1890s Populism. His treatment of Indigenous peoples is frustratingly superficial, in part because of the enormous advances in Indigenous history made since the book's publication. And the book has virtually no cultural history and moves too quickly through the twentieth century.

Like Campbell but unlike Fehrenbach, Haley, and Harrigan, I am a professional historian; and although I hope that this book will find an audience beyond universities and my fellow professional historians, *Texas: An American History* relies on generations of publications by academic historians. Readers familiar with particular books and articles will recognize passages in this book in which their work is being drawn upon. Walter Buenger and Arnoldo De León's edited volume *Beyond Texas Through Time: Breaking Away from Past Interpretations,* is an excellent guide to scholarship on major aspects of Texas history up to its 2011 publication date. For firsthand

ESSAY ON SOURCES 347

accounts of major events and leading political figures, I frequently referred to *Documents of Texas History* (1994), edited by Ernest Wallace, David M. Vigness, and George B. Ward.

Historical memory—how people have envisioned the Texas past, lifting up some stories and experiences while submerging others—is a major theme of this work. *Lone Star Pasts: Memory and History in Texas* (2006), edited by Gregg Cantrell and Elizabeth Hayes Turner, is an excellent starting point. Louis Mendoza's *Historia: The Literary Making of Chicana and Chicano History* (2001), Richard Flores's *Remembering the Alamo: Memory, Modernity, and the Master Symbol* (2002), William Carrigan's *The Making of a Lynching Culture: Violence and Vigilantism in Central Texas, 1836–1916* (2004), and Monica Muñoz Martínez's *The Injustice Never Leaves You: Anti-Mexican Violence in Texas* (2018) were other major inspirations.

The study of Indigenous people has gone through a renaissance in the twenty-first century. I found Carolyn Boyd's *The White Shaman Mural: An Enduring Creation Narrative in the Rock Art of the Lower Pecos* (2016) and Juliana Barr's *Peace Came in the Form of a Woman: Indians and Spaniards in the Texas Borderlands* (2007) to be particularly helpful guides to Indigenous Texas before and in the early stages of contact with Spanish colonialism. Andrés Reséndez's *A Land So Strange: The Epic Journey of Cabeza de Vaca* (2007) is an excellent recreation of Cabeza de Vaca's journeys and life, though there is no substitute for reading the original account, available in many English-language editions. David J. Weber's and Jesús F. de la Teja's books are the critical starting points for understanding Spain's northern frontier. Weber's last book, *Bárbaros: Spaniards and Their Savages in the Age of Enlightenment* (2005), along with Gary Anderson's *The Indian Southwest, 1580–1830: Ethnogenesis and Reinvention* (1999), Pekka Hämäläinen's *Comanche Empire* (2008), Brian DeLay's *War of a*

Thousand Deserts: Indian Raids and the U.S.-Mexican War (2008), and Paul Conrad's *The Apache Diaspora: Four Centuries of Displacement and Survival* (2021), are major works that show the extent to which "Spanish" and even "Mexican" Texas remained Native.

Reading Gregg Cantrell's *Stephen F. Austin: Empresario of Texas* (1999), Andrés Reséndez's *Changing National Identities at the Frontier: Texas and New Mexico, 1800–1850* (2004), and Raúl Ramos's *Beyond the Alamo: Forging Mexican Ethnicity in San Antonio, 1821–1861* (2010) was indispensable in understanding the larger patterns of Mexican life and politics that shaped Texas. Raúl Coronado's *A World Not to Come: A History of Latino Writing and Print Culture* (2013) and Andrew Torget's *Seeds of Empire: Cotton, Slavery, and the Transformation of the Texas Borderlands, 1800–1850* (2015) skillfully place Texas and the Texas Revolution in even larger orbits in both the Anglophone and Spanish-speaking worlds. The literature on the revolution itself is voluminous. William Davis's *Three Roads to the Alamo: The Lives and Fortunes of David Crockett, James Bowie, and William Barret Travis* (1998) remains a classic account focused on the Anglo side of the story, while Reséndez, Torget, and Stephen Harrigan's wonderful novel *The Gates of the Alamo* (2000) are particularly important in my account. And James Crisp's *Sleuthing the Alamo: Davy Crockett's Last Stand and Other Mysteries of the Texas Revolution* (2004) destroys some of the legends of the Texas Revolution even as it underscores the enduring drama and relevance of the 1830s for modern America.

The short but fascinating history of the Republic of Texas is well told in Ramos, Reséndez, Torget, and Sam Haynes's *Unsettled Land: From Revolution to Republic, the Struggle for Texas* (2022). Jesús de la Teja's edited volume *A Revolution Re-*

ESSAY ON SOURCES 349

membered: The Memoirs and Selected Correspondence of Juan N. Seguín (1991) powerfully captures Seguín's experiences. The winding road to annexation is explored in Joel Silbey's *Storm over Texas: The Annexation Controversy and the Road to Civil War* (2005) and Gary Kornblith's imaginative and thought-provoking article "Rethinking the Coming of the Civil War: A Counterfactual Exercise" (2003). Benjamin Lundy's tirade in 1836 against the Texas Revolution as a slaveholder's plot is still worth reading. Its magnificent nineteenth-century title—*The War in Texas; A Review of Facts and Circumstances Showing that this Contest is the Result of a Long Premeditated Crusade Against the Government, Set on Foot by Slaveholders, Land Speculators, & c. with the View of Re-Establishing, Extending, and Perpetuating the System of Slavery and the Slave Trade in the Republic of Mexico*—conveys its argument and tone.

Slavery as practiced in Texas has attracted the attention of superb historians. Randolph Campbell's *An Empire for Slavery: The Peculiar Institution in Texas, 1821–1865* (1989) is a foundational classic. Andrew Torget's *Seeds of Empire* offers the most compelling treatment of the role that slavery played in the politics of Northern Mexico, Anglo-American settlement, and the republic and early statehood. Former slaves' accounts of their own lives, given in testimony collected by a federal program in the 1930s, are rich and useful sources. Most Texas narratives are collected in Ron Tyler and Lawrence Murphy's collection *The Slave Narratives of Texas* (2006). The impact of the porous border between Texas and Mexico on slavery has started to receive the attention it deserves. Sean Kelly's article "'Mexico in His Head': Slavery and the Texas-Mexico Border, 1810–1860" (2003) is a powerful recreation of how Mexico became a beacon of hope for enslaved people in Texas. Sarah Cornell points to the limited nature of the freedom that those

350   ESSAY ON SOURCES

who escaped slavery found in Mexico in "Citizens of Nowhere: Fugitive Slavers and Free African Americans in Mexico, 1833–1857" (2013), while James Nichols uncovers persuasive evidence that indentured laborers in Mexico found similar opportunity by crossing from Mexico to Texas in his book *The Limits of Liberty: Mobility and the Making of the Eastern U.S.-Mexico Border* (2018). Alice Baumgartner links disputes over slavery and the U.S.-Mexico border to the coming of the U.S. Civil War in *South to Freedom: Runaway Slaves to Mexico and the Road to the Civil War* (2020).

The distinct history of German Texas continues to fascinate. Frederick Law Olmsted's classic travel account *A Journey Through Texas: Or a Saddle-Trip on the Southwestern Frontier* (1857) makes for great reading and is available in many modern editions. Wilhelm Steinert's depictions of Texas in *North America, Particularly Texas in the Year 1849: A Travel Account* is similarly edifying. For scholarly treatments of the subject, I recommend Walter Kamphoefner's *Germans in America: A Concise History* (2021) and Terry Jordan's *German Seed in Texas Soil: Immigrant Farmers in Nineteenth-Century Texas* (1994). Juan Cortina's life, including the roles that he and other Mexican Americans in Texas played in the Civil War, is compellingly treated in Omar Valerio-Jiménez's *River of Hope: Forging Identity and Nation in the Rio Grande Borderlands* (2013) as well as Jerry Thompson's biography *Cortina: Defending the Mexican Name in Texas* (2007). I first encountered Cortina in fictionalized form in the pages of Larry McMurtry's *Lonesome Dove* (1985); Carmen Boullosa's novel *Texas: The Great Theft* (2014) also has him as a central character. As with so many topics in Texas history, fiction is as effective as academic history, if not more so, in capturing truth.

My accounts of the Civil War, emancipation, and Juneteenth are deeply indebted to Stephen Harrigan's *Big Wonder-*

ESSAY ON SOURCES

ful Thing, where the telling of Sam Houston's dilemma is gripping; the Texas slave narratives; and Annette Gordon-Reed's *On Juneteenth*. María Esther Hammack's comments to journalists and forthcoming book *Channels of Liberation: Freedom Fighters in the Age of Abolition* and Emily Blanck's "Galveston on San Francisco Bay: Juneteenth in the Fillmore District, 1945–2016" (2019) helped me to understand how Juneteenth celebrations spread far beyond Texas. The homefront experiences of the Civil War are nicely explored in Deborah Liles and Angela Boswell's *Women in Civil War Texas: Diversity and Dissidence in the Trans-Mississippi* (2016) and Richard McCaslin's *Tainted Breeze: The Great Hanging at Gainesville, Texas, 1862* (1994). Key guides to Reconstruction in Texas include Barry Crouch's *The Freedmen's Bureau and Black Texans* (1992), Carl Moneyhon's *Edmund J. Davis of Texas: Civil War General, Republican Leader, Reconstruction Governor* (2010), and Jacqueline Jones's *Goddess of Anarchy: The Life and Times of Lucy Parsons, American Radical* (2017).

The expulsion of most Native peoples from Texas is well told in Gary Clayton Anderson's *The Conquest of Texas: Ethnic Cleansing in the Promised Land, 1820–1875* (2005). John Graves's story "The Last Running" was published as a stand-alone book of the same title in 1974 and is widely anthologized. Alex Hunt's vivid recreation of the Kiowa buffalo hunts and what they may have meant to the participants—"Hunting Charles Goodnight's Buffalo: Texas Fiction, Panhandle Folklore, and Kiowa History" (2004)—is indispensable. Goodnight's film *Old Texas,* available on the website of the Texas Archive of the Moving Image, is well worth watching. Accounts of the resurgence of Karankawas and Tāp Pīlam in *Texas Monthly* underscore the point that this expulsion was not nearly as complete as we think. Take a tour of the San Antonio missions sponsored by Tāp Pīlam and I bet that you'll agree with me.

352 ESSAY ON SOURCES

Joshua Specht's *Red Meat Republic: A Hoof-to-Table History of How Beef Changed America* (2019) was my starting point for understanding the environmental dimensions and the enormous impact of Texas cattle ranching outside the state. Owen Wister's "The Evolution of a Cow-Puncher" (1895), John Lomax's "Half-Million Dollar Song: Origin of 'Home on the Range'" (1945), and Teddy Blue Abbott's *We Pointed Them North: Recollections of a Cowpuncher* (1939) wonderfully capture the romance of cattle ranching and the great trail drives. Terry Jordan's *North American Cattle-Ranching Frontiers: Origins, Diffusion, and Differentiation* (1994) remains an authoritative account of cattle ranching. Andrés Tijerina beautifully evokes ranching culture and techniques in *Tejano Empire: Life on the South Texas Ranchos* (1998). Walter Buenger's *The Path to a Modern South: Northeast Texas Between Reconstruction and the Great Depression* (2001) and Rebecca Sharpless's *Fertile Ground, Narrow Choices: Women on Texas Cotton Farms, 1900–1940* (1999) are powerful reminders of the unchanging importance of cotton agriculture in the period whose mythology is more associated with ranching and oil.

Much of the specific material and general appreciation for the aims of Christian leaders after the Civil War come from Robert Wuthnow's *Rough Country: How Texas Became America's Most Powerful Bible-Belt State* (2014) and Joseph Locke's *Making the Bible Belt: Texas Prohibitionists and the Politicization of Southern Religion* (2017). Brenna Gardner Rivas's articles and forthcoming book on gun control helped me to think about the political implications of these cultural efforts. Bryan Edward Stone's *Chosen Folks: Jews on the Frontier of Texas* (2010) deepened my appreciation of the cultural pluralism of this time, as well as introducing me to the remarkable speech "The Moral Effect of the Possum." The amazing web-

ESSAY ON SOURCES 353

site hymnary.org allows you to trace where and when particular songs were included in church music books.

The literature on Populism is large and dynamic. Gregg Cantrell's *The People's Revolt: Texas Populists and the Roots of American Liberalism* (2020) informed my account more than any other work, though Charles Postel's *The Populist Vision* (2007) remains helpful to understand the movement's intellectual reach, especially that of figures like William Cowper Brann. Reading *Women and the Texas Populist Movement: Letters to the Southern Mercury* (1997), edited by Marion Barthelme, is a great way to see the passion behind the movement. Although Lawrence Goodwyn is not nearly as attentive to the racism of white Populists as Cantrell and Postel, and draws arbitrary distinctions between "real" Populism and a "shadow movement," his re-creation of Populist ideas about currency and interracial politics in *Democratic Promise: The Populist Moment in America* (1976) remains deeply compelling.

My first book, *Revolution in Texas: How a Forgotten Rebellion and Its Bloody Suppression Turned Mexicans into Americans* (2003), tells the story of Ranger and vigilante violence in South Texas. Monica Muñoz Martínez's *The Injustice Never Leaves You: Anti-Mexican Violence in Texas* (2018) captures the cultures of anti-Mexican violence and the ways that victimized families have remembered events like the Porvenir massacre. The *Texas Monthly* podcast "White Hats," on the history of the Texas Rangers, glosses these events and some of their reverberations very nicely. David Montejano's classic *Anglos and Mexicans in the Making of Texas, 1836–1986* offers a framework for understanding changes in race relations over a large sweep of Texas history. William Carrigan's *The Making of a Lynching Culture: Violence and Vigilantism in Central Texas, 1836–1916* is brutal but essential to understanding the lynching of Jesse

Washington and so many others. Patricia Bernstein's *The First Waco Horror: The Lynching of Jesse Washington and the Rise of the NAACP* (2005) showed me how essential campaigns against mob violence in Texas were to Black civil rights nationally. W. E. B. Du Bois's short story "Jesus Christ in Texas," first published in *Darkwater: Voices from Within the Veil* (1920), remains a searing indictment of white Texas culture in these decades.

My account of the campaign for women's suffrage is heavily indebted to Judith McArthur's *Minnie Fisher Cunningham: A Suffragist's Life in Politics* (2004). Sonia Hernandez's *Working Women into the Borderlands* (2014) is indispensable for understanding Jovita Idar and other Mexican feminists. Adrian Lentz-Smith's *Freedom Struggles: African Americans and World War I* tells the amazing story of Ely Green and other Black Texans who sought to use the war to advance their own struggles. J. Luz Sáenz's writings about the war and homefront can be read in *The World War I Diary of José de la Luz Sáenz* (2014), edited by Emilio Zamora. The campaign against German culture in Texas during the war is nicely captured in Mark Sonntag's "Fighting Everything German in Texas, 1917–1919" (1994).

Darren Dochuk's *Anointed with Oil: How Christianity and Crude Made Modern America* (2019) nestles the story of Texas oil in wider geographic and cultural contexts. *Oil in Texas: The Gusher Age, 1895–1945* (2002) by Diana Davids Hinton and Roger Olien was my key source for the industry's development. Brian Frehner wonderfully recreates oil exploration in *Finding Oil: The Nature of Petroleum Geology, 1859–1920* (2011). My descriptions of the culture of oil heavily rely on Alfred Crum's *Romance of American Petroleum and Gas* (1911), Joe Specht's "Oil Well Blues: African American Oil Patch Songs" (2011), and Mody Boatright's *Tales from the Derrick Floor: A People's History of the Oil Industry* (1970).

Darren Dochuk's first book, *From Bible Belt to Sunbelt:*

ESSAY ON SOURCES 355

Plain-Folk Religion, Grassroots Politics, and the Rise of Evangelical Conservatism (2010) is an excellent guide to the rise of political Christianity in twentieth-century Texas, especially when read alongside Joseph Locke's *Making the Bible Belt,* which recreates the anti-clerical tradition that ministers like Frank Norris had to destroy. The freedoms and debaucheries of urban life that so enraged Norris are nicely explored in Tyina Steptoe's *Houston Bound: Culture and Color in a Jim Crow City* (2015) and Patricia Evridge Hill's *Dallas: The Making of a Modern City* (1996). Michael Phillips's *White Metropolis: Race, Ethnicity, and Religion in Dallas, 1841–2001* (2006) conveys just how powerful the Klan was politically. The key reading for my re-creation of the 1936 Centennial Exposition is John Morán González's *Border Renaissance: The Texas Centennial and the Emergence of Mexican American Literature* (2009), augmented by Michael Phillips's *White Metropolis.* Robert Perkinson explores the relationship between Huddie Ledbetter and Alan Lomax in his *Texas Tough: The Rise of America's Prison Empire* (2010).

Emilio Zamora's *Claiming Rights and Righting Wrongs in Texas: Mexican Workers and Job Politics During World War II* (2009) is key to understanding how World War II supercharged pushes for civil rights. The story of Beatrice and Felix Longoria is powerfully told in John Valadez's PBS film *The Longoria Affair* (2009). Randolph Campbell's treatment of wartime mobilization in *Gone to Texas* provided helpful context for the World War II chapter. The details of Lyndon Johnson's early career, life in the Hill Country, and rural electrification are taken from Robert Caro's *The Path to Power: The Years of Lyndon Johnson* (1982), which is gripping despite the author's unduly negative take on Johnson and unduly positive evaluation of some of his chief opponents.

To understand the outsized national reputation of Texas in

the 1950s and '60s, there are still no better sources than Edna Ferber's *Giant* (1952), John Bainbridge's *The Super-Americans* (1961), George Stevens's movie version of *Giant* (1956), and Lawrence Wright's evocative coming of age story *In The New World: Growing Up with America, 1960–1984* (1987). Michael Phillips's *White Metropolis* and Edward Miller's *Nut Country: Right-Wing Dallas and the Birth of the Southern Strategy* (2015) were my guides to the intense conservatism of Dallas and the state as a whole. Annette Gordon-Reed's *On Juneteenth* is a great way of understanding some of the changes that civil rights brought to Texas. Frank Guridy's *The Sports Revolution: How Texas Changed the Culture of American Athletics* (2021) effectively highlights the role of college athletics in fostering civil rights. Brian Behnken's *Fighting Their Own Battles: Mexican Americans, African Americans, and the Struggle for Civil Rights in Texas* (2011) nicely captures overlapping and sometimes conflicting struggles to be treated with basic human decency, as does Max Krochmal's somewhat more optimistic *Blue Texas: The Making of a Multiracial Democratic Coalition in the Civil Rights Era* (2016). The interviews in Max Krochmal and Todd Moye's edited collection *Civil Rights in Black and Brown: Histories of Resistance and Struggle in Texas* (2021) and its companion website are gripping, as is, in its own strange way, the documentary *Dallas at the Crossroads* (1961).

Christian Wallace's article "Luckenbach Is a Hill Country Treasure. Can It Be Saved?" (2022) is a good entry point into the fascinating Hondo Crouch. Guridy's *The Sports Revolution* has great material on the Dallas Cowboys, as does the *Texas Monthly* podcast "America's Girls," which focuses on the team's cheerleaders. H. G. Bissinger's *Friday Night Lights: A Town, a Team, and a Dream* (2003) and the television series of the same name (2006–2011) are great explorations of high school football's near religious status. Most of my material on struggles for gay rights comes from Wes Phelps's landmark *Before Lawrence v. Texas: The Making of a Queer Social Movement* (2023). Joshua Prager's *The Family Roe: An American Story* (2021) is an excellent exploration of Norma McCorvey's life and extended family. The struggles over Barton Springs are nicely detailed in William Swearingen's *Environmental City: People, Place, Politics, and the Meaning of Modern Austin* (2010). There is a great book waiting to be written on John Mackey and Whole Foods; in the meantime, *Texas Monthly* reportage is a good place to start, especially Tom Foster's article "The Shelf Life of John Mackey" (2017). Uzma Quraishi's *Redefining the Immigrant South: Indian and Pakistani Immigration to Houston During the Cold War* (2020) is an excellent guide not only to South Asian migration but to the challenges and opportunities of cultural pluralism more generally. Chad Broughton's *Boom, Bust, Exodus: The Rust Belt, the Maquilas, and a Tale of Two Cities* (2015) captures some of the paradoxes, tensions, and opportunities that have come with the closer integration of Mexico and the United States in recent decades.

Dick Reavis's *The Ashes of Waco: An Investigation* (1998) places the story of the ill-fated siege of the Branch Davidians in the longer history of the Davidian religious movement. Lawrence Wright's *God Save Texas: A Journey into the Soul of the Lone Star State* (2018) is a thoughtful and provocative guide to Texas in the late twentieth and early twenty-first centuries. Increasing religious pluralism and the persistent strength of Christianity are nicely captured in the resources of the Pew Research Center's website.

Acknowledgments

Writing this book would have been impossible without the advice, expertise, and support of so, so many people. This started with the idea of the book itself: I will forever be grateful to Chris Rogers for approaching me to write a short, narrative-driven account of the sweep of Texas history, and then working with me so closely to finally bring it to completion. After Chris's retirement from Yale University Press, Adina Berk was generous in her support and guidance, to say nothing of being understanding about my many delays in finishing the book. Eva Skewes made sure that publications logistics worked out, and Erica Hanson did an amazing job of editing the manuscript. My colleague and chair, Brad Hunt, strongly supported the application for the research leave that finally let me finish it.

Many people were kind enough to read partial and complete versions of the manuscript. The two outside readers commissioned by the press, Gregg Cantrell and Rebecca Sharpless, provided exemplary and detailed feedback. Adam Goodman's enthusiastic response to early chapters came at just the right time to convince me that I could pull this off. Since this book is written for the general public, I am grateful for comments and engagement from lay readers: Ben Friberg (whose knowledge of Texas history is truly stupendous), Stephen Johnson, Andrew Johnson, Don Lassus, Ed Butler, and Beau Sample. The Windy City Writing group—Andrae Marak, Margaret Power, Teresa Prados-Torreira, Michael Staudenmaier, Ellie Walsh, Neici Zeller—helped with large chunks of the early chapters, as did Richard Ribb.

Guidance on specific chapters was generously provided by Cameron Maynard, Juliana Barr, Sebastian Wuepper, Brian Frehner, Johnny Nelson, Alex Hunt, Kat Walters, John Morán González, and Adrian Chavana. Michael Phillips, Jeff Littlejohn, Wes Phelps, Matt Babcock, and Joaquin Rivaya-Martínez confirmed some key factual details and saved me from factual errors. Countless Facebook friends weighed in with useful advice about a thorny issue around writing and audience in the introduction; Natalie Mendoza and Beth Lew Williams were particularly wise in their guidance.

I worked on this book for about seven years, with interruptions and delays for extended research for another project, work with Loyola's Faculty Council and chapter of the American Association of University Professors, a global pandemic, and living in Germany for seven months. Through all of this work and delay, my family constantly supported me, and so this book is for them.

Index

Page numbers in italics refer to maps

Abbott, Teddy Blue, 157, 158
Abilene, Kansas, 157
abolitionists, 94–95, 98, 114, 122,
    125, 132, 186
abortion, 302, 304–8, 330
Acapulco, Mexico, 47–49, 51–55
Acoma, New Mexico, 34–35
Adams, John Quincy, 94
agriculture: corn, 17–18, 23, 32,
    41, 245; cotton, 8, 19, 53, 69,
    98, 104, 110, 118, 132, 140, 153,
    182, 197, 223, 245; in early cul-
    tures, 17–18; and the economy,
    182–85; European contribu-
    tions to, 43; and the Grange,
    171; melons, 43; potatoes, 32;
    sugar cane, 53; sunflowers, 17;
    "three sisters" (corn, squash,
    beans), 17, 19, 43; tobacco, 32
air-conditioning, 241
aircraft industry, 256
Alabama, 53, 68, 285
Alabama-Coushatta people, 149

Alamo: cenotaph, 243; and the
    Daughters of the Republic of
    Texas, 243–44; first siege of,
    81–83; Long Barracks, 243;
    as mission, 40; place in Texas
    lore, 242, 273, 280, 281, 329;
    project to overhaul area around,
    337–38; second siege of, 83–86;
    story of, 2, 74–75, 80–86, 89,
    338–39
Alamo, The (film), 271
Alamo Defenders Descendants
    Association, 339
Alamo Plaza, 338
Albuquerque, New Mexico, 129
Alcohol, Tobacco, and Firearms,
    Bureau of (ATF), 323–24
alcohol prohibition and temper-
    ance movements, 168–70, 173,
    228–32, 234, 235
Alger, Bruce, 276–77, 278, 279
Alief (suburb), 319
Allred, James, 240, 262

361

Amarillo, Texas, 245
Amazon, 316
American Folklore Society, 250
American Football League (AFL), 299
American Revolution, 45, 56, 57
Anadarko people, 140
Anderson County, 340
Angola prison, 252
anti-clericalism, 173–74
Antietam, Battle of, 128
anti-monopoly laws, 191
anti-trust laws, 225
Apache people: attacks in Mexico, 113; and the Comanches, 51, 53, 54; and European settlers, 40, 43, 45, 48, 51–52, 76; Lipan, 54, 118; in New Mexico, 106; on reservations, 140
Apalachee people, 23
Aranama, 44
Arapaho people, 146
archaeology, 11
Argentina, 31, 110
Arizona, 34, 196
Arkansas, 42, 68, 118
Arlington National Cemetery, 254, 266
armadillos, 160
Army of New Mexico, 129
Army of Northern Virginia, 128
Arredondo, Joaquín de, 58, 59
Ashby, "Stump," 186
Asian Americans, 7, 318–20, 331, 340
Astrodome, 299
Athapaskan language, 19
Auburn, Texas, 173
Austin, Moses, 2, 62, 68, 94
Austin, Stephen F.: bringing colonists to Tejas, 2, 7, 62, 68,

69, 70–71, 74, 76–77, 107, 108, 243, 320–21; death of, 91; as "Esteban," 5, 60–61, 62, 68, 69, 71–72; as "father of Texas," 4, 5, 7; funeral and burial of, 2–4, 7, 294, 337; as immigrant to Mexico, 60–61; imprisonment in Mexico, 73–74, 78, 89; loyalty to Mexico, 71–72; in Missouri, 62, 94; as secretary of state, 91; on slavery, 69–70; and the Texas Revolution, 74–75
Austin, Texas: clubs in, 309; counterculture in, 315–16; Disciples of Christ in, 231; Huston-Tillotson University, 244; music scene, 317–18; Juneteenth celebration, 135; road to San Antonio, 234; urban growth in, 311–12, 313, 320–21
Austin City Limits (television show), 314–15
Austin College, 171
automobiles, 233–34, 241
Avavare people, 28
aviation, 206
Aztec Empire, 22, 23, 25, 32
Aztec Indians, 34

Bainbridge, John, 271–74
Baker, Don, 307
Banks, Jay, 288, 294–95
banks and banking, 171, 179, 220, 245–46, 258, 278, 311
Baptist General Convention of Texas, 170
Baptist Standard, 177, 228, 231
barbed wire fencing, 160–61
Barr, Amelia, 164
Barrow, Clyde, 193

INDEX

Barton, Billy, 309–10
Barton Springs, 309–11, 312, 313
basket weaving, 17
Baylor University, 170–71, 177, 188, 228, 230, 231, 303
Bean, Peter Ellis, 61
Beaumont, Texas, 124, 130, 217, 219, 220, 221–22, 224, 256, 286
Beavis and Butt-Head (television show), 317
Benavides, Santos, 132
Bevo (steer), 162
Bidai, 44
Big Bend National Park, 10, 259
"Big Inch" pipeline, 257
Birth of a Nation, The (film), 236
bison: declining numbers of, 11, 66, 103; giant, 15, 16; Goodnight's herd, 137–40, 149–50; hunted by Native Americans, 13, 14, 19, 49–50, 51, 102–3, 146–47; killed by white hunters, 147; Spaniards' view of, 25
"Black Giant" oil field, 217, 218, 219, 221, 224
Black people: as athletes, 286–87, 300–301; celebrating Juneteenth, 135–36; and the Civil Rights Movement, 289–95; and the Civil War, 124–25; as cowboys, 154, 159; education for, 166–67; enslaved Africans, 27, 32, 69; as farmers, 182, 185–86; as farm laborers, 245; folktales of, 244; free, 94, 247; freedom for, 124–25, 133–36, 141–42; incarceration of, 294; as landowners, 142–43; leaving Texas, 145, 236–37; in Mexico, 117–19; in the military, 209–10, 214, 244, 262, 264–65; musi-

cians, 251; in the NYA, 259; and the oil boom, 223; in the penal system, 252–53; in political office, 142, 170, 283–84, 293, 294; as Populists, 185–86; portrayal of, 247–49; and the prosperity gospel, 333; in Texas, 7, 84–85, 87, 333–34; in the Texas Revolution, 338; violence against, 143–144, 190, 198; voting rights for, 140, 141–42, 144–45, 190, 195, 200–201, 208, 285, 291. *See also* segregation; slavery
Blanton, Annie Lee, 205
"Blest Be the Tie That Binds," 167–68
Bolívar, Simón, 65
boogie-woogie, 235
boomtowns, 221–22
bootleg whiskey, 234
Bosque County, 250
bow and arrow, 17, 19
Bowie, James "Jim," 61, 75, 82, 83, 85
Bracero Agreement, 265–66
Branch, Jacob, 124, 125, 126, 134
Branch Davidians, 323–27
branding, 51
Brann, William Cowper, 176–77
Brazil, 94
Brazoria County, 4, 337
Brazos River, 69, 83, 88, 91, 140
Brewer, John Mason, 244
Brite Ranch, 197
British Empire, 64, 94
Brooks airfield, 206
Brown v. Board of Education, 284, 286, 290, 291, 302
Brownsville, Texas, 120–21, 132, 133, 194, 195
Bryan, William Jennings, 189

364 INDEX

Buchanan, Alvin, 304, 306
Buchanan lawsuit, 305
buffalo. *See* bison
Buffalo Bayou, 88
Buffalo Hump (Comanche
  leader), 104, 116
Buffington, Tom, 162
Bush, George Herbert Walker,
  274, 327–28, 329
Bush, George W., 256, 327, 328,
  329–30
Bush, Prescott, 274
Bywaters, Jerry, 244

Cabell, Earle, 277
Cabeza de Vaca, Álvar Nuñez, 22,
  23, 24–31, 45, 159
Cabeza Rapada (Comanche
  leader), 54
Caddo people: Comanches trad-
  ing with, 50, 53; decimated
  by European settlers, 42; and
  French exploration, 37, 40, 41;
  removal to reservation, 140,
  145; and Spanish exploration,
  33, 36, 39–40, 43, 45, 52; in
  Texas, 18–19; vulnerability
  to disease, 42–43
Caldwell County, 211
California, 34, 196, 237, 269, 305;
  Los Angeles, 231, 269; San
  Francisco, 135
Callahan, James, 118–19
Cameron, Texas, 180
Cameron County, 192, 197
Camisa de Hierro (Comanche
  leader), 54
Canada, 110, 125, 320
Canales, José Tomás "J.T.,"
  192–94, 200, 203, 209, 281
cannibalism, 26

Cantona, 44
capitalism, 178, 181, 263, 301, 315,
  316; conscious, 316
Caroline (Kiowa Indian), 137
Carroll, B. H., 170, 173
Carter, Amon, 242
Carter, Lucy (Parsons), 140–41,
  142
Casiano, José, 77
cattle, 51, 154–55, 242, 245; in
  Mexico, 155–56
cattle drives, 151, 157–60, 250
cattle industry, 151–62
Cavas, 44
Caynaaya, 44
Cedarstacker, Peter, 296
Centennial Commission, 242–43
Charlie (enslaved man), 125
Cherokee people, 96, 97, 101–2,
  103, 247
Cheyenne people, 103, 146
Chicago, Illinois, 235, 236
chili powder, 172
China, 129, 320
Chipps, Dexter, 227, 237
Chisholm Trail, 157
Cholomé, 44
Christians and Christianity: Bap-
  tists, 167, 168, 169, 175, 176–77,
  228, 230, 231, 332–33; Black
  churches, 142, 166, 169, 189;
  Catholics, 61, 62, 75, 121, 170,
  174, 195, 233, 277, 308, 319, 332;
  Church of Christ, 169; Cumber-
  land Presbyterians, 168–169;
  Disciples of Christ, 231; Episcopalians, 175; and European
  exploration, 22, 30–31, 34, 39,
  41–42, 44–45, 48, 52; Evangeli-
  cals, 308, 331, 332; Fundamen-
  talists, 227; German Lutherans,

211–12; importance to community, 167–68; Lutherans, 173; Methodists, 167, 169, 173, 175, 176, 230, 231, 331; Mormons, 332; Pentecostals, 331, 333; and politics, 173–76, 188–89, 229–31, 238; Presbyterians, 233, 331; prosperity gospel, 332–33; Protestants, 61, 170, 173, 188–89, 229, 277; revival meetings, 233; in San Antonio, 164; Seventh-Day Adventists, 326; Southern Baptists, 277, 331; spread of, 163–64, 166; and the temperance movement, 168–171, 228–30
Cíbola, 44
Circle of Friends (Dallas), 306
civil rights, 141, 177, 186, 199, 247, 249, 262, 267, 276, 277, 278, 279, 281, 283–95, 312, 319–20
Civil Rights Act (1964), 285, 293
Civil Rights Movement, 178, 186, 284
Civil War, 5, 124–36, 174, 182, 209; end of, 133; and the liberation of enslaved people, 124–25, 134–36; secession of Texas from the Union, 125–28; support for the Union in Texas, 130–33; Texan casualties, 28; Texan forces in New Mexico, 129; Union Army in Texas, 130
Civil War monument, 135
Clansman, The (Dixon), 236
Cleburne, Texas, 179
Clements, William, 328
Cleveland Browns, 269
climate change, 15, 226, 334–35

Clovis points, 16
Coahuila, Mexico, 2, 39–40, 43, 44, 66, 73, 74, 76, 77, 79, 136
Coahuiltecan people, 41, 44
Coahuilteco language, 44
Coke, Richard, 144, 173–74
Coleman, Preely, 124, 125, 134
College Station, Texas, 171
Collins, Phil, 338
colonialism, 44
Colorado, 196
Colorado County, 202
Colorado River, 87, 259
Columbia, Texas, 91
Columbus, Christopher, 12
Comanche people: bison hunting, 102–3; and German settlers, 116; and Mexico, 65–66, 113; Peneteka, 104–5; and the Republic of Texas, 97; on reservations, 140; and the Spanish, 45, 48–56, 65; in Texas, 66, 76, 79, 90–91, 104–6, 120, 138, 139, 146–47, 150
Comfort, Texas, 135, 296
Communism, 246, 275, 279–80
Compaq, 313, 314, 316
Compaq Arena, 333
computing industry, 312–13
Confederate Army, 138
Confederate States of America, 5, 6, 125–30, 242
Confederate Territory of Arizona, 129
conjunto music, 172
Connally, John, 268
Conroe, Texas, 285, 291
Cooke County, 130–31
co-ops, 261–62
copper, 19
Córdova, Vicente, 108–9

366 INDEX

Coronado, Francisco Vázquez de, 33
Corpus Christi, Texas, 130, 195, 256, 266
Corsicana, Texas, 217, 233, 249
Cortés, Hernán, 22
Cortina, Juan, 120–22, 132
Cortina's War, 120–21
Cos, Martín Perfecto de, 80, 82–83
cosmopolitanism, 241, 273–74
Cotulla, Texas, 258
cowboys, 152–54, 158–59, 161, 241; Black or Mexican, 154, 159
creosote bushes, 160
Criswell, W. A., 277, 278
Crockett, Davy, 75, 83, 85, 271, 272
Croix, Teodoro de, 45, 47–48, 53–54
Cronkite, Walter, 288
Crouch, John Russell "Hondo," 296–98
Crouch, Shatzi, 296, 297
Crum, A. R., 221
Cruz, Ted, 330
Crystal City, Texas, 290
Cuba, 22, 94, 276
culture: of cosmopolitanism, 273–74; music, 172, 233, 234, 235, 250–52, 309, 314–15, 317; paintings, 244; and social networks, 172–73; Texan, 281; violence and, 164–65, 176–77
Cunningham, Minnie Fisher, 204–8, 210, 215, 238
currency policy, 182–84

Dallas (television series), 9, 271, 302
Dallas at the Crossroads (film), 287–88

Dallas County, 329
Dallas Cowboys, 269, 299–301, 302–3, 313, 316
Dallas Cowboys Cheerleaders, 299, 301–2
Dallas–Fort Worth, Texas: aircraft factory in, 256; Black professionals in, 294; churches in, 333; Circle of Friends, 306; clubs in, 235, 251; computing industry in, 314; depictions of, 272; desegregation in, 287–89; Frontier Centennial Exposition, 242; gay pride parade, 306; image of, 298–99; Kennedy assassination, 9, 268–269, 273–78; Ku Klux Klan in, 236, 239; Love Field, 206, 268, 294; Native Americans in, 149; Oak Lawn neighborhood, 303; and the oil industry, 220; politics in, 277; population growth in, 234; radio in, 235; shopping in, 273; TESA chapter, 207; urban character of, 311
Dallas Nine painters, 244
Dallas Public and Private, 279
Darden, Ida, 279
Darwinism, 186
Daughters of the Republic of Texas, 243–44
Davenport, Samuel, 61
Davis, Edmund J., 141, 144
Davis Mountains, 325–26
Dealey, George, 238
death penalty, 252, 253
Debbie Does Dallas (film), 301–2
Debs, Eugene, 177
Deep Ellum, 234, 251
de Lara, Bernardo Gutiérrez, 57
Delaware people, 101

INDEX

de León, Alonso, 37–39
Delgado v. Bastrop, 289, 292
Dell, Michael, 312–13, 314, 316
Dell Computers, 312–14
Del Rio, Texas, 10, 149
Democratic Party, Democrats: conservative, 261, 263, 267, 331; in Dallas, 277; and the Black vote, 186–87, 291; and Christian voters, 306, 331; dominance of, 202, 257, 259, 262; elected officeholders, 110, 141, 178, 191, 275, 290, 327, 329; fraud and violence by, 189, 194, 200; and the Hispanic vote, 293, 330; liberal, 257, 327, 331; national, 189, 257, 275, 330; opposition to, 326; and the poll tax, 201; primaries, 201, 238, 264; 290, 291, 305; and the Roosevelt administration, 259, 261, 262; southern, 259, 277; in Texas, 144, 174, 178–79, 200–201, 265, 327–29, 331; white, 144, 174, 189–90, 201, 202, 236, 238, 257
desegregation, 291–92; in the defense industry, 265; of education, 284–89; of the military, 265; opposition to, 288–289; of public facilities, 287–288. *See also* segregation
de Soto, Hernando, 33
Detroit, Michigan, 236
DeWitt County, 165
Día de los Negros, 135
disease: anthrax, 103; brought by Europeans, 26, 33, 42–44, 50; dysentery, 26, 91; epidemic, 103; and extinction, 15; influenza, 33, 43; malaria, 33, 91; measles, 42; smallpox, 33, 42, 50; West

Nile virus, 335; yellow fever, 61, 91; Zika virus, 335
divining rods, 224
Dixon, Thomas, 236
Dobie, J. Frank, 242
Dodge City, Kansas, 157
doodlebugs, 224
Douglas, Aaron, 247, 248
Douglass, Frederick, 177, 186
draft boards, 213–14
Driscoll, Clara, 243–44
droughts, 244
drunkenness, 169, 173, 222
Du Bois, W. E. B., 249
Dust Bowl, 245
Duval County, 214
Duwali (Cherokee leader), 96, 101

Earl, Nancy, 294
earth ovens, 12, 13
education, 98, 144, 166–67, 318–19; for Black people, 142, 166–67, 171; Christian, 170–71, 173, 177; desegregation of, 284–89; funding for, 330; laws restricting, 339–40; segregation in, 166–67; state funding for, 191
Edwards, Haden, 71–72, 74
Edwards Plateau, 50
Eisenhower, Dwight D., 255, 279
electricity, 184, 241, 259–61, 264
Electronic Data Systems (EDS), 313
Ellis County, 167–68
El Paso, Texas (El Paso–Juarez), 36, 40, 149, 206, 287, 311
"El Paso Gas" (song), 222
Emancipation Park (Houston), 135
Emancipation Proclamation, 135

Emets, 44
England, 64, 94
English language, 75
entrepreneurs, 314, 316
environmentalism, 225, 276, 311, 315–16
equal rights amendment, 305
Ervipiame, 44
Estebanico (enslaved man), 27, 30
ethnic cleansing, 102
European explorers, 41–42
Evans, Hiram, 233, 235
expansionism, 110
Exxon, 220

Fair Park, 240, 241, 247–49
family feuds, 165
Fannin, James, 86
Farenthold, Francis "Sissy," 305
Farmers' Alliance, 179–81, 185–86, 187
Farmers' and Laborers' Protective Association (FLPA), 213
fascism, 265
Fayette County, 211
Federal Bureau of Investigation (FBI), 278, 323, 325
Ferber, Edna, 270, 279
Ferguson, James "Pa," 202, 237, 239, 257
Ferguson, "Ma," 238, 239, 257
firearms rights, 169–70, 323, 330–31, 336
First Baptist Church (Dallas), 277, 332
First Baptist Church (Waco), 170
First Baptist Church (Wichita Falls), 332
Flatlanders, 277
flint, 18
Florida, 22, 23, 34, 328

Folsom points, 17
football, 298–302
Fort Bliss, 206
Fort Ringgold, 206
Fort Worth, Texas, 220, 231. *See also* Dallas–Fort Worth, Texas
France: and the Louisiana Purchase, 55–56; in North America, 36–37, 38, 43; in Texas, 37–38
Fredericksburg, Texas, 116, 255
Fredonian Rebellion (Republic of Fredonia), 71, 74, 75
Freedmen's Bureau, 141, 143
Freeman, Elisabeth, 199–200
Freemasonry, 171–72
Freethinkers, 116, 176
French Revolution, 56, 57
Frontier Centennial Exposition, 242
frontier warfare, 53
Fundamentalist, The, 228

Gainesville, Texas, 131
Galveston, Texas: Black population in, 135, 209; in the Civil War, 130; education in, 171; growth of, 184, 312; immigrants in, 319; politics in, 142, 201; religion in, 231; shipyards in, 256; Spanish explorers in, 21, 27, 37, 46; TESA chapter, 207
Galveston Plan, 201
García, Hector P., 264, 265, 266
García, Pete, 292
Garfield, James, 174
Garland, Hamlin, 188
Garland, Texas, 256, 317
Garner, John Nance, 261–62
Gay, Bettie, 187
gay rights, 302, 303–8
Gebhardt, William, 172

INDEX

gender roles, 233
General Electric, 241
Geophysical Service Incorporated, 314
Georgia, 130, 232–33
German festivals, 172
German language, 210
Germany: immigrants from, 114–17, 119, 126, 131, 132, 164, 172, 175, 176, 179, 210–13, 215, 255, 319; prisoners of war from, 256; and World War I, 210–13; and World War II, 265
gerrymandering, 328
Gettysburg, Battle of, 128
G.I. Forum, 264
Giant (Ferber), 270, 271, 279
Giant (film), 270–71, 273, 274
"Git Along, Little Dogies," 250
Glenn, John, 256
Glorieta Pass, 129
Goliad, Texas, 71, 74, 86, 89, 242, 244
González, Henry B., 290, 292
González, Jovita, 250, 252
Gonzales, Texas, 79
Good Neighbor Commission, 266
Goodnight, Charles, 137–39, 140, 149–50, 160–61
Goodnight Loving Trail, 157
Gordon-Reed, Annette, 285, 294
Goyens, Bill, 247
Gran Círculo de Obreros Mexicanos, 172
Gran Liga Mexicanista, 200
Grand Prairie, Texas, 256
Grand State Farmers' Alliance, 179–81, 185–86, 187
Grange organization, 171
Granger, Gordon E., 134, 135
Graves, John, 150

Great Depression, 245–46, 259
Great Migration, 237
Great Western Trail, 157
Green, Ely, 210, 215
greenhouse gases, 334
Greenville, Texas, 255
Grimes County, 189
Groce, Jared, 69, 87
Guadalupe Hidalgo, treaty of, 121
Guadalupe River, 104
Guaraní Indians, 31
Gulf of Mexico, 21–23, 33, 38
Gulf Oil Company, 220, 225, 226, 241
gun ownership, 169–70, 323, 330–31, 336

Haiti, 55
Haitian Revolution, 56, 57
Hallettsville, Texas, 212
Hamer, Frank, 192–93
Hamill, Al, 219
Hardin, John Wesley, 165
Harpers Ferry, 122
Hasinai confederacy, 42
Hawaii, 254
Haywood, Felix, 117
hematite, 11
Henry, Vida, 214
Hickey, Thomas "Red Tom," 212–13, 215
Hidalgo, Miguel, 56–57, 58
Higgins, Patillo, 221, 223–24
Hill Country, 115, 131, 176, 179, 210, 258, 260, 296, 319
Hill of Heroes, 3
Hobby, Ovetta Culp, 255
Hobby, William, 211
Hogg, James, 187, 191, 225
Hogue, Alexandre, 244
Holley, Mary Austin, 68

"Home on the Range," 151–52, 154, 250
hometown groups, 164
homosexuality, 303, 332. *See also* gay rights
Hondo, Texas, 296
Hood, John Bell, 128
Horse (Kiowa Indian), 137
horses: brought by Europeans, 23–24, 29, 32, 35, 43, 51, 155; Comanche use of, 49–50, 53, 102–3
Houston, Sam: as governor of Texas, 122, 126–27, 128, 131; and Native Americans, 96–97, 101–2; as president of Texas, 5, 89, 91, 93, 109; as Texas hero, 75, 100–101, 126, 127, 272; and the Texas Revolution, 80, 83, 86, 87–88
Houston, Texas: Black population in, 202, 209, 294; as capital city, 91; churches in, 333; clubs in, 235; depictions of, 272; gay pride parade, 306; Kennedy in, 276; Ku Klux Klan in, 239; mayor of, 329; Montrose district, 303; Native Americans in, 149; and the oil industry, 217, 220; people from, 255, 283–84, 327–28; politics in, 202, 207; population growth in, 234; as port city, 220; shipyards in, 256; suburbs of, 319, 320; TESA chapter, 207; urban character of, 311
Houston Oilers, 286, 299
Houston Riot, 214
Houston Rockets, 333
Houteff, Victor, 326
Hubbard, Texas, 227

Hughes, Sarah, 275
Huichols, 19–20
Humble Oil Company, 226
Hunt, George (Kiowa leader), 137–38
Hunt, H. L., 278, 299
Hunt, Lamar, 299
hunting: of bison, 13, 14, 19, 49–50, 51, 102–3, 146–47; by colonists in Texas, 67–68; by early cultures, 15–18, 20; by Native Americans, 45, 50, 51, 102–3
Huntsville, Texas, 252, 253
Hurricane Harvey, 334
hurricanes, 22
Huston-Tillotson University, 244
hydroelectric dams, 259–60

Iconoclast, The, 176–77
Idar, Clemente, 207, 209
Idar, Jovita, 200, 207
Idar, Nicasio, 207
immigrants: Asian, 311, 331; Czechoslovakian (Bohemian), 164, 172, 179; European, 164; German, 114–17, 119, 126, 131, 132, 164, 172, 175, 176, 179, 210–13, 215, 255, 319; from the Middle East, 311, 331; Nigerians, 7, 311, 319, 321; Polish, 209; South Asian, 7, 318–20; to Texas, 5, 66–67, 75–76, 114–15; Vietnamese, 7, 311, 319–20, 325
Imperial penitentiary, 253
Impressionism, 244
Incan Empire, 32
Indiana, 232
Indian Territory, 96, 102, 146
Indigenous people. *See* Native Americans

INDEX

industrial infrastructure, 256–57
Iraq war, 329–30
Iturbe, Agustín de, 62

Jackson, Andrew, 93
Jakes, T. D., 333
Japan, 254–55, 265
Jefferson, Thomas, 55
Jeffress, Robert, 332
Jennings, Waylon, 297
Jewish residents, 175, 233, 237, 273, 331
Jim (enslaved man), 70–71
"Jim Crow" system, 202, 232, 236, 253, 258, 259, 262, 264–65, 284, 287, 288, 292
Jim Wells County, 267
Joe (enslaved man), 85
Johnson, Alex, 232, 236
Johnson, Claudia Taylor ("Lady Bird"), 275, 277
Johnson, Lyndon Baines ("LBJ"): civil rights record, 266–67, 281, 285; and the Hill Country, 260; and Kennedy, 275–76, 277; as president, 268, 274, 281–82, 329; and the Roosevelt administration, 258–59, 262–63; and Vietnam, 279–82, 319
Johnson, Sam, 192
Johnson, Wesley, 135
Joiner, Columbus Marion ("Daddy"), 221, 224, 278
Jordan, Barbara, 202, 283–84, 289, 293, 294
Judge, Mike, 317
Jumano Indians, 36, 40, 44
Juneteenth, 135–36, 247

Kadohadacho confederacy, 42
Kansas, 34, 145

Kansas City, 235
Karankawa people, 21, 24, 25–27, 38, 40, 43, 148–49
Kearby, Jerome, 187
Kelly airfield, 206
Kennedy, Jacqueline ("Jackie"), 268, 273, 275
Kennedy, John F., 274–76, 281; assassination of, 9, 268–69, 273, 274, 275, 276, 277–78
Kennedy, Robert F., 269
Kickapoo people, 101, 149
Kilby, Jack, 314
Kilgore, Texas, 216
Kinchlow, Ben, 159
King, Martin Luther, Jr., 284
King of the Hill (television show), 317
King Ranch, 158, 258, 270, 272
Kingsville, Texas, 157, 197
Kiowa George (Kiowa Indian), 137
Kiowa people, 104, 137–40, 146, 149–50
Kleberg, Richard M., 258, 259
Kook, Guich, 297
Koresh, David, 323–27
Ku Klux Klan, 144, 232, 235, 236, 237–39, 277, 319–20; "Second Klan," 232–33

La Bahía, Texas, 59
labor strikes, 246
labor unions, 246, 263, 278
Lakewood Church (Houston), 333, 334
Lamar, Mirabeau, 97–102, 104, 105, 106–7, 109–10, 129
Lampasas, Texas, 179
Lampasas County, 165
landforms, *14*

372 INDEX

Landry, Tom, 300, 316
Langtry, Texas, 16
Laredo, Texas, 58, 107, 121, 195, 197, 200, 207, 320
La Salle, René Robert Cavelier, Sieur de, 38, 41
las Casas, Juan Bautista de, 56–57
Las Cruces, New Mexico, 129
"Last Longhorn, The," 161
"Last Running, The" (Graves), 150
Latin America, 8, 56, 64, 94, 110, 293. *See also* Mexico
Lawrence v. Texas, 302, 303
Lawson, Renee, 315
Ledbetter, Huddie "Lead Belly," 251–53
Lee, Robert E., 123, 128, 130, 133
LeVias, Jerry, 286, 289
Liberal Hall, 176
liberalism, 258, 261, 272, 279
Light Crust Doughboys, 262
Lincoln, Abraham, 113, 132, 135
Linnville, Texas, 104–5
Little Rock, Arkansas, 288
livestock industry, 51; cattle, 151–62; longhorn cattle, 155, 156, 157–62
local option laws, 229
Lockhart, Matilda, 104
Lockhart, Texas, 105
Lodge, Henry Cabot, 275
Lomax, John, 152, 153, 154, 160, 250–52
Lone Star Ammunition Plant, 256
Longhorn (Kiowa Indian), 137
longhorn cattle, 155, 156, 157–62
Longoria, Beatrice, 254, 266–67
Longoria, Felix, 254, 264, 265, 266–67

Longview, Texas, 216
Los Angeles, California, 236, 269
Louisiana, 42, 52–53, 59, 68, 118, 130, 193, 234
Louisiana Purchase, 55–56
Love Field, 206, 268, 294
Lowber, James William, 231
Loyalists, 262
Luckenbach, Texas, 297–99
"Luckenbach, Texas" (song), 297–98
Luckenbach World Fair, 297
LULAC (League of United Latin American Citizens), 249, 250, 289, 292
Lundy, Benjamin, 94–95, 114
Luz Sáenz, José, 209, 210, 215
lynchings, 187, 191, 194, 198–200, 252, 253, 295, 340

Mackey, John, 315–16
Macune, Charles, 180, 183
Mailer, Norman, 280
mammoths, 15
manganese, 11
Mansfield High School, 288, 289, 294–95
Marcus, Stanley, 273
Marfa, Texas, 270
Marian (enslaved person), 68
marriage: and divorce, 188, 235, 274, 275; same-sex, 302, 330, 332
Maryland, 287
Masonic lodges, 171–72
massive resistance, 287
mastodons, 15, 16
Matagorda, Texas, 37–38, 64
Matamoros, Texas, 113
Maverick, Samuel, 156
McCarthy, Joseph, 278

INDEX 373

McCluskey, Henry Jr., 303–7
McCorvey, Norma, 304–5, 306, 308
McLaren, Richard, 325–26, 327
McMurtry, Larry, 150
McVeigh, Timothy, 325, 326
Meacham, H. C., 237
Medina, Battle of, 58
Medina River, 58, 63
megafauna, 15–17
Mescale, 44
Mesilla, New Mexico, 129
Mesoamerica, 7
mesquite, 14, 159–60
Meusebach, John, 116
Mexican Americans, 195–97, 202–3, 242; as agricultural workers, 265–66; and the Centennial exhibit, 247, 249–50; as "Chicanos," 293; and the Civil Rights Movement, 289; festivals and food, 172; infant mortality, 246; in the military, 209, 262, 264–65; in the penal system, 253; in political office, 289–90, 292–93, 330; and the prosperity gospel, 333; rights for, 209; in San Antonio, 246; strikes by, 246; supporting Bush, 330. See also Tejanos
Mexican American studies, 340
Mexican Republic, 57–59
Mexico: and the Alamo, 338; Bracero Agreement, 265–66; Comanche raids, 103; connection to Texas, 2, 7, 8, 19–20; fight for independence, 56–57; freedom from slavery in, 117–19, 125; independence from Spain, 48, 62; laws against slavery, 78, 94; limiting migration to Texas,

77–78; Texas independence from, 4; trade with, 320; Texas war with, 80–81; U.S. war with, 110, 112–13, 121, 122
Middle East, 329–30
Midland, Texas, 268, 272, 274, 285
Mier, Texas, 107
Mier y Terán, Manuel, 75, 76, 77–78
Milam, Ben, 82–83
military aviation, 206
military infrastructure, 255–56, 264–65
minimum wage, 259, 263, 266, 278
Minute Women USA, 279
Mission San Antonio de Valero, 40. See also Alamo
Mississippi, 53, 285, 287
Mississippi River, 33, 38–39, 55
Mobil, 220
Mokeen (Kiowa Indian), 137
Momaday, N. Scott, 150
monetary policy, 182–84
monopolies, 171, 191, 217, 224, 225, 266, 278, 312
Montgomery bus boycott, 284
Moody, Dan, 237, 238, 239
Mopechucope (Comanche leader), 116
Morfi, Agustín, 45
Mount Carmel, 323–27
Muk-wah-ruh (Comanche leader), 104
murals and muralists, 244, 259
Murchison, Clint Jr., 299, 300
Murphy, Audie, 255
museums, 243

Nacogdoches, Texas, 50, 57, 59, 71, 101, 108–9, 247

374 INDEX

Naduah (Cynthia Ann Parker), 147–48
Napoleon Bonaparte, 55
Narváez, Pánfilo, 24
Natchitoches confederacy, 42
National Association for the Advancement of Colored People (NAACP), 199–200, 265, 288–89, 290, 291, 292
National Football League (NFL), 299
nationalism: Mexican, 61; Texas, 84
National Youth Administration (NYA), 258–59
Native Americans: artworks of, 10–12; confederacies established by, 42; confrontations with Europeans, 52; early cultures, 12–19; enslavement of, 30, 34, 35, 43–44; and Europeans, 40–46; on the Gulf Coast, 21–24; and Sam Houston, 96–97, 101–2; leaving Texas, 145–46; and Mirabeau Lamar, 101–2, 104, 105; in Mexico, 19–20; in the military, 209; removal from Texas, 145–50; on reservations, 138, 139, 140, 145–47, 149, 157; in South America, 31; in Texas, 7, 35, 40–46, 48–59, 90–91, 242, 238; and Texas oil, 217; treaties with, 146–47; violence against, 145–46, 149
natural foods movement, 315
Navajo people, 106
Navarro, José Antonio, 61, 77, 84, 107
Navarro family, 77, 79, 107, 132
Neff, Pat, 230, 251, 252, 253

Negro Folk Songs as Sung by Leadbelly (Lomax), 251
Neighbors, Robert, 145, 146
Neiman Marcus department store, 272–73, 279
Nelson, Willie, 167, 297, 298, 315
New Braunfels, Texas, 172
New Deal, 258–59, 261–64, 278
New France, 37, 41
New Mexico, 34, 36, 37, 43, 49, 54, 91, 105–6, 129, 140, 149, 196, 234
New Orleans, Louisiana, 55, 57, 63, 64, 73, 77, 132, 145, 156, 235
New Spain, 45, 47. *See also* Spanish Empire
Nigerians, 7, 311, 319, 321
Nimitz, Chester, 255
Nixon, Richard, 275, 277, 283
Norris, Frank, 227–30, 237, 239, 277, 331
North American Free Trade Agreement (NAFTA), 320
North Carolina, 118, 328
Nueces River, 105, 107, 112, 121, 131
Nueces Strip, 105
Nueva Vizcaya, 43
Nuevo León, 43, 44, 66
Nuevo México. *See* New Mexico
Nuevo Santander, 66

Obergefell v. Hodges, 307
O'Daniel, Wilbert Lee "Pappy," 262, 263
Ohio, 328
oil, discovery of, 5, 216–26, 242, 312
"Oil Man Blues," 221
Oklahoma, 126, 212, 226, 232, 234; Indian reservation in, 138–39,

140; Native Americans in, 42, 149

Oklahoma City bombing, 325, 326

Old Texas (film), 139

Operation Showtime, 324

ordnance factories, 256

Oregon, 232

Osage people, 103

Osteen, Joel, 332–33

Oswald, Lee Harvey, 276, 277

Palace Theater, 236

Palo Duro Canyon, 138, 147, 259

Pamaque, 44

Pampopa, 44

Pantex, 256

Papanac, 44

Paraguay, 31

Paris, Texas, 230

Parker, Annise, 329

Parker, Bonnie, 193

Parker, Cynthia Ann, 147–48

Parker, Quanah, 147, 148

Parsons, Albert, 141, 145

Parsons, Lucy Carter, 140–41, 142, 145

Paso del Norte, 36, 45. *See also* El Paso, Texas

Pastía, 44

Patrick, Dan, 330–31, 339–40

Patrons of Husbandry (Grange), 171

Paul Quinn College, 142

Payayas, 44

Peattomah (Kiowa Indian), 137

pecans, 14

Pecos River, 10, 12

penal system, 252–53, 294, 336

People's Party. *See* Populist Party, Populists

Permian Basin, 220

Perry, Rick, 326

Peta Nocona (Comanche leader), 148

petrochemical industry, 256

petroleum industry, 5, 216–26, 242, 245, 256–57, 312; pipeline construction, 257

Philippines, 265

piney woods, 13, 33, 244

Plains Indians, 139, 147

Plan de San Diego, 196–97

plantations, 7, 53, 69, 143

politics: gerrymandering, 328; poll taxes, 201–2, 289; and religion, 173–76, 188–89, 229–31, 238, 277; whites-only primaries, 201, 291

Polk, James K., 109–10, 112–13

Polk County, 290

Populist Party, Populists, 178–85, 189–91, 201–2, 212, 224, 225, 232, 238, 258, 261, 281, 284, 290, 322, 331; Black, 185–86; and religion, 188–89; white, 181, 185, 186–87, 190, 194, 200; women, 187–88, 206

Port Arthur, Texas, 256

Porvenir, Texas, 197

Possum and Tater Club, 175

Potter's House, 333

pottery, 19, 20

Prairie View, Texas, 171

Prairie View A&M, 291

Presidio, Texas, 36

Presidio County, 340

prickly pears, 14

printing press, 64

prison system, imprisonment, 252–53, 294, 336

privacy rights, 304

Prohibition, 228–32, 234, 235

prosperity gospel, 332–33
prostitution, 222
Pueblo Indians, 18, 34, 50, 106
Pueblo Revolt, 36, 37

racial equality, 259
racism, 270, 271, 274, 287, 292
radio, 234–35, 241, 261
Railroad Commission, 191
railroads, 184, 191, 195, 225
Rainey, Homer, 263–64
ranching, 51. *See also* cattle industry; longhorn cattle
Rayner, John B., 185–86, 189
Raza Unida Party, 293
Reagan, Ronald, 328
real estate development, 309–11
Rebel, The (newspaper), 212–13
religion: Buddhism, 331; Freethinkers, 116, 176; Hinduism, 319, 331; Indigenous, 19–20; Islam, 319, 331; Judaism, 175, 233, 237, 273, 331; pluralism, 175; and politics, 277. *See also* Christians and Christianity
Religious and Benevolent Association, 176
Republican Party, Republicans, 144, 179; Black members, 170; and Christian voters, 306, 331, 333; conservative control of, 331; dominance of, 141, 279, 327, 328–32; elected officeholders, 144, 276, 326, 327–28, 332; and Hispanics, 333; national, 141, 143; violence against, 164
Republican Women's Clubs, 278–79
Republic Hill, 294
reservations, 138, 139, 140, 145–47, 149, 157

revival meetings, 233
Rice University, 286–87, 289, 318
Richard (enslaved man), 68
Richards, Ann, 327
Richmond (enslaved man), 68
Richmond, Virginia, 128
Rio Grande, 12, 36, 55, 70, 91, 105, 107, 117, 120, 121, 124, 130, 132
Rio Grande City, 121, 122, 206
Rio Grande Valley, 34, 159, 195
River Walk (San Antonio), 259
roadside markers, 242–43
Robertson, Felix D., 238
Robertson County, 189
Robinson, Texas, 199
Rockefeller, John D., 217, 225
rodeos, 154, 253
Roe v. Wade, 302, 303, 305, 306, 307, 308
Roosevelt, Franklin D., 245–46, 257, 260, 265; and the New Deal, 258–59, 261–64, 278
Roper, Daniel, 240
Ross, Lawrence "Sul," 147–48
roughnecks and roustabouts, 218, 219, 221, 223
Ruby, George Thompson, 142, 145
Ruiz, Francisco, 84
Ruiz family, 107
Runaway Scrape, 86–87
Rural Electrification Administration (REA), 260
Rusk County, 224

Sabine Pass, 217
Sabine River, 56, 57, 130, 134
Sahmount, Luther, 137
Salado, Texas, 171
Saltillo, Mexico, 73, 76
Sam (enslaved man), 85
Sana, 44

INDEX

San Antonio, Texas: airfields in, 206; Black people in, 70; churches in, 332; and the Comanches, 50, 54; Germans in, 117, 212; in the Great Depression, 246; integration in, 287; Kennedy in, 276; Ku Klux Klan in, 239; missions, 40, 149, 155, 159; occupation by Mexican army, 109; people from, 329; population growth in, 234; restaurants in, 172; River Walk, 259; road to Austin, 234; Seguín as mayor of, 108–9; settlers in, 61, 62, 63, 64, 65, 66; slavery in, 77; Spanish in, 45, 50, 54, 56–57, 58, 59; TESA chapter, 207; and the Texas Revolution, 81–83; urban growth in, 184, 311, 312. *See also* Alamo
San Antonio River, 40
San Diego Chargers, 286
San Francisco, California, 135
San Jacinto, Battle of, 2, 88, 89, 98, 242
San Jacinto monument, 243
San Sabá valley, 52
Santa Anna, Antonio López de, 2, 58, 79, 80, 83, 85–88, 108, 116
Santa Fe, New Mexico, 129
Save Our Springs, 311, 315–16, 321
Schramm, Earnest "Tex," 299, 300
Scott, Garrett, 190
secessionists, 125–28
Second Texas Cavalry, 132
segregation, 178, 179, 195, 202, 262, 292; in education, 166–67, 186, 202, 203, 266, 284, 290; in government programs, 259; in the military, 209, 214; in the oil industry, 223; protests against, 209–10, 287; in transportation, 186. *See also* desegregation
Seguín, Erasmo, 61
Seguín, Juan, 61, 83, 88, 90, 108, 109, 338
Seguín family, 74, 77, 79, 88, 107, 132
Seminole people, 119
sexual abuse, 323
sexuality, 233, 301, 302, 305, 306, 308, 331; homosexuality, 303, 304, 305–7, 332
sharecroppers, 143, 213
Shaw, J. D., 176
Shawnee people, 101, 103
Sheppard, Morris, 231, 235
Sherman, William Tecumseh, 113
shipyards, 256
Shivers, Allan, 288
Shoshone people, 49
Shuler, "Fighting Bob," 230
silver mining, 34, 37
Sinaloa, Mexico, 29–30
Six Flags Over Texas, 125
slavery, 7, 8, 9, 62, 253; abolition of, 209; German view of, 117, 119; and Indigenous people, 30, 34, 35, 43–44; Mexican opposition to, 69–70; portrayal of, 248; on Southern plantations, 53; in Texas, 68, 69–70, 77–78, 85, 90, 93–96, 111, 114, 117–19, 127–28, 338, 339, 340, 338
Smith, A. Maceo, 247, 248
Smith, Lonnie, 291
Smith, Robert Lloyd, 202
Smith v. Allwright, 291
Smithwick, Noah, 82, 86–87
Socialist Party, 212–13
Sons of Hermann, 172

South Asian people, 7, 318–20
Southern Conservative, The, 279
Southern Methodist University (SMU), 231, 285–86, 289
South by Southwest festival, 317
Southwestern University, 171
Soviet Union, 276
SpaceX rockets, 6
Spain: alliance with Comanches, 54–55, 65; and the Caddo people, 39; civil war in, 66. *See also* Spanish Empire; Spanish explorers and colonists
Spanish Armada, 33
Spanish Empire, 29–31; and Indigenous people, 40–46; in North America, 47; in Texas, 32–46, 48; war with England, 54. *See also* New Spain
Spanish explorers and colonists, 21–22, 217; Cabeza de Vaca's expedition, 21–31; Coronado, Francisco Vázquez de, 37; Cortes, Hernán de, 22; as healers, 28–29, 42; looking for French colony, 36–38
Spanish language, 61, 154, 195
spear points, 16
Spindletop oil strike, 5, 219–22, 223, 225
Sprecht, Theodore, 116
Standard Oil Company, 217, 223, 224–25, 226
Staubach, Roger, 300
Sterling, Ross, 218, 226
Stevens, George, 270
Stevenson, Adlai, 275–76
Stevenson, Coke, 266
stills, 234, 235
stock market crash, 244, 251

Storey, C. H., 233, 235–36
subtreasury plan, 183–84
suburbs, 255, 317, 319
suffragists, 204–5, 207–8
Sugarland (suburb), 319, 320
Sul Ross State University, 243
Sun Dance, 138–39
Sun Oil Company, 220
Super-Americans, The (Bainbridge), 271–74
Super Bowl, 299
Swartz, Mimi, 329
Sweatt, Heman, 291
Sweatt v. Painter, 291
Swiss farmers, 65

Taino people, 22
Tamaulipas, 44
Taovaya people, 52
Tāp Pīlam Coahuiltecan Nation, 149, 339
Tejanos: at the Alamo, 81–83, 85; alliance with Anglo-Americans, 108; Austin's alliances with, 69–70, 74, 78, 79; and the Civil War, 126, 131–33, 134; and the Comanches, 116; and Cortina's war, 120–21; culture of, 172, 250; derivation of name, 39, 76; revolt against Spain, 57, 59, 63, 65; settling in Texas, 68, 197, 76, 77, 80; and slavery, 119; as Texas heroes, 338; and Texas independence, 84, 88, 90, 91, 108–9, 112; violence against, 108–9, 340. *See also* Mexican Americans
telephones, 184
temperance movement, 168–70, 173

INDEX

Temperance Family Visitor, 169
Temple Baptist Church (Detroit), 230
Temple Rodef Shalom, 175
tenant farmers, 213
Tenayuca, Emma, 246
Ten Bears (Comanche leader), 147
terrorism: domestic, 325; white, 144, 236
Texaco, 220, 224, 225, 226, 272–73
Texanization, 329
Texas: declaration of independence and constitution, 84, 107; flag of, 97; Indigenous and Spanish, *35;* Independence Day, 97–98, 127, 245; natural environments of, 13–14; origin of name, 39; Panhandle, 19, 33, 34, 50, 137, 139, 147, 149, 160, 161, 220, 245, 277; population growth in, 113–14, 272; Republic of, 8, 88–99, 101–7, 127, 243, 325–26; Revolutionary (with Mexican land grants), *81;* stereotypes of, 9, 268–82; U.S. annexation and statehood, 5, 75, 90, 93–94, 100, 109–11; and World War I, 205–6
Texas A&M University, 98, 162, 171, 202, 203, 234, 255
Texas Board of Education, 340
Texas Brigade, 128
Texas Centennial Central Exposition, 240–44, 247–50
Texas Christian University, 171, 231
Texas Club (San Francisco), 135
Texas Equal Rights Association, 206

Texas Equal Suffrage Association (TESA), 204–5, 207, 208
Texas Folklore Society, 244, 250
Texas Highway Department, 242
Texas Instruments (TI), 313, 314
Texas Methodist Historical Association, 163
Texas People's Party, 185. *See also* Populist Party, Populists
Texas Rangers: fighting Cortina, 120–21; fighting Native Americans, 118–19, 138, 146; and Thomas Hickey, 213; preventing anti-Black violence, 252, 288; statue at Love Field, 294; and the Texas Centennial Exposition, 240, 241; in Uvalde, 335; violence by, 340; violence against Hispanics, 192–94, 197, 200, 281
Texas Revolution, 2, 4, 6, 74–88, 114, 126, 241–42, 271, 340
Texas Southern University, 318
Texas State Cemetery (Austin), 3, 243
Texas State Fair, 240
Texas Surgical Society, 28
Texas Tech University, 243
Texas Western University, 286
Texeira, Antonia, 177
Texians, 76, 79–80, 83–84, 85, 88, 98
Thomas, Ann, 87
Thomas, Cullen, 242
Three Rivers, Texas, 264
Tigua people, 149
Tijerina, Felix, 292
Tivi (enslaved person), 68
Tlaxcalan Indians, 34, 65
tobacco, 32

Tohana, 44

Tonequoah (Kiowa leader), 137–38

Tonkawa people, 45, 52, 140, 145

Tower, John, 327, 328

trade: among Indigenous cultures, 18–19, 27, 41–42, 50; between Indigenous cultures and Europeans, 37, 41–42, 50, 52; in the Spanish Empire, 32–33

Travis, William Barret, 75, 83, 85, 329

Trespalacios, José Félix, 63–64

Truman, Harry, 265

Trump, Donald, 329, 332

turquoise, 19

Umlauf, Charles, 273

"Unclouded Day, An," 167

underground railroad, 117

unemployment, 246

unionization, 246, 263, 278

Union Loyal League, 131

United Daughters of the Confederacy, 208

United Nations, 275

United States: annexation of Texas, 5, 75, 90, 93–94, 100, 109–11; opposition to annexation, 94–97. *See also* Civil War

U.S. Constitution, 283; Thirteenth Amendment, 142, 144; Fourteenth Amendment, 142, 144, 290; Fifteenth Amendment, 142, 144, 201

U.S. Supreme Court, 284, 290–91, 307, 328

University of Houston, 318

University of Mississippi, 287

University of North Texas, 205

University of Texas, 98–99, 142, 162, 202, 211, 234, 250, 251, 263, 272, 284, 314; in Austin, 171, 203, 286, 296, 297, 312, 314; in Dallas, 317; at El Paso, 243, 286; Law School, 291, 304

urbanization, 311–14

Uruguay, 31

Ute people, 49, 106

Uvalde, Texas, 261, 335–36

Valdez, Lupe, 329

Vela, Isidro, 132–33

vice squads, 303–4

Victoria, Texas, 81, 104

victory gardens, 204, 206

Vietnamese residents, 7, 311, 319–20, 325

Vietnam War, 279–80, 293, 319, 329

vigilantes, 197, 285, 340

Villa of Béxar, 40. *See also* San Antonio, Texas

Vinson, Eddie, 221

violence: against Indigenous people, 145–46, 149, 164; anti-Black, 143–44, 164, 190, 212, 232–33, 236; anti-German, 212; anti-Mexican, 200, 209, 212; at the border, 193–98; Christianity as counter to, 167–68; colonial, 293; as cultural standard, 164–65; homicides, 335–36; Houston riot, 214; mass shootings, 335–36; mob, 198–200, 209, 252; political, 189–90, 202, 275–76, 279; racial, 285, 288–91, 292, 294, 340; by the state, 324–25, 340; in Texas history, 340; by the

INDEX

Texas Rangers, 192–94, 197, 200, 281, 340. *See also* lynchings
Virginia, 130, 287
Viva Texas: The Story of the Mexican-Born Patriots of the Republic of Texas, 249–50
Voting Rights Act (1965), 285, 293

Waco, Texas, 140–41, 170, 172–73, 175, 176, 198–200, 340; and the Branch Davidians, 323–27
Waco people, 140
Waco University, 170
Wade, Henry, 304, 306, 307
Wade, Melvin, 186, 188–89
Walker, Jerry Jeff, 297, 298, 303
Wallace, Henry, 262
Washington, George, 7, 65, 278
Washington, Jesse, 198–99, 340
Watergate hearings, 283–84
Waterman, Texie, 301
Waxahachie, Texas, 210
Wayne, John, 271
weaving, 17
Weddington, Sarah, 304–5, 306, 308
Weiner, Ted, 273
West Texas A&M University, 243
West Virginia, 333
White, Bob, 290–91, 294
White Man's Union, 190
White Shaman mural, 10–13, 15, 18, 19–20
white supremacy beliefs, 141, 144, 326, 339; enforced by law and violence, 190, 202; Ku Klux Klan and, 232, 239; Populists and, 186–87; and slavery, 127
Whitman, Walt, 177
Whole Foods, 315–16

Why Are We in Vietnam? (Mailer), 280–81
Wichita Falls, Texas, 220, 236
Wichita people, 43, 45
wildcatters, 221, 271
wild west tradition, 241
Wiley College, 142
Willet, Slim, 222
Williams, Charles T., 273
Wilson, Woodrow, 197, 200, 211
Wisconsin, 212, 328
Wister, Owen, 153, 160
women: as authors, 250; of color, 284; Dallas Cowboys Cheerleaders, 301, 302; Daughters of the Republic of Texas, 243–44; discrimination against, 305; flappers, 228; from Mexican families, 61, 107, 195, 246; Native American, 41; political activism of, 275, 278–79, 302, 305; in political office, 284; and the Populist Party, 179, 187–88, 206–7; as property holders, 84, 305; and religion, 169; rights of, 7, 187–88, 207, 274; voting rights for, 191, 194–95, 205, 206–7, 208, 210; and war efforts, 204–5, 210, 255, 256
Women's Army Corps (WAC), 255
World War I, 195, 204–6; Blacks in the military, 209–10, 214; and German immigrants, 210–13, 215; opposition to, 213–14
World War II, 254, 255–57, 262–67
Wright, Lawrence, 280
Wyoming, 238

Xarame, 44
XIT Ranch, 158

Yarborough, "Smilin" Ralph, 276
Yojuane, 44
Young, William, 131
Ysleta, Texas, 36

Ysleta del Sur Pueblo, 149
yucca, 11

Zacatecas, Mexico, 34, 79
Zapata County, 133
Zavala, Adina de, 243–44
Zavala, Lorenzo de, 79, 84, 107–8
Zilker, A. J., 310